AN ECONOMIC HISTORY OF INDIA

From Pre-Colonial Times to 1986

DIETMAR ROTHERMUND

CROOM HELM
London • New York • Sydney

© 1988 Dietmar Rothermund
Croom Helm Ltd, Provident House,
Burrell Row, Beckenham, Kent, BR3 1AT

Croom Helm Australia, 44–50 Waterloo Road,
North Ryde, 2113, New South Wales

British Library Cataloguing in Publication Data

Rothermund, Dietmar
    An economic history of India : the
    colonial period to 1986.
    1. India—Economic conditions
    I. Title
    330.954′03   HC435
    ISBN 0–7099–4228–1

Published in the USA by
Croom Helm
in association with Methuen, Inc.
29 West 35th Street
New York, NY 10001

Library of Congress Cataloging-in-Publication Data
Rothermund, Dietmar.
    An economic history of India.

    Bibliography: p.
    Includes index.
    1. India — Economic conditions. I. Title.
HC435.R56 1987   330.954   87-30125
ISBN 0-7099-4228-1

Photosetting by Mayhew Typesetting, Bristol, England
Printed and bound in Great Britain
by Billing & Sons Limited, Worcester.

Contents

Preface

India's economic history is like a fascinating drama: an ancient peasant culture was subjected to a regime of military feudalism, which achieved its greatest success under the Great Mughals. The Mughal agrarian state and its revenue base were then captured by the East India Company. This capitalist organisation was engrafted on the agrarian state. In this way a parasitical symbiosis was established which benefited the alien usurpers and paralysed the host, who survived under conditions of a low-level equilibrium. In the twentieth century India came under the influence of the world market to an increasing extent. The First World War, the Great Depression and the Second World War made a strong impact on India. As there was no national government, these external influences remained unchecked by any national economic policy and India was fully subjected to them. Throughout the period, the vagaries of the monsoon played their fateful role, as India depended almost exclusively on rain-fed agriculture. The independent republic emphasised irrigation and industrial production so as to escape from this fate. After some progress was made, a serious drought proved to be a severe setback. In subsequent years, the Indian economy grew only at a moderate rate, just enough to support the growing population, which will be about one billion by the end of the present century. A recent upswing in industrial growth and surplus production of the major foodgrains seems to usher in a brighter future, but many problems have still to be solved.

The interpretation of India's economic history has always given rise to lively debates. In the nineteenth century, Indian nationalists like Dadabhai Naoroji, Mahadev Govind Ranade and Romesh Chunder Dutt discussed the economic consequences of British rule. Karl Marx also commented on the British impact on India. To him, the British appeared to be the executors of the predetermined course of world history: they were breaking the crust of tradition and subjected India to capitalism. Nationalist and Marxist economic historians have made further contributions to these debates. British authors have often tended to highlight the positive aspects of British rule in India (law and administration, infrastructure, etc.) and have denied or ignored the negative aspects. In recent years, the predominance of nationalist and Marxist opinions in India have provided a challenge to Western scholars, who have based their arguments on neoclassical economic theory and have tried to refute the views of Indian scholars. These debates have stimulated research, and many important dissertations, monographs and articles have appeared which have greatly enriched our understanding of Indian economic history.

The publication of the *Cambridge Economic History of India* in two volumes, to which 28 authors have contributed a large number of impressive analyses, is a milestone which marks the progress that has been made in this field. However, no attempt has been made by the editors of this important work to provide a synthesis, nor do the contributors seem to have had a chance to read each other's chapters. In this way these chapters remain rather isolated. Furthermore, such a book necessarily requires a regional and sectoral division of the subject matter. This kind of division makes it difficult to envisage economic history as a process in which there is an interaction of various different factors. For example, in 1853 Karl Marx published his often-quoted prediction that by building railways in India the British were ushering in a phase of rapid industrialisation. He expected linkage effects as engines and rails, etc. would be manufactured in India and ancillary industries would necessarily arise. From the perspective of 1853 this was a reasonable prognosis. Marx could not know that only a few years later the steamer and the telegraph and the opening of the Suez Canal would reduce the distance and the freight rates and increase the flow of information and the transport of goods to such an extent that infant industries in India would no longer be protected by the high cost of transportation. Marx could not foresee that British capital was not exported to India to the extent that the first rush of railway investment might have indicated in 1853. He also could not know that rising agrarian prices and an even greater increase in land prices would soon offer more attractive lines of investment to Indian capital than the investment in industrial production, which was risky and would yield a profit only after some time.

In order to portray India's economic history as a process, this book has to follow a chronological order. The earlier periods of India's economic history before British rule have been outlined only in a summary fashion and the nineteenth century has also been treated rather briefly; the main emphasis is on the first half of the twentieth century, which was punctuated by two world wars and the intervening depression. The year 1947, in which India achieved independence, has not been regarded as a convenient terminal point for this economic history of India. The economic development of the republic has been discussed here with a view to show the continuity of the structural problems, which would not suddenly disappear with the end of colonial rule. The Indian economy has been analysed by many scholars in recent years, but modern economists rarely show an interest in historical perspectives; therefore an attempt has been made here to place their findings in such a perspective.

Agriculture, which still supports about three-quarters of India's population, is a main focus of our interest in this book. Although industry was rather insignificant in the years before 1947, it has nevertheless been discussed in detail because of its later importance and also because industrialisation, or rather the lack of it, has been a main point in all debates concerning India's economic history under British rule. Currency and monetary policy are discussed in detail in this book because they are of central importance for the British control over the Indian economy. Questions concerning money and credit are usually discussed only in the specialist publications and technical details often discourage the general reader from reading such books and papers. Accordingly, this subject is often not well integrated in the surveys of economic history. In this book an attempt has been made to discuss monetary policy in its general political and economic context.

An awareness of the political history of India is, of course, a precondition for the understanding of India's economic history. The present book is published as a companion volume to *A History of India*, which I wrote together with Hermann Kulke. The reader may refer to that book for further information. In stating this, however, I do not wish to indicate that the present book cannot stand on its own. I have briefly outlined the respective political constellations which conditioned economic development in this book in order to provide some basic orientation for the reader.

No footnotes have been added to the text of this book, but the reader will find all the relevant references in the annotated bibliography at the end of the text. This bibliography is limited to books and articles which have been used for the preparation of the respective chapters.

I wish to acknowledge the debt of gratitude I owe to my Indian and British colleagues for all that I have learned both from their published work and from many discussions with them. I am also indebted to my students at Heidelberg University who have asked many questions in the lecture courses and seminars which I gave on this subject. The German Research Council (Deutsche Forschungs-gemeinschaft) provided me with several travel grants for the years and months I spent in India. None of these grants were specifically related to the present book, but they helped me to acquire the knowledge I needed for this work. Last, but not least, I wish to mention the South Asia Institute of Heidelberg University, where I have worked since 1963 in an interdisciplinary environment which enables me to benefit from the advice and criticism of my colleagues.

Dietmar Rothermund
Heidelberg

1

The Structure of the
Traditional Economy

1.1 APPROPRIATE TECHNOLOGY AND THE FAMILY UNIT

The traditional Indian economy was characterised by what we would call today an 'appropriate technology' geared to small-scale production in family units of peasants and artisans. Land and labour as factors of production were abundant, and therefore the third factor — capital — which is substituted for the other factors whenever they are scarce, was not required. There was, of course, some capital formation in trade and also in terms of the construction of wells and tanks for local irrigation, but there was no capital accumulation that would lead to a concentration of the ownership of the means of production. The tools and implements were simple and could be made locally and cheaply. The manufactures sponsored by some rulers for the making of arms or of luxury goods were very rare indeed. Wealth was sometimes amassed by successful merchants or victorious warlords, but such wealth was usually lost as quickly as it had been gained.

In agriculture, the small family farm was predominant. Land was not yet a commodity that was freely bought and sold. The peasant family who tilled the soil was in greater demand than the land, 'which belonged to him who first cleared it', as ancient law codes proclaimed. Landlords were not landowners; they only had the right or privilege to collect taxes from the peasants. They kept some of these dues for themselves and handed over the rest to the ruler or another privileged person in the hierarchy of those who lived on the work of the peasantry. If these dues were too high, peasants would flee and look for the protection of a less rapacious lord. Nobody ever thought of organising agricultural production on a large scale with hired wage labour. The vagaries of the monsoon would have made

1

such an operation very risky. It was much better to let peasant families bear the risk, and usually also the entire cost of production, and get hold of their surplus when the harvest was in.

A strong ruler would tend to eliminate middlemen and concentrate the collection of surplus in his capital city, but there were several problems which he would face when doing this. Such concentration was impossible without coercion and this meant overheads in terms of armed retainers, weapons, horses, etc. The growth of such overheads would then lead to more taxation and more coercion, which would finally meet with resistance. Moreover, the concentration of the collection of surplus in kind was difficult because of the cost of transportation, and the high degree of monetisation which was required for the large-scale collection of revenue in cash could not be attained in many periods of Indian history. Decentralisation prevailed most of the time. Medieval Indian kings normally controlled only a circle of about 100 km radius around their capital in terms of direct taxation; from more distant parts they could at the most extract some tribute. These kings were used to granting a great deal of local autonomy to their subjects; they emphasised their ritual sovereignty and bestowed land on temples and brahmins, who in turn provided moral support for their rule. They also profited from the control of ports and trade routes. Urbanisation and monetisation were limited and money circulated only in the centres of trade and pilgrimage.

1.2 MILITARY FEUDALISM, URBANISATION AND MONETISATION

The traditional structure of the medieval kingdoms was rudely shaken when Northern India was conquered by Islamic horsemen, whose new strategy of swift cavalry warfare soon spread throughout India, as no ruler could hope to survive unless he adopted the new style of warfare and military organisation. Horses were rare in India and horsebreeding somehow did not meet with great success; thus horses for the cavalry had to be imported at great cost from Persia and Arabia. This required increased taxation and the man on horseback was a more formidable tax collector than his pedestrian predecessors. Local autonomy was crushed by the man on horseback. New urban centres arose in the countryside; they housed the garrison of the cavalry, the treasury of the tax collector and served as market places too. Increased international trade brought precious metals to India and this contributed to the spread of monetisation, which enabled the tax collectors to get their revenue in cash.

The military commander and tax collector, who ruled the countryside from his garrison town, was usually a stranger with no local roots. In the north, he would be a Turk or Afghan; in the south, Telugu warriors had penetrated the Tamil country. Whenever central control was reduced, such a commander could turn into an independent warlord and start a dynasty of his own. In order to guard against such a challenge, the central rulers tried to concentrate a larger military force in their capital. The type of urbanisation bred by this system of military feudalism was a strange one: there were no patricians, no municipal autonomy in these towns. The military elite was in complete control and civil administration was already subject to the control of military officers.

The universal spread of cavalry warfare and the distribution of the cavalry units in various garrisons made the assertion of central control more and more difficult. Only the introduction of an even more powerful force could help to support a new central dynasty. The Mughal field artillery was such a force and the Great Mughals saw to it that it remained under their direct control. This type of armament was very expensive and although the Mughals were successful in conquering most of India with their guns, they finally exhausted the land-revenue resources on which their empire was based. The enormous overheads of innumerable soldiers, courtiers and administrators were too much for the revenue-paying peasant, who had to sell an ever-increasing proportion of his produce in order to pay his revenue in cash. This monetisation under a military feudal regime did not lead to a genuine commercialisation, just as the new pattern of feudal urbanisation did not lead to the rise of a bourgeoisie. The Indian traders who bought and sold grain and provided credit to the ruling elite could never hope to achieve a corporate autonomy. They were very astute in going about their business, but the conditions under which they had to operate were not conducive to the growth of genuine capitalism. The sluggishness of the seasonal circulation of money in the vast agrarian economy also handicapped the financial operations of the traders. Sometimes they emerged as large-scale revenue contractors, but more often they were cautious and did not want to get involved in such risky business. Knowing the rapacity of the military elite, they hid their wealth and adapted themselves to the prevailing conditions. In addition to the appropriate technology, which has been mentioned above, there was thus an appropriate capitalism of merchants, who

3

were used to dissimulation rather than to an active assertion of their influence.

1.3 LONG-DISTANCE TRADE AND FRAGMENTED MARKETS

The political unification of most of India under Mughal rule did not imply the emergence of an integrated market economy. There were many regional markets, which remained isolated from each other owing to the high cost of transportation. Only expensive goods with little weight such as textiles or precious raw materials such as indigo were traded over long distances and also entered the international market via maritime trade. Bullock carts, which are now the universal means of transportation, were rare in Mughal India because there was a lack of adequate roads. Pack animals were the only means of transportation. Long-distance trade in grain was impossible under such conditions. Only the Great Mughal could afford to hire thousands of pack animals to transport grain for his army when it was deployed on distant battlefields. Only where coastal and river transport by ship was possible did grain shipments occur over long distances, such as Bengal rice being sent to Sri Lanka or up the Ganges to North Indian markets or rice from Gujarat reaching ports in East Africa or in the Persian Gulf. Inside the country, grain rarely ever reached the next regional market, even when there was a famine and prices were rising. Thus there coexisted long-distance trade routes for certain commodities and regionally fragmented markets for most other goods.

The lucrative and risky long-distance trade and maritime trade were well financed. Rich merchants as well as high officers and princes participated in these ventures. There were even speculative ventures such as the initial stages of freight insurance, when merchants not directly involved in the respective trade themselves undertook to bear the risk of loss in transit for a share of the profit of the sale of goods after their safe arrival. Futures trading was also widely practised. Islamic merchants who wished to abide by the religious injunction against the taking of interest nevertheless managed to provide credit and to get debts serviced by including the interest rate in the price fixed in advance for a future sale. Large-scale transactions were facilitated by the circulation of promissory notes (*hundi*), which were sometimes handed on like bank notes before they were encashed. Each merchant who passed them on to another would endorse them and with such additional endorsements they were even more welcome to the next recipient. Thus there was a well-developed trade and a great deal of sophistication in dealing with money and credit, but all this was never institutionalised or guaranteed by any authority. Credit was based on personal relations and not on an impersonal legal system. Therefore all established channels of trade were well financed, but new ventures and investments would rarely find the necessary credit. Among the most well-established branches of trade was the export trade, and especially trade with Europeans who brought precious metals to India, for which there was such an enormous demand.

1.4 THE SILVER STREAM AND STATE FINANCE

The monetisation of the land revenue was very important for the rulers of a great agrarian state because only cash could be easily transferred from the local to the central level so as to support a powerful government and a large army. As India had no silver mines and paper money was not yet in circulation (except for the private promissory notes), the monetisation of the revenue depended directly on the influx of silver from abroad. In their own interest, the Great Mughals had standardised and improved the minting of coins in their empire. Their silver rupee was of good quality and was universally accepted. Anybody could go to the mint and could get silver converted into rupees at a small charge of 5.6 per cent. By means of a clever device the Mughals assured the steady circulation of these coins: the rupee was accepted at its full value only in the year in which it was minted; in subsequent years there was an increasing discount. People who hoarded money thus had to bear a certain loss, unless they replaced the coins in their hoards every year. If they forgot to do this or if they inherited an old hoard, they had to take it to the mint to get new coins, because the discount on the old coins in the market would far exceed the charges of the mint master. In this way the rupees were kept in constant circulation, and the mints and the treasury were assured of a steady flow of money. But the system in which this circulation took place kept on growing at a fairly rapid rate. New regions were made to pay revenue in cash, government expenditure increased and the population grew too. Around 1600, India had a population of about 150 million; 200 years later there were about 200 million. This meant that India's capacity for the absorption of the silver stream coming from the West was also growing, but the stream was so big that it led to a price

5

inflation, in spite of this absorptive capacity. Spurts of inflation could be noticed in times when the import of silver was particularly large.

The output of the American silver mines was transferred to India with a certain time-lag. Thus the price inflation that could be noticed in Spain in the early sixteenth century spread to India only a few decades later. From 1500 to 1600 the circulation of coins increased in Spain from 5 to 91 million ducats (that is, eighteen times), whereas prices increased fourfold. The pattern of inflationary price increases was regionally differentiated. In the coastal regions of Spain prices were three times higher than in the interior of the country. Merchants accumulated capital, whereas the real income of the higher nobility declined and its dependence on the king increased.

The high level of prices in Spain encouraged imports and contributed to an outflow of precious metals. A large amount of this Spanish money found its way to India. In the period from 1591 to 1639, the circulation of silver coins trebled in India. The conduct of Mughal public finance was an additional factor that could contribute to spurts of inflation. It is said that Jahangir, who inherited Akbar's throne and treasury in 1605, spent about 60 million of the 70 million rupees he found in that treasury. The great stream of imported silver of the early seventeenth century was thus augmented by Jahangir's lavish expenditure. Jahangir died in 1627 and his successor Shah Jahan then tried to replenish the treasury by saving 5 million rupees per year. The deflationary effect of this measure was not immediately felt, as imports of silver remained fairly high. Prices doubled in India in the period from 1595 to 1637. Some reduction in the circulation of money could only be noticed around the middle of the seventeenth century, although during its last decades the stream of silver increased once more and Aurangzeb's enormous expenditure on his wars contributed to a new spurt of inflation.

These spurts of inflation ruined Akbar's rational system of land revenue assessment and of carefully graded salary scales for the hierarchy of imperial officers. Just as the higher nobility of Spain felt the pinch of declining real incomes, the Mughal mansabdars found it difficult to make both ends meet. Instead of revising Akbar's system, however, his successors merely adjusted it in a piecemeal fashion. The very rationality of the system thus proved to be a handicap. Inflationary pressure and increasing government expenditure led to a stepping up of the land revenue demand. Modern states can ride the tide of inflation by collecting customs duties, income tax, sales taxes, etc., whereas Mughal public finance was tied to land revenue, a sluggish and regressive tax which cannot be revised in a short period of time. Mughal finance was thus faced with a dilemma: the silver stream which came into the country by means of trade was welcome, because it enabled the monetisation of the land revenue, but at the same time this stream of silver led to an inflation that could not be tackled with the existing methods of taxation. Therefore it was necessary to rely even more on the land revenue, which was ill suited for the purpose of coping with the problems of public finance in a period of inflation.

The agrarian state of the Mughals was unable to meet the challenge of these new economic conditions. As far as external relations were concerned, the Mughals were practically liberal free traders, but in internal affairs they unwittingly followed the doctrine of the physiocrats, who believed that there should be no other tax than the tax on agriculture, as this tax was anyhow passed on to the consumer and was thus the most universal tax imaginable. The Mughals in fact succeeded in adjusting the land revenue to the rising level of prices, but in collecting this revenue they faced more and more resistance. The bulk of the peasantry in subsistence agriculture did not profit from the rise in prices. They were forced to sell some of their produce only in order to meet the revenue demand. That demand was regulated by the needs of the central government, whereas the price the peasant received was dictated by the conditions of the local market, which was not yet integrated into a national market. Tensions increased in that way. Rebellious peasants got hold of guns, which could be produced by the local blacksmith, in spite of strict orders of the Mughal government against this type of manufacture of arms. However, this 'appropriate technology' of rural resistance could not be easily checked. The Mughal empire, which owed its rise to the stream of silver and the introduction of new arms, was challenged by the consequences of the developments that were the secret of its own success. Military feudalism was at the end of its tether. Finally, the bourgeois servants of the East India Company stepped in where the Mughals had failed.

2

The Development of Maritime Trade
and the Beginnings of Colonial Rule

2.1 MEDIEVAL CORPORATE EMPIRES AND MARITIME TRADE

From ancient times, India had had active maritime trade relations with many countries around the Indian Ocean. In the medieval period, South Indian states were particularly involved in this trade. Kings used to get a good deal of their income from trade and could thus afford to maintain a large army and to build a powerful navy without exhausting their land revenue base, which was mostly confined to the fertile core area of their dominion. The peasantry enjoyed a great deal of local autonomy, while the king's power grew nevertheless.

Around 1000 AD there was a remarkable change in the structure of Asian maritime trade. The previous pattern of pre-emporia trade changed into the new pattern of emporia trade. Whereas in the phase of pre-emporia trade goods were shipped directly from the place of origin to that of final consumption, the rise of emporia, particularly along the Indian coasts, implied new practices of re-export, breaking bulk, assorting shipments according to the demands of various ports of call, etc. This major change in the pattern of Asian maritime trade was related to the simultaneous rise of powerful corporate empires in several parts of Asia. The Chola empire of South India, the Khmer empire of Cambodia and the empire of Champa in Vietnam, and China under the Sung dynasty emerged in the amazing eleventh century AD, which witnessed a rapid extension of rice cultivation and a large-scale increase both in local and long-distance trade. The goods traded were no longer only a few luxury items, but a wide variety of commodities such as processed iron, spices, sandalwood, camphor, pearls, textiles, as well as horses and elephants. Customs duties played a major role in the budgets of these corporate empires, which differed from the land-revenue-based agrarian states of a later period. The political order of these medieval corporate empires was not so much that of territorial sovereignty, but of a corporate network of rulers, merchants, temples, priests and/or royal officers. A brief survey of the rise of the Chola empire and of China under the Sung dynasty will illustrate this new development.

The Chola empire experienced a sudden spurt of expansion under the powerful rulers Rajaraja I and Rajendra I in the early eleventh century AD. The power of these rulers was partly based on the control of the fertile rice basin of the Kaveri delta, but also on their intimate links with prosperous and influential merchant guilds which controlled long-distance trade. In fact, Chola imperial expansion was planned according to the advice of such merchants. It was a merchant who told Rajaraja about the weakness of Sri Lanka's king and suggested a military intervention. The main thrust of the Chola expedition was then aimed at the Pollonaruva-Trincomalee region, which was obviously of strategic importance for the South-East Asian trade. At the same time the complete control over the Gulf of Mannar gave the Cholas and their merchants a monopoly of the pearl trade, as this region was famous for its pearl fisheries. The Cholas had trade relations with China, Burma, Srivijaya and other South-East Asian realms. Rajaraja's embassy, which reached China in 1015 AD, advertised his realm as an important member of the new emporia network. For the most part, these maritime trade relations were peaceful, but Rajendra's naval expedition against Srivijaya in 1025 AD clearly demonstrated that diplomacy could be backed up by military intervention. The issue at stake was undoubtedly the access to the Chinese market, which developed very fast under the Sung dynasty.

At the end of the tenth century the Sung dynasty suddenly rose to prominence and established its stronghold in a fertile area on the lower Yellow River, where Kaifeng was their first capital. Under this dynasty, China experienced a veritable renaissance in the eleventh century AD. Pressed by the powerful hordes of the northern steppes, the Chinese turned towards the sea. New varieties of rice imported from Champa enabled them to have two harvests a year in the fertile southern provinces. The circulation of coins and the volume of trade increased by leaps and bounds in the eleventh century, which was a golden age in medieval Asia. The printing of banknotes and the circulation of cheques and other negotiable instruments ('flying money') greatly expanded the scope of monetisation and commercialisation. Chinese reformers conceived of an expanding economy which would increase both the standard of living of the people and the income of the state. Mandarins and merchants prospered in this state and became the main supporters of its corporate structure. The Chinese junks, which were the most advanced vessels of their day and age, crossed the high seas. The nautical use of the compass was introduced by the Chinese at that time. (The Venetians adopted it only several centuries later in order to cross the Mediterranean in the cloudy winter, thus sending out two fleets to the Levant per year rather than only one.) In the eleventh century Asia was definitely ahead of Europe in most respects, and its corporate empires, whose power was based on an ample supply of rice and a buoyant trade, were much more splendid even in cultural terms than the realms of the West.

This close relationship of emporia trade and imperial splendour did not last very long. The advance of land-based conquerors who introduced a kind of military feudalism led to the demise of the old type of corporate empires. When these empires declined, their navies also disappeared and the Indian Ocean emerged as an enormous free trade zone not controlled by any sea power whatever.

2.2 ASIAN FREE TRADE IN THE INDIAN OCEAN

The free trade of the Indian Ocean was dominated by individual merchants and sometimes by individual pirates, who could do whatever they liked in the absence of any sea power. These merchants made their arrangements with small coastal rulers, who could not afford to ask for more than a moderate rate of customs duties, as trade could easily shift to another port. In fact sometimes an audacious shipowner could himself rise to the position of such a local ruler, as the example of the Sultan of Honavar shows, who was a powerful figure on India's western coast in the days of Ibn Battuta's memorable visit. The father of this sultan had been a shipowner and he himself was initially a kind of pirate. He subdued several coastal rulers on the Malabar coast and established his headquarters in the small port of Honavar. Since this place was not far from Vijayanagar, the new centre of a military feudal regime, the Sultan paid tribute and owed allegiance to King Harihar of Vijayanagar, who obviously did not interfere with the Sultan's maritime operations. Honavar did not have a rich hinterland and depended even for its food supply on maritime trade. This was typical for such emporia, which often received long-distance grain shipments. The division of labour and the integration into a common maritime market often established closer connections among such coastal enclaves than those they had with their immediate hinterland. The men on horseback who ruled the hinterland were busy collecting their land revenue and did not bother to disturb the coastal enclaves. As they depended to a large extent on imported horses, they appreciated the services of maritime horse-traders, who had settled in such enclaves.

In the fifteenth century, the Portuguese entered the Indian Ocean and soon noticed that they could dominate it in the absence of any other sea power. They also learned the tricks of various trades; after they had captured Goa, which was a horse-traders' station, they soon emerged as major suppliers of horses to Vijayanagar, with whose rulers they were on very good terms. Their main concern was, of course, the pepper trade. Initially they had hoped to seal off the Red Sea route and to deprive Venice and the Levant of all alternative supply. When this did not work and when the rising Ottoman empire provided protection to the old trade routes, from which a good deal of protection rent could be derived, the Portuguese adjusted to the new situation and preferred to collect customs duties in the ports they controlled, rather than to make vain attempts at diverting the Asian spice trade to the Atlantic. As the volume of Portuguese trade remained fairly modest when compared to the vast volume of Indian Ocean trade, and as their sea power was also rather limited, they did not bring about a major structural change of that trade. It was left to the Dutch to do this when they barged into the Indian Ocean in a massive way at the beginning of the seventeenth century.

2.3 THE DUTCH INVASION

The Dutch East India Company imitated the Portuguese precedent in many ways, but from the very beginning the Dutch operations were of a far greater magnitude. With their enormous shipbuilding industry and an immense fleet of trading vessels with which they already dominated the shipping trade in Europe, they could easily divert a great number of ships to the Indian Ocean. They not only captured the spice trade, but also entered the textile trade in a big way. Moreover, they also participated to an ever-increasing extent in the 'country trade', as the trade among Asian countries was called. Often Asian merchants would entrust their shipments to the

Dutch, rather than to indigenous shipowners; they were then sure that their goods were safe and would not be intercepted by pirates. The Dutch were after all the greatest pirates in the Indian Ocean, but whereas it was impossible to entrust goods to ordinary pirates, one could always rely on a contract made with the Dutch.

The Dutch method of selling the goods they bought from Asia at a free auction in Amsterdam enabled them to diversify their trade very quickly. The Portuguese, with their restrictive royal pepper monopoly, could never have conceived of establishing a trade with Indian textiles as the Dutch did, and their textile trade soon surpassed their spice trade. At an auction it was possible to test the market for whatever one could think of and buyers from all over Europe flocked to these auctions in Amsterdam. Another element of the Dutch success was the financial revolution, which had preceded the rapid expansion of their international trade. This financial revolution was initially due to Habsburg imperial rule and the unlimited need of the Habsburg rulers for funds with which they could pay for their ambitious campaigns. The financial innovations they introduced in the Netherlands were supposed to mobilise resources for this purpose, but instead of benefiting the alien rulers, they added to the financial strength of the local bodies in the Netherlands, whose bonds were then freely traded in an expanding market. The British financial revolution of the eighteenth century was thus preceded by a Dutch financial revolution of the sixteenth century.

The East India Company that was established in London in 1600, two years before the Dutch company, was initially much less important. The amount of trading capital and the number of ships were much smaller than the enormous Dutch resources. The mode of operation was, however, very similar. The pattern of the auctions in London followed that of the auctions in Amsterdam. This also enabled the British to shift from the spice trade to the textile trade, and to add the tea trade later on. But the lack of capital and the more limited volume of trade forced the British to introduce some important innovations, which then distinguished their mode of operation from that of the Dutch. Instead of sending convoys of cheap slow ships, they concentrated on more expensive fast ships, which were well armed and could sail alone. At first such ships were built at the company's own dockyard, but in the last decades of the seventeenth century the company adopted the policy of leasing rather than owning ships. In this way most of the capital of the company could be invested in trade rather than in expensive ships.

The risk of the underutilisation of such ships was shifted to private shipowners, who in turn charged high freight rates whenever they could lease a ship to the company. Due to these high rates, such ships were only suitable for the intercontinental route and had to stick to a strict timetable. If they missed the proper season and were detained in the Indian Ocean, this was a loss to the company for which a regional tour in the country trade could never provide adequate compensation. Accordingly, the country trade was left entirely to private traders, who were sometimes called 'interlopers' by the representatives of the company, but who actually contributed a great deal to British expansion in the Indian Ocean. Their trading activities often had an ancillary function: for instance, they took Indian raw cotton or opium to China and paid their sales proceeds into the company's treasury in Canton in return for drafts on Calcutta or London, thus providing the company with local cash for buying tea.

Among these British private traders there were many aggressive people who were quick to advise the company to use its resources and manpower for an active intervention in Asian affairs, the more so since they did not need to pay for such ventures. But even among the directors of the company there were daring men who thought of the land revenue resources in India, which could be captured by territorial conquest. When Sir Josiah Child first proclaimed such intentions and the company even dared to wage a war against the Great Mughal in 1686, this dangerous move proved to be premature. The Mughal empire was at the height of its power under Aurangzeb at that time. The British suffered a severe setback and this greatly benefited their Dutch rivals.

Despite all these dramatic activities, the Europeans nevertheless remained marginal figures in Asia. There were Indian shipowners who had more ships in the Indian Ocean than the European companies. The European demand for Indian goods did not introduce any changes in the Indian production, as it could be met in the traditional way. Only the silver that was brought from Europe had a major impact on the Indian economy, as we have seen. But not all of this silver was brought by European traders. Indian trade with Arabia and the Persian Gulf also resulted in remittances in silver, which had come from America via Europe to Western Asia. Similarly, Indian trade with East Asia resulted in such remittances. Some of this silver had come directly from America via the Pacific to China and South-East Asia. Japan had silver mines and some Japanese silver also entered the East Asian market, until the Japanese government declared a silver export embargo in 1668. On the other hand, some silver also travelled to the East from India, especially to China, whose absorptive capacity was as great as India's.

To this multiplicity of the flow of silver corresponded a great variety of export centres in the seventeenth century. Many ports on India's west and south-east coasts were involved in the export trade and there were numerous settlements of artisans engaged in production for this trade. This situation changed in the eighteenth century, when the British concentrated on Bengal, which had not played a major role in the textile trade in earlier times.

2.4 THE BRITISH IN BENGAL

In the seventeenth century, Dutch and British textile imports consisted mostly of colourful printed cotton piece-goods, for which Gujarat and the Coromandel coast were the best centres of production. The campaigns of British textile workers had finally resulted in an embargo on the import of printed cotton textiles. Only white cotton material, which could then be further processed at home, could be imported in the eighteenth century, and for this kind of material Bengal was an ideal centre of production, as the fine white cotton textiles of Bengal were well known. It seems that these fine textiles with fashionable printed patterns added in England were in great demand, because the textile trade with Bengal increased by leaps and bounds in the early decades of the eighteenth century. In the years before 1725, it amounted to an annual value of £200,000 sterling; about five years later it had doubled, while at the same time the British textile trade with the other provinces of India, which had surpassed the Bengal trade earlier, had dwindled to only one third of that with Bengal. This also implied that the stream of silver with which the British paid for these textiles was now mainly entering Bengal. This influx strengthened the position of the Nawab of Bengal, who was practically independent from Mughal rule by that time. He centralised the organisation of his government and abolished Mughal fiefs. The collection of revenue in cash increased. The method of auctioning the right of the collection of revenue to the highest bidder was introduced at that time by the Nawab of Bengal, long before the British adopted it too.

While the British had stuck to their coastal bridgeheads in most other parts of India, this increasing trade with Bengal took them farther and farther into the interior of the country. Factories were opened in places as far as Patna. Contracts were first made with leading weavers, but then agents of the company bypassed such middlemen and got in touch with the individual weavers. With this greater involvement in inland trade and production, the British acquired a much more intimate knowledge of internal conditions in India and they were also enticed to intervene in Indian affairs. The increasing British demand did make a difference to textile production in Bengal; many weavers worked exclusively for the export trade and thus became completely dependent on it. When the industrial revolution reversed the flow of goods later on and the British stopped buying Indian textiles and started selling their products, the weavers in other provinces could still produce for the Indian home market and withstand the pressure of industrial competition, whereas the weavers of Bengal lost their jobs and had to return to agriculture or starve. In 1740 nobody was able to foresee this cruel fate which was in store for the Bengali weavers. Employment expanded rapidly and the value of the textiles bought by the British reached about £500,000 sterling per year. Accordingly, British influence in Bengal increased day by day.

The Nawab watched this development with mixed feelings. These strangers brought silver into the country, and he welcomed that, but their company was like a state within his state and he had reasons to be alarmed. As long as the strong Nawab Alivardi Khan was alive, the balance of power was somehow maintained, but his weak successor, Siraj-ud Daulah, took offence at the British fortification of Calcutta and when they refused to remove it, he sacked the town. Robert Clive then relieved the town and pursued the Nawab, bribed his treacherous commander-in-chief and thus won the Battle of Plassey. The Nawab was killed and the traitor was made Nawab, for which he was beholden to Clive. The Great Mughal in Delhi, who had lost all control over Bengal long ago, thought that he could reassert his influence by coming to terms with Clive. He offered the Diwani of Bengal (revenue administration and civil jurisdiction) to the East India Company, leaving only the military command and penal jurisdiction to the Nawab. Clive was willing to accept this offer, but he felt that the crown rather than the company should take on this responsibility. When he made this suggestion to William Pitt, that astute statesman advised against it. New power and patronage would have accrued to the ambitious King George III in this way and he could have freed himself from the financial control of Parliament by drawing upon the revenues of Bengal. Therefore Pitt felt that these revenues should flow into private pockets rather than enrich the king. Thus the Great Mughal's offer was not accepted when it was first made, but when Clive returned as Governor of Bengal and the offer was repeated in 1765, he did accept it on behalf of the East India Company, which acted as a buffer between the declining Mughal empire and the rising bourgeois democracy of Great Britain. The revenues of Bengal flowed into private pockets instead of accruing to the crown: Pitt's astute advice had prevailed.

This new arrangement helped the company at a crucial time. The stream of silver from Europe had dried up and the revenues of Bengal could now be used to pay for tea in China. The silver that had been brought to India by the company was now extracted again. The British were not yet territorial rulers and they emphasised that they were collecting taxes and exercising their jurisdiction on behalf of the Great Mughal. They even minted coins in his name. Earlier, they had often faced great difficulties in getting access to the mint and had to pay handsome fees to the mint master and various brokers; now they controlled the mint themselves. Soon they also moved the Bengal treasury from Murshidabad, where the powerless Nawab resided, to Calcutta, where it was under direct British control. The plunder of Bengal was well organised. The revenues were used not only to finance the company's trade, but also to finance the further conquest of India.

2.5 THE EVOLUTION OF A PARASITICAL SYMBIOSIS

The East India Company as a modern capitalist corporation of an advanced bourgeois nation entrenched itself like a parasite in the agrarian state dominated by a decaying military feudal regime. The parasite adjusted to the system of its host and benefited from it without changing it very much. The company was well geared to function in this way. It had developed a modern bureaucracy in the course of its trading operations. This bureaucracy had all the characteristics of a modern civil service: a structured hierarchy and definite career patterns, free transferability, regular accounts and files regarding all administrative transactions, etc. Moreover, the company had a corporate memory. It could learn and correct mistakes; even a mediocre member of its service could contribute efficiently to this process — perhaps even more so than the brilliant exception to the general rule.

Nevertheless, the company was lucky enough also to attract brilliant men like Clive and Hastings, who served their distant masters well and did not become empire builders on their own account. These men came to India at a very young age. They learned quickly and were soon promoted to positions of great responsibility. Hastings' career is a good example. He arrived in India at the age of 18, serving as a writer in Calcutta; he was then put in charge of the factory at Cosimbazar, was imprisoned by the Nawab in 1756 and after being liberated became the British Resident at the court of the Nawab at Murshidabad when he was only 25 years old. Later on, he served for some time as member of the council of the Governor of Madras and at the age of 39 he was appointed as Governor of Bengal. Three years later he became the first Governor General. Civil servants of this stature rose from the ranks of young merchants to the position of statesmen without transgressing the framework set by their society and its political system. Indian military feudalism also produced brilliant men, such as Murshid Quli Khan, a brahmin converted to Islam who rose in the service of the Great Mughal because of his administrative abilities and who finally became Nawab of Bengal, asserting a de facto independence from his master. However, the meteoric rise of a man like Murshid did not contribute to the strength of the Mughal empire, whereas men like Clive and Hastings increased the power of the company, which made the transition from a company of traders to a territorial government rather swiftly. There were, of course, individual cases of rampant corruption and maladministration, but by and large the company's bourgeois discipline prevailed and did not give way to the chaos of unbridled individual avarice.

The company soon managed to collect much more revenue than its military feudal predecessors had ever done, and even in military affairs it proved to be superior to them. This was not due to any technological superiority: all the weapons the company used were well known to Indian rulers, who had often more of them at their disposal than the company had. Better organisation and discipline were the only secrets of the company's success. Most Indian generals did not know how to coordinate cavalry, artillery and infantry on the battlefield. The daring cavalry dashed ahead, the artillery was left behind and often fired only some desultory shots in order to show its presence, which was more a matter of prestige than of strategic function. The straggling infantry, ill-trained and ill-equipped, was often more of a nuisance than of use in the decisive battle. Moreover, Indian rulers and generals were not good at financing wars: they might win a battle, but then proved to be unable to pay their troops. The parsimonious directors of the East India Company in London would not spend much on military ventures and therefore their servants in India were bound to calculate very carefully; they did not invest much in cavalry and artillery, but rather relied on a well-trained infantry, which was regularly paid and drilled and could mow down the Indian cavalry by shooting with machine-like precision. The military feudal man on horseback was a valiant fighter, but he was an individualist at heart who looked for his counterpart on the other side with whom he could engage in a duel worthy of a warrior. He was usually generous and improvident and left the accounts to his scribes. Thus he was at a loss when he had to face a company of scribes who knew much better how to make both ends meet. The methods of the counting house and the tough discipline of the drill sergeant thus proved superior to Indian valour. The man on horseback who literally looked down upon scribes and humble foot soldiers would never understand the secret of the company's success.

After having overcome the defensive mechanisms of its host, the parasitical company could go about its business without encountering major difficulties. If the industrial revolution had not followed the establishment of British territorial rule in India within a fairly short time, the company would probably have organised commodity production in India on a large scale. This did not happen, however, and India became a dependent agrarian state. The sequence in time would tend to suggest that the plunder of this agrarian state directly contributed to the industrial revolution in England. The capital amassed in Bengal — so it seems — was invested in industries at home. In fact this direct connection did not exist. Industrial enterprises in England were initially of small dimensions and did not need much capital. They were mills in the literal sense of the term, mechanical looms and tools driven by water power. The industrial entrepreneurs did, of course, depend on a growing demand and a well-financed trading network, which guaranteed a rapid turnover of the goods they produced. This well-financed trading network and the expanding British home market did indeed benefit from the influx of Indian wealth. Pitt's wise suggestion that the revenues of Bengal should be turned into private capital rather than into crown capital, which would have been wasted on patronage and luxury consumption, proved to be the right one in this respect. This merchant capital also contributed to the stability of a political system in which Parliament had emerged as the guarantor of public finance. In India, however, the company did nothing to stimulate the economy and simply collected tribute as its military feudal predecessors had done, but whereas these predecessors had spent that tribute in India, the company transferred most of it abroad.

3

The Agrarian State and the Company: Parasitism and Paralysis

3.1 EXPLOITATION, DEFLATION AND THE LACK OF BUYING POWER

Territorial rule by a trading company, and the introduction of British law and of a modern bureaucracy, could have ushered in a rapid commercialisation, a development of India's home market and general economic growth. The rise of Indian merchants in the eighteenth century, when Mughal power was declining, could have added to this type of development. There was a 'commercialisation of power' in the eighteenth century, when traders often emerged as important creditors and bidders for the right to collect taxes in many small Indian states. The East India Company was also involved in this game in a big way. But in spite of all this 'commercialisation of power', traders and rulers remained tied to the sluggish rhythm of the economy of agrarian states subjected to the vagaries of the monsoon and the slow seasonal circulation of the currency. The East India Company did not try to introduce any major changes in the Indian economy. For a long time it even retained the duties on internal trade and the taxes on artisans, etc., which impeded the production and circulation of commodities. The company also copied the land revenue system of its respective predecessors and, in spite of all kinds of *obiter dicta* in the files of British administrators, they did exactly what these predecessors used to do, only they were more exacting in collecting whatever was assessed. The province of Orissa may serve as an example to illustrate this point. It yielded 400,000 rupees of land revenue per annum after having been conquered by the Marathas, who were known for their eagerness to extract as much revenue as possible; after the company took over this province (1804–15), however, it managed to collect

750,000 rupees annually.

The famous Permanent Settlement of Bengal, which was fixed once and for all in 1793, was not at all generous by the standards of the time. It was based on the rule that the zamindar, who used to be only a tax collector and who now became a landlord in the British sense of the term, would keep only 10 per cent of what he collected from the peasants, who were now called tenants and who paid rent rather than revenue to the landlord. Much has been written about the philosophy behind the Permanent Settlement, but little attention has been paid to the actual conditions prevailing at the time it was introduced. The population of Bengal had been decimated by the severe famine of 1770. There was a scarcity of tillers of the soil and the zamindars complained about 'absconding peasants' whenever they had to meet the British revenue demand. Warfare in Southern India had to be financed by the company and therefore it was in dire need of a predictable revenue income. The Permanent Settlement was the best solution of the immediate problem. The zamindar now had the exclusive responsibility for meeting the revenue demand and his estate would be auctioned if he did not pay up in time. Complaints about 'absconding peasants' became irrelevant, as the authorities were no longer concerned with the contractual relations between 'landlord' and 'tenant'; the landlord could turn to the civil courts for that. But they did treat the revenue demand that the landlord had to meet as a contractual obligation and subjected him to the fuller rigour of British law, which protects the creditor and sees to it that contracts are strictly observed. The revenue settlement, however, was not subject to the scrutiny of civil courts and the zamindar could not hope to delay a forced sale by appealing to a court. He had to accept the terms of the contract imposed upon him or quit.

By injecting the dynamics of British contractual law into the Indian land revenue system, the new rulers toned up that system in a big way. This also applied to the regions of India to which the Permanent Settlement was not extended and where the peasants were assessed directly. These revenue-paying peasants were defined as government tenants whose land was also subject to forced sale when they did not meet their contractual obligation of paying the revenue punctually. In keeping with the philosophy of the freedom of contract, the peasant was free to relinquish the land, if he felt that the revenue demand was too high, but as he had nowhere else to go this option was not open to him. If he did forfeit his land, he usually stayed on to till it for somebody else.

Earlier regimes had always regarded land revenue as a tax that varied in accordance with good or bad harvests. By turning this tax into a contractual rent to be paid to the government regardless of such vagaries and enforcing this demand with the rigour of British law, the company had created the necessary conditions for its symbiosis with the agrarian state. Much of the silver pumped into India earlier was now extracted again and transferred abroad. This caused a severe deflation in India, where money was now scarce and prices remained depressed throughout the first half of the nineteenth century. This also set a limit to the upward revision of the revenue demand in the provinces to which the Permanent Settlement had not been extended. Wherever the revenue assessment was enhanced, this meant a further reduction in the buying power of the peasantry. This in turn limited the demand for imported goods, and British industry therefore found less of a market in India than it might have hoped for. Indigenous weavers, who could produce cheap textiles because their food and the raw material they required was cheap in this period of depressed prices, could withstand British competition. Only Bengal, where most weavers had produced for the export market, was severely affected and the bones of Bengali weavers did indeed bleach in the plains of India, as Lord Bentinck remarked. Nevertheless, those weavers who survived in other provinces did so only under miserable conditions. It has sometimes been stated that imported British industrial yarn enabled the Indian weavers to stay in business quite comfortably. This imported yarn was only of marginal significance, however; in most parts of the interior of India indigenous yard was still predominant. Moreover, textiles made of Indian yarn were more durable when subjected to the drastic treatment meted out to all textiles by India's vigorous washermen.

Under such conditions of exploitation, deflation, depressed prices and reduced buying power, the parasitical company could live on its paralysed host for some time, but there were no prospects of economic growth. There was a considerable time-lag in the regional penetration of India, but by 1840 most provinces had been subjected to British rule and the revenue administration had covered every nook and corner of the vast land. The fact that the British moved in as heirs to regimes that had put up a fierce and costly resistance to them meant that they also inherited a revenue demand that was pitched very high. Tipu Sultan in Southern India, the Marathas on the Deccan and the Sikhs in the Punjab had all geared up their revenue machinery in order to find the means for fighting the British. Although their resistance proved to be futile in the end, they

21

did pave the way for the exploitation of the respective regions by the company.

3.2 FOREIGN TRADE UNDER COMPANY RULE

Internal economic conditions were bad under company rule, and there was also not much scope for 'export-led growth', although the company was interested in promoting exports in order to facilitiate the remittance of tribute from India to Great Britain. In 1813 the trade monopoly of the company had been abolished by Parliament and in 1833 its trading activities had been terminated altogether, but nevertheless it had to find ways and means to make remittances to London in order to pay a dividend to its shareholders.

An important subsidiary role was played by the agency houses, which had grown up in Calcutta in this period. Initially they had served the purpose of supplying imported provisions to the servants of the company; they had then diversified their operations and had acted as bankers and as contractors in the export trade. After 1813, they became more active as the monopoly of the company had been abolished; they entered the field of indigo processing and marketing and advanced money to the cultivators so as to tie them to specific performance and fixed prices. From 1814 to 1821, the export of indigo increased and the agency houses were drawn more and more into this business. They had little capital, however, and much of it was sunk in processing plants, which could not be readily sold, if the market collapsed. The market did in fact collapse very suddenly, when indigo prices were halved in the period from 1825 to 1831. Most agency houses were bankrupt by 1831. They had tried in vain to shift the risk to the Indian cultivators and had instigated the Governor General to promulgate an ordinance which obliged these cultivators to produce indigo at such low prices that they would suffer a loss. This was done by defining their position in analogy to that of the British wage labourer of the time, who could be imprisoned, if he failed to fulfil his contractual obligations. However, even this highly unjust and oppressive measure could not save the agency houses from their fate, which they had conjured up by speculative overtrading and an excessive reliance on an under-capitalised credit structure.

A new chance for venturesome enterpreneurs was provided in 1833, when the company had to stop all its commercial activities and had to sell its indigo establishments, silk processing plants, etc.

Figure 3.1: Foreign trade of British India, 1814–54

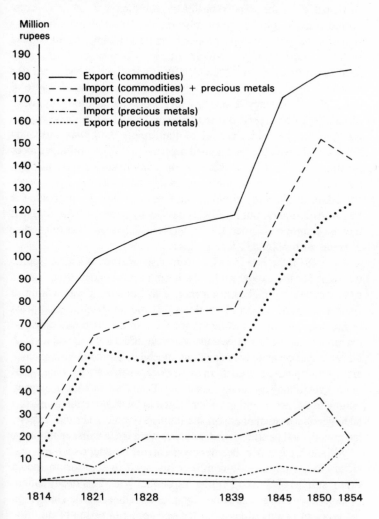

Source of data: K.N. Chaudhuri, *The Economic Development of India, 1814–1858* (Cambridge, 1971), p. 25.

At this stage a remarkable Bengali businessman, Dwarkanath Tagore, the grandfather of poet Rabindranath Tagore, founded a new style of agency house with a British partner (Carr, Tagore & Co.) and acquired many of the plants and equipment of the East

India Company. He also organised a local steamship company and participated in the export business. He then got other Calcutta businessmen to join him in establishing the Union Bank, which was supposed to give credit on proper banking principles to all comers without indulging in speculative ventures. There was indeed a great need for such a bank in Calcutta. The agency houses had acted like banks for their own specific ventures and had collapsed because of this. The Presidency Banks of the East India Company were something like government treasuries and could not act as commercial banks. The initial capital of the Union Bank was raised by Dwarkanath, who pledged landed property worth one million rupees for this purpose. Being involved in the bank in such a way, he often treated it as his house bank, although this was not appropriate according to the original plan. The Union Bank did not escape the fate of bankruptcy, but it did survive Dwarkanath by two years and thus he cannot be blamed for its demise, which was due to another crisis in British India's foreign trade.

After 1833, the East India Company also emerged as a major source of credit for the export trade. As it could not conduct trade on its own account, but had to remit money to London, it was willing to finance even the export of products that did not fetch a good price in London, as long as this facilitated the remittance transactions. At the same time, the Indian peasants were subjected to increased revenue demands and became more and more indebted. The combined revenue and credit squeeze forced them to produce whatever they were asked to do, even if they had to do so at a loss. With the East India Company willing to finance anything which helped to facilitate remittances, this added up to a system of export-led immiserisation rather than export-led growth, and parasitism and paralysis were made worse in this way.

Although the export business was carried on under such inauspicious circumstances, the company managed to sponsor an Indian export surplus of about 40 million rupees per year. This steady pattern of exploitation was maintained in spite of rather drastic changes in the types of commodities exported and in the direction of the flow of the precious metals. Initially, the export of indigo to Europe was the main item; this was then replaced by the export of opium and raw cotton to China. In this way the indigo crisis of the 1830s did not lead to a crisis as far as the transfer of remittances was concerned. A detailed analysis of India's trade with Great Britain and China in the years 1829–38, which constituted 80 per cent of India's total foreign trade, shows this very clearly (Table 3.1). The export of goods to Great Britain was nearly halved from 1829 to 1831 and had to be

Table 3.1: British-India's trade with Great Britain and China, 1829–38 (million rupees)

(a) Great Britain

Year	Export to GB	Import from GB	Net export of precious metals to GB	Balance (1)
1829	60	30	8	+ 38
1830	46	34	5	+ 15
1831	35	30	17	+ 22
1832	43	29	12	+ 24
1833	39	26	5	+ 18
1834	42	28	1	+ 15
1835	52	31	—	+ 21
1836	62	38	—	+ 24
1837	47	32	1	+ 16
1838	51	35	—	+ 16
Total 10 years	477	313	50	+209

(b) China

Year	Export to China	Import from China	Net export of precious metals from China	Balance (2)	Balance (1 + 2)
1829	30	8	14	+ 8	+ 46
1830	29	8	10	+ 11	+ 26
1831	40	5	6	+ 29	+ 51
1832	34	5	6	+ 23	+ 47
1833	47	5	13	+ 29	+ 47
1834	37	6	12	+ 19	+ 34
1835	56	5	14	+ 37	+ 58
1836	67	5	12	+ 50	+ 74
1837	45	4	17	+ 24	+ 40
1838	45	5	21	+ 19	+ 35
Total 10 years	430	56	125	+249	+458

Source: K.N. Chaudhuri, cf. Bibliography, Section 3.2.

supplemented by the export of precious metals, which increased considerably. At the same time, the import of silver from China decreased, but the export of goods to China was stepped up so that India attained a very favourable balance of trade. Exports to China increased rapidly in subsequent years, while imports of Chinese goods were kept at a low level, although imports of precious metals from China were augmented. By the end of the ten years under consideration, India had exported a total amount of 50 million rupees in precious metals to Great Britain and imported precious metals worth 125 million rupees from China. However, if we look at the export and import of commodities, we notice that

25

India had exported goods worth 900 million rupees to the two countries and had imported goods worth only 370 million rupees from them. If we add the surplus of 75 million rupees in precious metals, we get a total amount of 445 million rupees; thus 455 million rupees of export surplus were available for the transfer of remittances.

Opium played a major role in this change of pattern of the export trade. Just like indigo, opium was produced in the family farms of peasants, who received advances and were under the strict supervision of the opium agents of the company. The trade with opium in India was a government monopoly and the company tried to prevent smuggling as far as possible. The opium was then sold to private exporters in Calcutta at a price fixed by the company. In China the import of opium was illegal and therefore the company left this part of the trade gladly to private traders. In order to keep the price at a high level, the company exercised strict controls and even destroyed surplus opium. The peasants who produced opium did not get much more out of this than those who produced indigo.

Raw cotton, which was also exported to China, was a comparatively 'free product'. Nevertheless, the revenue and credit squeeze also played a role in the marketing of cotton. In contrast with the trade in indigo and opium, which was in British hands, the cotton trade was for the most part in Indian hands and was concentrated in Bombay, not in Calcutta. Bombay was also the export centre for opium smuggled from the Malwa highlands. The centres of production of this smuggled opium were mostly located in princely states and were therefore not controlled by the company's opium agents. The Parsis, who later on emerged as the pioneers of industrial capitalism in India, accumulated a great deal of their capital in the cotton and opium trade in Bombay.

Opium played its leading role only until 1834; at that time indigo emerged once more as the main export commodity and thus contributed to the rise of Bengali merchants, who now did the business earlier done by the agency houses. By 1839 indigo was far ahead, whereas opium had suffered a severe setback (the Opium War occurred in 1840–2). Subsequently there was another dramatic change: opium exports increased once more and indigo declined, amounting only to 10 per cent of the value of Indian exports in 1850, whereas opium made up 35 per cent. Opium maintained this lead for quite some time and indigo receded even further. Raw cotton, however, maintained a steady intermediate position, making up between 15 and 20 per cent of the total value of exports (see Figure 3.2).

Figure 3.2: Composition of British India's exports, 1828–57

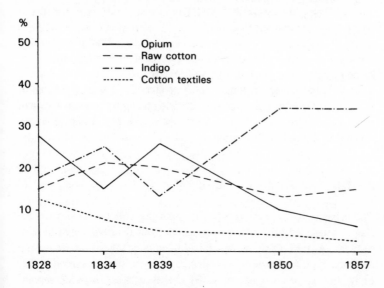

Source of data: K.N. Chaudhuri, *The Economic Development of India, 1814–1858* (Cambridge, 1971), p. 26.

The steady pattern of the raw cotton trade was very important for the rise of Bombay, whereas the violent fluctuations of the Calcutta export market ruined a large number of firms there. The first victims were the British agency houses, but the Indian firms that prospered in the 1830s soon faced the same problems and collapsed. Wise men withdrew from this business and invested their money in landed estates, where they could look forward to a steady rental income. In Bombay such a withdrawal was neither necessary nor possible, because the Permanent Settlement had not been extended to the Bombay Presidency. In Bengal, however, investment in landed estates became more and more attractive in the course of the nineteenth century. The effects of the famine of 1770 had long since been forgotten, the population had increased once more and with it increased the demand for agricultural land. The prices of landed estates rose steadily and therefore this type of investment was safe and predictably profitable. The great zamindars built city palaces in Calcutta and left the administration of their estates to agents or country cousins. They rarely invested anything in the improvement of agriculture, nor did they play the role of the dual landlord who channels agricultural income into industry. Dwarkanath Tagore, who pledged his estate to found the Union Bank, was the great exception. The collapse of this bank and the decline of the Tagore family's fortune was certainly not an encouraging example for other potential investors. Rabindranath Tagore later on remembered with some nostalgia the glorious times of Dwarkanath. In Rabindranath's days Calcutta could no longer have produced a Dwarkanath, as it was dominated by the powerful British managing agencies which gave no chance to Indian entrepreneurs except perhaps that of serving as humble subcontractors.

3.3 THE PRICE RISE IN THE 1850s

The crisis of 1847, which brought about the collapse of the Union Bank, coincided with a crisis in Europe, but it lasted much longer in India. Agrarian prices, which had been very low in earlier years, declined even further until a sudden change reversed this trend in the early 1850s. Several unconnected events ushered in a period of rising prices. The British attack on Upper Burma in 1852 created a demand for rice in many districts of Eastern India, where rice prices rose accordingly. In 1853, railway construction was started in India in a big way. British capital flowed to India, and many Indian labourers were employed in building the tracks. From 1853 to 1856 altogether about £5 million sterling in silver was remitted to India for this purpose. In 1854, the Crimean War cut off Europe's supply of Russian hemp and Indian jute emerged as a substitute, which was suddenly in great demand. Finally, in 1857, the Mutiny completely upset the pattern of exploitation of India by the East India Company. Communications were disrupted, some regions were cut off and thus prices rose in others. The re-conquest of Northern India required a great deal of military expenditure. The company could not remit money to London, but had to spend it in India and although it was victorious in the end, its coffers were empty and its system of extracting surplus from India had collapsed.

The price rise that had been effected by the cumulation of these various events had a number of different consequences. The peasants who experienced a doubling of prices within a few years could increase their income considerably, as the revenue demand could not be adjusted to the new price level within such a short period of time. Indian traders also prospered. But the weavers and other artisans who had been able to compete with imported industrial products as long as low prices for food and raw materials had enabled them to produce their goods cheaply could no longer make both ends meet. The import of industrial goods increased and industrial import substitution also became feasible in India. The establishment of the first Indian cotton textile mill in Bombay in 1855 has to be seen in this context. India was at the threshold of a new age. The parasitical East India Company had lost its mandate. Queen Victoria, when proclaiming her direct rule over India in 1858, pronounced words that gave great hopes to her Indian subjects. Finally, however, parasitism prevailed in spite of such proclamations. The extraction of surplus from India could be organised even more profitably in a period of steadily rising Indian prices than in the earlier period of deflation and depression, which was characterised by a much more primitive mode of exploitation.

India's economic development from 1858 to 1914 will be described in Chapters 4 and 5; the first of these chapters will be devoted to the evolution of the Indian home market under the tutelage of the world market, and the second will deal with the special problem of India's retarded industrialisation. The analysis of this specific problem requires a prior understanding of the general forces at work in the Indian market, to which we shall turn our attention in the following chapter.

4

The Evolution of an Indian Market
in the Nineteenth Century

4.1 THE POLITICAL UNIFICATION OF INDIA

In the course of the early decades of the nineteenth century the
British had conquered almost all of the economically more attractive
regions of India. Some princely states remained like insects enclosed
in amber. They controlled territories that were in general much less
attractive for the British as revenue collectors. Indirect rule was less
costly and more appropriate in such cases.

The provinces of British India that had initially different traditions due to the regimes that preceded British rule evolved in due
course a rather unified pattern of administration and jurisdiction.
English became the universal medium of communication. British
courts proliferated; the officials collected court fees that did not only
pay for the judicial establishment, but yielded a handsome revenue
to the government. Law commissions had unified the law of the land
and in this respect British India was ahead of Great Britain, where
old legal traditions could not be streamlined to such an extent. The
currency system had also been unified under British control, and
from 1835 the silver rupee was the only legal tender. Everybody
could take silver to the mints and get coins, just like under Mughal
rule. But whereas this access was free only in theory and less so in
practice under Mughal rule, when mint masters and brokers often
acted in collusion so as to extract some illegal gains from those who
were in a hurry to get coins, this access was less cumbersome under
British rule.

What the British failed to give to India was an adequate modern
banking system. The Presidency Banks established by the East India
Company in Bombay, Calcutta and Madras were very much
restricted in their banking business, as they were only supposed to

serve as reliable keepers of the government's money. Branches of the major British exchange banks were established in the big ports to facilitate exchange transactions. Their banking business was usually restricted to the short-term financing of maritime trade. Indian banks established along the lines of British commercial banks often proved to be unreliable and collapsed, as they were frequently used for financing speculative ventures of their major constituents, who had little respect for the principles of sound banking. Nevertheless, at least some progress was made in the direction of institutionalised banking under a new legal system, whereas earlier only personal trust in individual bankers had been the mainstay of the Indian credit network. However, this did not yet liberate India from the fetters of the sluggish circulation of the silver currency. Under such conditions, money supply always proved to be a bottleneck and liquidity had to be the major concern of every businessman. Many years later, Keynes castigated the Indians for their inordinate love of liquidity, which according to him was a major obstacle to economic development in India. Although he analysed the seasonal circulation of the Indian currency and was aware of its inherent problems, he did not explain the quest for liquidity in terms of the whole economic and fiscal system, but attributed it to an emotional craving. Similarly, most British commentators who expressed their opinions about peasant indebtedness in India would refer to individual improvidence, rather than to the compulsion of the system under which the peasants had to work.

The political unification of India under British rule also enhanced inter-regional communication. The restrictions of trade caused by internal customs, etc. were removed. But before railway construction was started nothing much had been done about the improvement of infrastructure; therefore the cost of transportation had remained high and market integration had not progressed. River transport was the only exception and Calcutta's dominant position was mainly due to its connection with the Ganges as a major trade route. Other parts of the interior remained isolated as long as the railways did not reach them. Prices fluctuated according to the vagaries of the seasons in many small regional markets, which were unconnected with each other. This, of course, also benefited some local producers and especially the artisans who produced for the local market. As the extension of railways in Great Britain had just reached its zenith when the political unification of India was completed, there was a strong motive for transferring this type of development to India. It so happened that Lord Dalhousie, who had played a major role in organising the expansion of the railway network in Great Britain, came to India as Governor General and pursued a vigorous policy of annexation in order to complete India's political unification. He drafted an important minute in which he outlined an ambitious plan for an Indian railway network. This plan was certainly ahead of its time as far as India's stage of economic development was concerned, but it neatly coincided with developments at home in Great Britain. In the 1840s, annual British investment in railways at home had amounted to about £15 million sterling; this rate of investment had decreased considerably in the 1850s, as the British railway network had almost reached its limits. However, the British public was by now used to investing capital in railways and together with America it was India which became the major target of British capital export for railway construction.

4.2 THE RAPID EXTENSION OF INDIA'S RAILWAY NETWORK

When Lord Dalhousie wrote his minute in 1853 proposing the construction of 5,000 miles of railway track in India, the first Indian track connecting Bombay with Thane had just been completed. The first contracts with the East Indian Railway Company (EIR) and the Great Indian Peninsular Railway Company (GIPR) had been signed in 1849. The EIR was supposed to penetrate the interior starting from Calcutta and the GIPR from Bombay. Thus Dalhousie was not the first person to plan a railway network for India, but his contribution was the magnitude of his design and the idea of attracting the investment required for it by providing a government guarantee of a fixed return on the capital so invested. The Secretary of State, Charles Wood, who sanctioned Dalhousie's plan, even thought at the time about the prospects of procuring Indian cotton as a substitute for American cotton, as if he had had a premonition of the American Civil War, which did cut off the American cotton supply a few years later. In 1860 the railway reached Solapur on the Deccan, in the heart of a major cotton tract that did emerge as a source of alternative supply of this important raw material at the time of the Civil War. Dalhousie and Wood were proved to be right in what would have seemed to be pipedreams in 1853.

Indian railway construction would probably have attracted British capital even without the government guarantee of 5 per cent. Without this guarantee, however, the railway companies concerned would obviously have calculated much more carefully and would have built only such routes that promised an immediate return. With the generous guarantee, they had a motive to extend the network as rapidly as possible without regard for the profitability of the respective lines. The interest rate in Great Britain was about 3 per cent at that time and therefore a minimum of 5 per cent was a very attractive proposition. The Indian taxpayer had to foot the bill for this debt service and he was not asked what he thought about it. By 1869, a total of 4,225 miles of railway track had been completed, and an amount of 890 million rupees had been invested in this network, for which 44 million rupees' interest had to be paid annually. This amounted to about 10,000 rupees of annual debt service for each mile of railway track. Until 1900 the Indian railways were always in the red and Indian nationalists bitterly criticised the British Indian government for squandering money on the railways, whereas a similar amount spent on irrigation would have benefited Indian agriculture and enhanced its productivity. The British did not heed this criticism: they did not spend much on irrigation and went ahead with railway construction at such a rapid pace that there were about 25,000 miles of railway tracks by 1900, an impressive achievement indeed, but a very costly one too.

The expansion of the Indian railways created an enormous demand for steel (rails, bridges, etc.), engines and wagons and even English coal. As all this was imported from Great Britain, there were no linkage effects in India. Much of this could have been produced in India. The first Indian railway engine was built in Bombay in 1865 at a reasonable cost. But for the entire period from 1865 to 1941, only 700 engines were built in India, whereas British firms exported about 12,000 engines to India. The opening of the Suez Canal in 1869 reduced the distance between Great Britain and India considerably and freight rates were cut down so that engines and rails could be transported at a low cost. Until the beginning of the First World War, coal imported from England was cheaper in Bombay than Bengal coal in Calcutta, which was mostly consumed by the East Indian Railways. The rapid expansion of the railways therefore did not contribute to a 'take-off' of the Indian economy; railway construction did not become the 'leading sector' of the Indian economy. At the most there was some increase in local employment of construction labour. The capital transferred from Great Britain, of which a certain share was turned into wages of labour, did increase buying power and thus contributed to the rise of food prices. Furthermore, prices rose in all those areas that were

Table 4.1: Influence of the railway connection on rice prices

District/subdivision	Average price (seers per rupee)		Price fluctuation (standard deviation divided by mean value)	
	Before railway	After railway	Before railway	After railway
Dinajpur/Sadar	30.8	20.2	8.6	3.9
Mymensingh/Nasirabad	20.3	13.7	9.2	5.1

Source: M. Mukherjee, cf. Bibliography, Section 4.2.

reached by the railway. The fluctuation of prices after good or bad harvests was very much reduced, as external demand could make itself felt immediately.

A study of certain Bengal districts shows this development very clearly. Table 4.1 shows a comparison of rice prices before and after the railway reached Dinajpur and Mymensingh. (The railway reached Dinajpur at the end of the 1870s and Mymensingh in the 1880s.)

In both cases the prices rose by about 50 per cent, while their fluctuation was halved. The difference between the prices in the two districts before they were reached by the railway was due to the fact that Mymensingh was reached much later and that the prices were rising generally in this period.

In the period before 1885, prices showed great fluctuations everywhere whenever the harvest deviated from the average. After 1885, the grain prices rose steadily and fluctuations were greatly reduced. The depreciating silver currency, which will be discussed below, was also of great significance in this context. It is remarkable, though, that this reduction of fluctuations did occur at a time when the actual volume of grain shipments by railway was still rather moderate. The utilisation of the railway network did not expand nearly as fast as the network itself. By 1885 there were 10,000 miles of railway track, but only 12 million tons of freight were transported by the railways annually and only one-third of this total volume consisted of grain shipments for export abroad. For the reduction of price fluctuations, however, potential movements of grain were more important than actual ones. In places connected by railway one only needed to consult the table of freight rates in order to find out to what extent the local price could deviate from that elsewhere without creating an immediate demand for shipments. Moreover, the railway was accompanied by the telegraph as it penetrated the interior of India and thus commercial intelligence

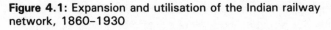

Figure 4.1: Expansion and utilisation of the Indian railway network, 1860–1930

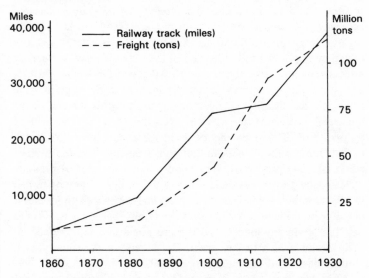

Source of data: V.B. Singh, ed., *The Economic History of India (Bombay, 1965)*, p. 336.

could be transmitted very fast. It is said that in Russia in those days one could find the Berlin grain prices posted even in small railway stations. India began to be linked to the world market in a similar way.

The freight rates of Indian railways had some peculiar features. They were still fairly high in 1885, but there were three different categories of rebates, which allowed for substantial reductions in the freight rate, particularly if one could claim rebates under all three categories:

(1) for shipments over long distances;
(2) for shipments to or from one of the big ports;
(3) for shipments that did not need to be transferred from one line to another (e.g. from East Indian Railways to Great Indian Peninsular Railways).

Long-distance grain shipments from Northern India to Calcutta or shipments of imported industrial goods from Calcutta to Northern

35

India could thus benefit from favourable rates, whereas short hauls in the interior would be much more expensive, as none of the three rebates would be applicable. The freight-rate structure therefore encouraged linkages with the world market and worked against regional integration within India. As long as freight rates were fairly high they impeded a full utilisation of the railway network, but they protected in this way the artisans of the interior from industrial competition and also prevented the depletion of stocks of grain in the country. This situation changed drastically towards the end of the nineteenth century. From 1880 to 1900 freight rates were reduced by one third. The shipments of grain for export increased in this period from 3 million to 10 million tons annually. The depletion of stocks of grain progressed very rapidly in this way. Most peasants were indebted to moneylenders-cum-grain-dealers. They often had to turn over their whole harvest to them and then ask them for credit in cash or in kind in order to feed their family. Such peasants could not store grain any longer, and if there was a famine, they had no savings with which to buy grain. By the end of the century such famines decimated the Indian population.

After the turn of the century the railway network was not extended for some time; freight rates, however, were slashed and the volume of freight doubled within a decade. In this way the railways managed to make a profit after a long period of deficits. Passenger traffic also increased. In 1871 the Indian railways had transported only 19 million passengers annually; in 1901 there were 183 million passengers. This new intensity of communication was not only important as far as economic development was concerned; it also hastened political development. The Indian National Congress, which was convened for the first time in Bombay in 1885, could not have met without the railways, which tranported delegates from all provinces. The growing Indian press also depended for its circulation on the railways. The British linked India with the world market by building this great railway network, but they also facilitiated the communication of the critics of their rule. In a similar way, the extension of the British legal network nurtured a large body of Indian lawyers from whose ranks arose the most ardent and effective critics of British rule. In his manifesto *Hind Swaraj*, Mahatma Gandhi decried both railways and lawyers, but being himself a lawyer by profession and a man who was destined to traverse India by train perhaps more often than any other national leader, he ought to have avoided this sweeping condemnation of his profession and his means of transportation.

4.3 THE GROWTH OF FOREIGN TRADE

There was a steady expansion of foreign trade in the second half of the nineteenth century. India had to have an export surplus in order to provide the means for the transfer of tribute and other remittances, as has been mentioned above. The stationing of British troops in India after the Mutiny, the debt service for the railways, and the expansion of the British Indian administration enhanced the amount to be transferred, which was termed 'Home Charges'. From £10 million sterling per year in 1870 these charges increased to £25 million per year by the end of the nineteenth century. In earlier times this transfer had been effected by means of silver remittances or by using the India-China-Great Britain triangle. In the late nineteenth century such means would have been insufficient. India absorbed enormous quantities of silver, as we shall see below, and the opium trade with China was still going on, but it no longer played such an important role as in earlier times. Instead, India exported more and more agricultural produce to Europe and imported industrial goods from there.

The British cotton textile industry had its major export market in India from 1870 to 1895. Therefore the representatives of that industry watched everything concerning that market with keen interest. In 1870 British textiles worth £80 million sterling were exported to India, but then there was a recession in 1879 and the value of these exports declined to £65 million. The British textile lobby then forced the government to remove the Indian cotton import duties, which had been imposed for purely fiscal reasons and not as a protective tariff. In spite of this success, the textile magnates still complained in 1882 about stagnating Indian demand. This lack of demand was only natural, as Indian buying power could not increase under a regime of constant exploitation. Compelled always to have an export surplus, India could not import too much. Moreover, a good deal of India's import capacity was taken up by the import of large quantities of silver. In the two decades from 1868 to 1887, India imported precious metals worth 1.8 billion rupees and commodities worth 8.2 billion rupees (see Table 4.2). The import of precious metals thus amounted to 18 per cent of India's total imports. This, of course, greatly benefited London's silver traders, because Indian demand helped to maintain the world silver price, which was under great pressure at that time. Textiles and silver were India's main imports, and all other imports were insignificant when compared to these two major items.

Table 4.2: Foreign trade of British India, 1868–87 (million rupees)

Year	Commodities		Net import of precious metals	Export surplus	Percentage surplus
	Export	Import			
1868	508	356	107	44	8.7
1869	530	359	135	35	6.6
1870	524	328	129	66	12.6
1871	553	333	38	181	32.7
1872	631	308	101	222	35.2
1873	552	304	32	214	38.8
1874	549	316	39	194	35.3
1875	563	346	65	151	26.8
1876	580	371	31	177	30.5
1877	609	353	74	181	29.7
1878	651	393	152	106	16.2
1879	608	365	31	211	34.7
1880	671	397	97	177	26.4
1881	745	503	75	166	22.3
1882	819	469	102	246	30.0
1883	834	500	124	210	25.2
1884	880	527	118	234	26.6
1885	832	531	119	180	21.6
1886	838	518	143	176	21.0
1887	884	586	93	203	22.9
Total 20 years	13,370	8,171	1,811	3,388	25.3

Source: K.N. Chaudhuri, cf. Bibliography, Section 4.3.

India's exports increased rapidly in the late nineteenth century and there was also a remarkable trend towards diversification. In addition to raw cotton there was now also raw jute, which emerged as a major export commodity. Tea, which had earlier only been grown in China, was now produced in the tea plantations of Assam and Northern Bengal. Burma, which belonged to British India at that time, exported a great deal of rice and North India exported more and more wheat. With the exception of tea, which was grown in plantations, all these other items were produced in small family farms. A comparison of the pattern of exports in 1871 and 1901 (see Table 4.3) shows that the five major cash crops changed ranks to a considerable extent. Opium, indigo and raw cotton, which had been of major importance in the first half of the nineteenth century, still made up 60 per cent of all exports in 1871, but in 1901 their share had dwindled to 20 per cent. Tea and jute, which constituted just 7 per cent in 1871, attained 19 per cent in 1901. Moreover, the total value of exports doubled in those 30 years, but the share of the five cash crops listed here in the total value of exports was reduced from 68 to 39 per cent.

A more detailed analysis of this shift in the pattern of exports is presented in Table 4.4. Decennial averages have been calculated for this purpose in order to exclude short-term fluctuations. Industrial products such as cotton and jute textiles attained more and more importance in this period, a fact which will be discussed below in the context of India's industrialisation. Grain exports also increased considerably. The seven items listed in Table 4.4 amounted throughout to about 60 per cent of the total value of exports.

The diversification of exports was greatly encouraged by the expansion of the railway network, which opened up regions for export production that had remained isolated before. However, the different provinces of British India did not participate in export production at the same rate. A comparison of the value of exports from the four major ports of British India (Table 4.5) shows that Eastern India exported much more than Western India, and thus contributed much more to India's export surplus. Calcutta, as the gateway of the north-east, had the lion's share of this export, and Calcutta's export surplus always amounted to one-third of the value of its exports. Madras had only a modest share, but its export surplus reached nearly one-half of the value of its exports. Bombay exported almost as much as Calcutta in the 1880s and the export surplus also amounted to about one-third of the value of its exports, but subsequently there was a drastic change and the export surplus was greatly reduced. In Karachi the contrast was even more striking, but this was due to the fact that a great deal of material for the northern railways was imported via Karachi, whereas only wheat was exported from there. If the export surplus is taken as an indicator for the degree of exploitation, it appears that Eastern India was much more exploited than Western India. In the early twentieth century this contrast became even more obvious. When discussing the pattern of India's industrialisation, we shall relate this to the fact that Bombay had an industry geared to production for the home market and contributing to import substitution, whereas Calcutta's industry was entirely dependent on the export market.

India's foreign trade was both a mechanism for the transfer of surpluses abroad and an engine for the development of India's home market. The surplus that was extracted from India was not the kind of surplus that originates as a spillover of a home market saturated with indigenous products, which thus permits a profitable participation in a worldwide division of labour. The forces of the world market penetrated India, extracted cheap raw materials and made a formative impact on the home market, which grew up under the

Table 4.3: The change in the composition of exports, 1871 and 1901 (million rupees)

Year	Raw cotton (%)	Raw jute (%)	Opium (%)	Tea (%)	Indigo (%)	Total five products	Total of exports (= 100%)
1871	191 (35)	20 (5)	117 (20)	11 (2)	32 (6)	371 (68)	524
1901	101 (9)	109 (10)	94 (9)	97 (9)	21 (2)	422 (39)	1077

Table 4.4: Major export commodities, 1870–1909 (million rupees)

Annual average for each decade	Raw cotton	Cotton textiles	Raw jute	Jute products	Opium	Rice	Tea
1870–9	137	18	34	5	122	60	22
1880–9	144	54	56	16	112	87	44
1890–9	119	94	87	44	83	129	75
1990–9	201	123	154	124	93	176	94

Source: K.N. Chaudhuri, cf. Bibliography, Section 4.3.

Table 4.5: Regional origin of British India's exports, 1871–1911 (million rupees)

Year	Calcutta (1)		Madras (2)		Export surplus total (1 + 2)	Bombay (3)		Karachi (4)		Export surplus total (3 + 4)
1871	241	(73)	67	(31)	(104)	221	(101)	11	(6)	(107)
1876	302	(110)	76	(39)	(149)	225	(71)	13	(3)	(74)
1881	340	(119)	83	(36)	(155)	320	(109)	33	(13)	(122)
1886	375	(119)	103	(43)	(162)	370	(95)	38	(−3)	(92)
1891	432	(156)	116	(53)	(209)	384	(103)	62	(1)	(104)
1896	484	(167)	116	(54)	(201)	326	(−21)	54	(2)	(−18)
1901	589	(214)	141	(60)	(274)	438	(106)	119	(33)	(139)
1906	771	(273)	190	(85)	(358)	510	(82)	173	(37)	(119)
1911	924	(303)	240	(84)	(387)	580	(58)	240	(83)	(141)

Export surplus is given in parentheses.
Source: A.K. Bagchi, cf. Bibliography, Section 4.3.

tutelage of the world market. The progress of monetisation and the operation of the revenue and credit systems facilitated this extraction. The influx of a stream of silver was required for this monetisation, and the sluggishness of the circulation of the currency always produced a scarcity of money which, in turn, enhanced the pressure of the revenue demand and the compulsions of indebtedness, which caused the peasant to produce for the market. This system had prevailed even in earlier times, but the first half of the nineteenth century was a period of deflation and depression, which imposed restrictions on the parasite and its host. In the second half of the century the parasite injected a stream of silver into the host, stimulated its activity and could benefit from it much more. There was no long-term planning in this process. The metaphor of the parasite and its host is meant to highlight the kind of interaction between them. The parasite always adjusted to new conditions and used them to its advantage. The influx of silver provided a new dimension to the parasitical symbiosis which had been established at an earlier time. The linkages between the home market and the world market were strengthened by this medium of circulation in a way that was not to India's advantage.

4.4 THE SILVER CURRENCY AND WORLD MARKET INTEGRATION

Silver had always played a decisive role in India's economic development as well as in India's relations with Western nations. The Great Mughals had welcomed the flow of silver from the West and their empire was thriving for some time on the land revenue collected in silver rupees. The British had extracted silver from India in order to pay for tea in China, from where the silver then returned once more to India in the early nineteenth century. However, these silver imports were hardly sufficient to solve the problem of endemic deflation in India at that time. A new epoch had started with the British investment in Indian railways, when silver once more flowed from the West to the East. Subsequently the great increase in the production of the American silver mines had given rise to a veritable torrent of silver. Soon the old silver/gold ratio of 15 : 1, which had prevailed for a very long time, was upset and many European countries that had been on a silver standard demonetised silver and adopted a gold standard. Thus even more silver was available for shipment to the East, where the British Indian mints remained open to all those who wanted to convert silver into rupees.

The British welcomed this flow of silver for two reasons: India's almost unlimited capacity for the absorption of silver helped to support the silver price in the world market, and the increase in the circulation of silver coins facilitated the collection of land revenue. The rapid depreciation of the rupee (in 1874 R1 = 22d; 1894 R1 = 13d) was initially accepted with equanimity. It amounted to an export bonus for India's raw produce and it shielded the Indian home market against the fall in the (gold) prices of agricultural produce in the world market, which occurred in the late nineteenth century. British civil servants in India who complained about the devaluation of their salaries could be pacified by being granted an exchange allowance. The only bottleneck was the payment of the Home Charges, which were fixed in gold, whereas the Indian revenues were collected in silver. Soon the British Indian government could not make both ends meet any longer. The land revenue could not be enhanced to keep pace with the depreciation of silver. Customs duties could have been raised immediately and Indian nationalists would have welcomed the protective effect of such a measure, but the doctrine of free trade as well as powerful vested interests in Great Britain were opposed to it. This gave rise to a new type of parasitical paralysis. Whereas in the early nineteenth century deflationary stagnation was the main cause of such a paralysis, this new type of paralysis was due to the fact that the British Indian government was not permitted to adopt the fiscal measures that would have been required to master the transfer crisis under inflationary conditions. The income of the British Indian government from customs duties declined from 25 million rupees in 1873 to 16 million rupees in 1893, while the income from land revenue could only be enhanced from 200 million to 250 million rupees in the same period. The Home Charges, however, increased from £13.5 million to £15.8 million sterling in those two decades. The first amount corresponded to 147 million rupees in terms of the exchange rate prevailing at that time (R1 = 1s 10d), whereas the second amount corresponded to 270 million rupees (the exchange rate then was R1 = 1s 2d). This was more than the total income from land revenue and customs duties. The bankruptcy of the British Indian government was imminent.

In 1893 the Indian mints were closed to the public; from then on rupees could only be coined at the behest of the Secretary of State for India. The token value of these coins no longer corresponded to their intrinsic value. In order to prevent a further automatic devaluation of this currency, the Secretary of State had to follow a deflationary policy. From 1876, when silver had begun to depreciate, until 1893, when the mints were closed, the silver currency circulating in India had increased from 1.2 billion to 1.8 billion rupees. The rate of growth of the circulation of money had been twice as high as the rate of population growth. This had greatly contributed to the monetisation of the economy. Furthermore, India had set the world silver price as well as the world wheat price, the one by absorbing silver, the other by exporting wheat at the cheapest rate. The liberal economists had never conceived of this strange kind of equilibrium: they had always taught that the flow of the precious metals would raise the wage level in the recipient country to a point where a reverse flow would set in, thus maintaining a perfect equilibrium. In Asia the influx of silver did not lead to this kind of development, and whatever else the flow of silver may have done, it only benefited Europe and America.

4.5 THE EMERGENCE OF AN INDIAN HOME MARKET

The railways, the stream of silver and foreign trade all contributed to the emergence of an Indian home market under the tutelage of the world market. There had been an export boom in the early nineteenth century, as we have seen, but it collapsed in the 1830s. Moreover, there was a lack of infrastructure and of capital at that time and no major changes could take place. In the 1860s, however, a new phase of development was ushered in and new actors appeared on the scene. In the first half of the nineteenth century the Bengali merchants, together with the British merchants of Calcutta, had organised the trade in the Gangetic basin. Most of them had lost their money and had faded away. Now a new group came from the northwest and penetrated the Gangetic basin: the Marwaris. Some of them settled in Calcutta and managed to find a niche in the new economic order. As moneylenders and grain-dealers, they got used to making full use of the British law, which protected the creditor against the debtor. The major lines of trade were now controlled by the British merchants of Calcutta and London, and by the British exchange banks, shipping agents, etc. The Marwaris were satisfied to act as subcontractors. They worked mostly in the Indian home market and avoided the export business, which was risky and tightly controlled by the British. Indian businessmen could not hope to rise in this world of intercontinental connections. In Calcutta, everybody must have been very well aware of this. In Bombay, which experienced a sudden spurt of growth due to the railways and the cotton boom at the time of the American Civil War, there was a speculative euphoria which for a short time even encouraged small merchants to try their luck in the export business. British importers in London and Liverpool were eager to receive consignments of raw cotton in those days; they paid handsome advances to these small merchants as soon as the consignment was dispatched and shared the profit with them later on, once the consignments were sold in Great Britain. As soon as the Civil War was over this boom collapsed and international competition increased. The small traders were undercut by the big exporters, who eliminated middlemen and set up cotton presses in the areas of production. The bales were then sent to Bombay to be shipped immediately. Indian merchants could at the most play a role as cotton buyers in the villages of the interior, combining the roles of moneylender and trader in order to get a good grip on the producers. The Marwaris were adept at this game, but the major profits were reaped by the big British export merchants.

The Marwari was the prototype of the buyer-cum-creditor who served as a pioneer in developing the Indian market as a dependent adjunct of the world market. Marwaris were everywhere, not only in Northern India and Calcutta, but also on the highlands of the Deccan, where Ahmednagar became a veritable headquarters of Marwari traders and moneylenders. Such centres served the purpose of refinancing the rather modest operations of the individual Marwaris scattered in many villages in the countryside. The Marwari network also transmitted commercial intelligence and whatever cash crops were in demand in the world market could be produced, as the peasants were at the beck and call of their Marwari creditors. Even the peasant who was not totally indebted to his moneylenders could be enticed to produce the required cash crop by being offered a tempting advance. The peasant rarely had access to a truly free market, because the cost of transportation and the cost of storage and credit were too high for the individual producer, who could rarely afford to hold on to his produce until he could sell it at a good price in the best market. Most peasants had to sell their produce immediately after the harvest at a price dictated by their creditors. The demand for rent and revenue helped to push the peasant into the clutches of the moneylenders. The threat of forced sales for arrears of rent or revenue would guarantee that the moneylender paid the peasant's dues so as not to forfeit his security. Therefore the revenue authorities actually appreciated the activities of the moneylender and hesitated to support any legislation aimed at curtailing his sphere of operations. Only after endless debates about the political dangers of the transfer of land and the threat of peasant uprising did the British Indian administration finally sponsor Relief Acts for indebted peasants and Tenancy Acts, which protected tenants against eviction and the enhancement of rent. In 1875 peasants of the Deccan highlands had attacked their Marwari moneylenders. They had torn up and burnt the bonds that they could capture. The Deccan Agriculturalists Relief Act, which was passed subsequently, enabled judges to 'go beyond the bond' by inquiring into the conditions under which it had originated rather than just taking it at its face value. This was a difficult proposition. Moreover, the definition of an agriculturist created problems, because a moneylender who held some land could also claim to be an agriculturist.

The British sponsors of that act had hoped that it could be applied to all of India, but it remained restricted to the Deccan districts, for which it was first enacted. When similar problems came up in the Punjab, an altogether different strategy was adopted. The Punjab Land Alienation Act prohibited the transfer of land to non-agriculturists and these were not defined in general terms, but by appending a list to the act that specified the castes and communities that were deemed to be agriculturists and non-agriculturists. Land could only be transferred within these categories; non-agriculturists were, of course, permitted to alienate land to agriculturists, but not vice versa. This act was also thought to be of more general application by those who sponsored it, but it remained confined to the Punjab. Its grossly discriminatory provisions were deeply resented by many people in India, but the Punjab peasants considered it to be a privilege bestowed upon them and resented any attempt to amend it.

Most British Indian provincial governments were afraid that such legislative interference with the freedom of contract would endanger their revenue system and therefore they refrained from passing such legislation. Some of them, however, did go in for tenancy legislation, which stipulated that a tenant could not be evicted as long as he paid his rent and that this rent could not be enhanced beyond a certain specified rate The definition of this rate and the period for which no further enhancement was permitted differed from province to province, but on average the rate of permissible enhancement amounted to 1 per cent per year. In periods of rising prices, this meant that the occupancy right of a tenant was soon much more valuable than the landlord's right with regard to the same unit of land. In some provinces the transfer of such an occupancy right was prohibited; in others it was permitted, but required the permission of the landlord, who could then recover what he had lost in terms of rent enhancement by asking for a handsome fee (*salami*) when assenting to the transaction. As the landlord did retain the right of evicting a peasant who owed him arrears of rent, conflicts could arise whenever prices were falling and the peasant's income would be suddenly reduced. This did not happen until the Great Depression hit India in the 1930s, and thus most of this type of tenancy legislation did serve its purpose for quite some time after its enactment.

The British had passed all this legislation not in order to improve Indian agriculture, but simply for political reasons, as they wanted to preserve and extend the social base of their power. Initially, they had thought of the landlord as the most suitable support of this kind. But when trouble was brewing, they protected those peasants who held their land immediately from the landlords, but did not bother to extend the same type of protection to subtenants and other tillers of the soil, who could be fully exploited by those whose rights had been defined and improved by agrarian legislation. Orthodox adherents of economic liberalism criticised all these arbitrary restrictions of the freedom of contract, and their arguments could not be easily controverted by the sponsors of this type of legislation, unless they simply pointed to the political expediency of such measures.

If one considers the compulsions that led to this kind of legislation, one could perhaps presume that the market forces that had been unleashed under British rule had led to the rise of capitalist agriculture, which would have induced landlords to evict tenants and cultivate their land with hired labour. Rising prices and an increasing production of cash crops for export could have enticed such landlords or other entrepreneurs to consolidate large holdings and operate them along such modern capitalist lines. But this did not happen; the vagaries of the monsoon made large-scale operations very risky and it was better to let numerous small peasants bear this risk and restrict oneself to extracting whatever surplus one could get from them. In this field, government, landlord and moneylender competed with each other. In those provinces where the government had assessed peasants directly (ryotwari settlement), the revenue authorities found it difficult to enhance the revenue so as to keep up with rising prices. Such revenue settlements were usually revised

47

only once in 30 years on the basis of average prices prevailing in the decade before the respective revision. Landlords and moneylenders could enhance their demand much more quickly, unless they faced the restrictions of Tenancy Acts or Relief Acts. Peasants who were evicted by landlords and debtors whose mortgage was foreclosed were usually not driven off the land, but remained there, tilling it as before, but under less favourable conditions.

The steady increase of the Indian population and the prevailing pattern of subdivision of holdings inherited by several sons led to a rapid growth of the number of share-croppers, who tilled the land of others for which they received one-half or less of the respective produce. Share-croppers will always try to maximise their production per unit of labour rather than in terms of the yield per acre. They are bound to cultivate the land extensively rather than intensively, as the peasant who owns a small family farm would do. This led to the strange phenomenon that the growth of an Indian market was accompanied by declining yields per acre. One may, of course, ask why those who let their land to share-croppers put up with this type of extensive cultivation, instead of adopting more intensive types of cultivation with hired labour. In answering this question we may again refer to the vagaries of the monsoon and the spread of risks. Those who let their land to share-croppers rarely contributed any capital or implements and were satisfied with their share of the produce, which they received as an assured rental income without doing anything for it.

The lure of an assured rental income also supported a booming land market, which was in striking contrast with the stagnant or even declining yield per acre. The creditworthiness of landowners increased in this way and the amounts one could raise by means of a mortgage increased in the same way. The evolution of the Indian market thus had the strange effect that the price of land increased much more than its productive capacity would have warranted. This development was encouraged by a constant rise in the prices of produce. But even at the time of the rapid decline of these prices in the Great Depression of the 1930s, the price remained fairly stable. Land as security and as a source of rental income was much more in demand than the precious metals. A rising population would guarantee that the value of land was bound to rise.

An increasing population, an expanding export of produce and the stream of silver also gave rise to a steady increase of prices. In addition, there was a ratchet effect, which prevented the fall of prices in years of a plentiful harvest, after they had risen in years of scarcity. All traders were interested in high and stable prices and would store grain so as to prevent a fall in prices. As long as the terms of trade for Indian agriculture did not change very drastically, this system could be maintained.

5

The Limits of Industrialisation under Colonial Rule

5.1 BASIC PROBLEMS OF INDIA'S INDUSTRIALISATION

The British industrial revolution had set a precedent which other countries could follow. In doing this they even had a certain advantage; they at first imported British industrial products, then they erected tariff walls behind which they could nurture their infant industries, which would initially go in for import substitution and later on progress to production for export. On the European continent, investment banking helped to raise capital for much larger plants than those that had been built by the pioneers of the industrial revolution. Theoretically, India could have pursued the same course: there was some scope for import substitution as well as for production for export. In the latter field, only jute and leather provided some opportunities of progressing from raw material exports to processed goods, whereas opium, grain and other produce did not provide such opportunities. A jute industry did in fact emerge in India, whereas the new process of chemical treatment of leather actually meant a setback for Indian tanneries. Earlier they had produced semi-finished leather for export, but as the new process required a continuous treatment from the raw hide to the finished product, India could provide raw hides only and the indigenous tanneries lost most of their export business.

In the field of industrial manufacture for export, protective tariffs were, of course, irrelevant, but for infant industries producing for the home market they were essential. The British Indian government would not grant such protection to Indian industries, even tariffs that were imposed for purely fiscal reasons had to be abolished or else they had to be neutralised by a countervailing exercise duty. Only the advantages of being close to the Indian market and of employing cheap labour could give some encouragement to Indian industry. However, the opening of the Suez Canal reduced the first advantage to a considerable extent, and the passing of the Factory Act of 1882 made it more difficult for Indian industrialists to exploit cheap labour. This act was not passed for philanthropic reasons, but at the insistence of British industrialists, who had to put up with similar restrictions at home.

India's infant industry also faced the problem of an endemic shortage of capital. Money was always in short supply in India and interest rates were high when compared with the low rates prevailing in contemporary Great Britain. The stream of silver that had poured into India had facilitated the monetisation of the land revenue, but it had also been continuously absorbed in this way. A genuine inflation, which would have made investment and debt service easy, did not occur in India. Indian entrepreneurs did not have ready access to the British capital market with its low and stable interest rates, but even if they had had this access, the depreciation of the rupee would have made the debt service rather burdensome. Indian silver capital found better opportunities of investment in trade and in the land market and shunned industry, which required heavy investment and long-term commitment. We shall return to this fundamental problem below. At this stage, it may suffice to state that the lack of industrial capital was due to the general conditions prevailing in India under colonial rule. Some capital could be mobilised for the cotton textile industry, where the amount to be raised for building one mill was comparatively moderate; the iron and steel industry, however, required a much greater investment per unit and this proved to be a major obstacle for a long time. The export-oriented industry, which grew in response to foreign demand and could therefore also attract foreign capital, did not face these problems. Even in this field, though, the investment was fairly modest, as we shall see. Because the problems of the import-substituting industry were so different from those of the export-oriented one, and because these industries were also located in different centres — Bombay and Calcutta — we shall discuss them separately in the two subsequent sections of this chapter.

5.2 THE COTTON TEXTILE INDUSTRY

The first Indian cotton textile mill was founded in Bombay by C.N. Davar, a Parsi entrepreneur, in 1854 and it started production in

1856. There had been some earlier attempts, but they had failed. There were good reasons for these failures and for the sudden success of Davar's venture. As we have seen above, the Indian cotton textile industry not only had to face the competition of foreign mills, but also of indigenous spinners and weavers, who could make both ends meet as long as food and raw cotton were both very cheap. The sudden price rise in the 1850s had changed these conditions drastically, and from then on industrial production was a viable alternative.

C.N. Davar was a very enterprising man who had started a bank, a cotton press operated by a steam engine, a local steamship company, etc. in Bombay. He found enough partners for the establishment of his cotton mill. In fact some of them went ahead and started more mills, as soon as the first experiment had succeeded. These first mills were spinning mills and not weaving mills; they manufactured yarn for the hand-loom weavers and exported much of it also to China. This early expansion of the 1850s came to a sudden halt when the American Civil War greatly increased the price of raw cotton and all available capital was invested in the cotton export trade. When this boom collapsed after the end of the war, the crisis which ensued discouraged new investment in the textile industry. It took some time before another spurt of industrial expansion could be noticed in Bombay. In the 1870s, raw cotton was once more very cheap in India and investors were ready to take the risk of starting new cotton mills. From 1872 to 1878, altogether 32 new mills were established and the industry expanded beyond Bombay. At the same time the Bombay spinning mills were also supplemented by weaving mills.

The interest in weaving mills increased when Bombay's yarn export to China was diminishing because of Chinese and Japanese competition in the 1880s. Before this had happened, Indian yarn had almost completely replaced British yarn in the East Asian market, but now it was India's turn to be crowded out of the market. Therefore the total numbers of spindles in Indian cotton textile mills only increased from 2 million to 6.8 million in the period from 1883 to 1913, whereas the number of looms increased from 16,000 to 100,000 in the same period. Bombay remained the major centre of the Indian textile industry; by 1913, it had only 31 per cent of all Indian cotton textile mills, but 44 per cent of all spindles, and 47 per cent of all looms, and it employed 42 per cent of the 250,000 millhands working in the Indian cotton textile industry.

The Indian textile industry could withstand the tough competition of the British textile industry, because it had made a virtue out of necessity and had specialised in the production of cheap grey cloth, for which Indian short staple cotton was good enough and which could be produced at a low cost with rather unskilled labour, of which there was plenty in India. The imported machines could be fully utilised by working them in several shifts. The combination of spinning and weaving mills in India, which did not exist in the British textile industry, provided the Indian mills with more flex-ibility in times of crisis, when the demand for yarn receded. A large British firm in Bombay, Greaves, Cotton & Co., which operated only spinning mills, had to close down these mills in due course as they proved to be unprofitable.

Greaves, Cotton & Co. was an exceptional firm in Bombay, because it was British-owned, whereas the other mills were Indian ones. The Parsis had been the pioneers in this line, but they were soon followed by entrepreneurs of other communities. The Parsis had acted as catalysts in the channelling of capital into the textile industry. They were concentrated in Bombay, where they had accumulated capital in trade and shipbuilding. In starting the textile industry, they were not at all exclusive and gladly involved partners of other communities in this new enterprise. When C.N. Davar established his first mill, he had 50 partners, of whom the majority were Parsis, although there were also two British businessmen and several Hindus. In Bombay, the Parsis maintained their leading role in this industry for a long time. In 1924, there were 81 textile mills in Bombay, of which 22 belonged to Parsis; these 22 mills, however, were among the largest, as they together had one-third of the spindles and looms and also employed about one-third of the Bombay millhands. Hindus, Muslims and Jews owned 19, 15 and 14 mills respectively, and only 11 mills were in the hands of European entrepreneurs.

Bombay had monopolised the Indian textile industry in its early phase, but by 1924 only one-third of all Indian cotton textile mills were located in Bombay; another third was in Ahmedabad, where Gujarati entrepreneurs dominated the industry. In terms of spindles, looms and employment the Ahmedabad mills were, of course, still much smaller than the Bombay mills. In Northern India, Kanpur had emerged as a major centre of the cotton textile industry. British entrepreneurs were dominant there. Some small centres also arose in the south, in Madras and Madurai. Solapur on the Deccan also became a major textile town in the late nineteenth century. It had first served as the railhead for the cotton of the Southern Deccan in the days of the cotton boom during the American Civil War, and it had then made the transition from a centre of trade and transport to an industrial centre. The first mill, the Sholapur Spinning and Weaving Mill, was established there in 1877, two more mills followed before the end of the century and three more before the beginning of the First World War. A peculiar feature of this industrial centre was the coexistence of large mills with a major concentration of hand-loom weaving establishments. They were for the most part not competing with each other, as mills and hand-looms specialised in different products.

Eastern India was a barren territory as far as the cotton textile industry was concerned. By 1911 there were only 22 cotton textile mills in Bengal, Bihar and Orissa. Bengal acquired some more mills later on, but in Bihar and Orissa they disappeared. When compared to those of Western India, all these mills of Eastern India were negligible.

In spite of the vigorous growth of the textile industry in Western India, this industry did not become a leading one in terms of linkage effects. There was a growing demand for textile machinery, but all of this machinery was imported and none of it produced in India. The large number of Indian millhands did not contribute to the development of a skilled labour force in India; they remained at the most semi-skilled and as there were no other industries that provided alternatives of occupational improvement, they had no incentives to move on to higher skills and better jobs. There were good economic reasons why Indian industrialists were interested neither in the production of Indian textile machinery nor in the training of a skilled labour force. A textile machine factory would have required a major investment and it could hardly have been started without an initial protective tariff, which the British would not have granted; if they had consented to it, textile machinery would have become more expensive and the millowners would have resented that. For similar reasons, Indian industrialists were also not interested in the training of skilled labour. They left the recruitment of millhands to agents (*moccadam*), who could always draw upon the large reserve army of job seekers who would gladly work even for a few days, if some regularly employed workers did not turn up because they were ill or had returned to the countryside to look after their family or help with the harvest. The moccadam usually received fees both from the millowner and from the millhands whom he hired; he often also owned the humble quarters in which the millhands were housed. Large numbers of workers came all the way from Northern India to work in the Bombay mills; to them their moccadam was also an interpreter and guide who helped them to adjust to a new environment. For the millowner, it was much easier to deal with the moccadam than with the amorphous mass of millhands.

Trade unions did not thrive under such conditions. Bombay did have some of the earliest trade unions in India, but collective bargaining was irrelevant and union leaders could at the most create some trouble from time to time. Just as there was no collective bargaining on behalf of the workers, there was no labour market policy on which all millowners could have agreed. The Bombay Millowners Association (BMOA), which was founded in 1875, wanted to introduce a uniform wage scale in the 1890s, but it did not succeed in this, nor could it persuade the millowners to adopt a common policy with regard to the restriction of production so as to stabilise prices. The industry was born and bred in an atmosphere of tough competition and this also meant competition among Indian millowners. One element of this competition was the ruthless exploitation of an unskilled and fluctuating labour force in whose training, discipline and stability the millowners were not at all interested. Whenever they were asked by official committees of inquiry, the millowners always used to complain about the millhands, who lacked skills and would run off to their villages every so often without regard for discipline and orderly production. Such complaints, however, were a matter of routine; in fact, the labour force was by and large much more steady and disciplined than the millowners made them appear to be. There was also never a shortage of millhands, with the exception of such catastrophic events as the plague epidemic of 1898.

The development of the Indian cotton textile industry shows the potentialities and limitations of industrialisation under colonial rule very clearly. Under conditions of tough competition in a free trade empire and under the constraints of a lack of capital, a niche was nevertheless found and the exploitation of cheap labour enabled the millowners to stay in business. In this way they also showed a remarkable flexibility. Most of them managed to make the transition from the production of yarn for the indigenous hand-looms and for export to the production of cheap grey cloth for the home market. There was certainly not a lack of entrepreneurial skill in India, as has sometimes been argued by those who wish to explain the stunted growth of Indian industries. This skill also consisted of adjusting to the constraints imposed by the colonial system and avoiding an exposure to incalculable risks. Visionaries like Jamshed Tata, who sponsored an Indian steel industry in spite of all these constraints, were rare indeed. However, without the windfall gain made by this industry in the First World War, this venture would probably have failed and Jamshed Tata would have been remembered as a reckless gambler rather than as an industrialist with a vision of the future. Jamshed Tata had been very lucky right from the beginning of his career. In the Abyssinia War of 1867–8, he and some partners had obtained a very profitable contract for the supply of provisions to the British Indian army. He had then invested his share of these profits in a cotton textile mill and had later on built two more mills in Bombay and in Nagpur. Thus he was well placed to make the transition from textiles to steel, to which he applied all his energy and acumen. He actually did not live to see the opening of his steel mill at Jamshedpur in Bihar in 1907, but without his daring vision this mill would never have been started.

However, this example of the transition from textiles to steel remained the only one; it was the great exception to the rule that India's textile industry did not give rise to any further industrialisation. The same rule also applied to the jute industry of Calcutta, which showed a similar pattern of growth to the cotton textile industry of Western India and also did not have any major linkage effects which would have contributed to an industrial 'take-off'.

5.3 THE JUTE INDUSTRY

Dundee in Scotland had been the major centre of the jute industry in the early nineteenth century. Indian jute as a cheap substitute for hemp and linen had been processed there for some time, even before industrial production was started in 1840. In the subsequent 30 years, Dundee had a monopoly in the field of industrial jute products. The Crimean War of 1854 interrupted the supply of Russian hemp and the demand for jute products increased very rapidly. Dundee could not cope with this demand and as raw jute was mainly grown in Bengal, it was only natural to think of establishing a jute mill in Calcutta. This was done in 1855 by George Acland, who thus did for the Indian jute industry what C.N. Davar did for the Indian cotton textile industry at almost the same time.

Jute was grown in the rice fields of the East Bengal districts of Dacca and Mymensingh in peasant family holdings. Whenever the demand for jute was slack, rice could be substituted for it. On the other hand, when jute was required, the peasants could be made to cultivate it by means of the usual advances and the pressures of rent and debt service, even if the cultivation of rice would have been more profitable. Raw jute had different grades of quality and it soon became a regular practice to export the higher grades of raw jute, while the lower grades were used for the manufacture of rough gunny bags in Calcutta's jute mills. The first large-scale jute spinning and weaving mill was built in Calcutta in 1859 by the Borneo Company, a British trading company. Acland's mill had only been a spinning mill and the manufacture of gunny bags in Calcutta had to wait for the establishment of the Borneo Company's mill, which was soon followed by four others. In 1873, these five weaving mills had together 1,000 looms and did very well. Most of their production was used for packing agricultural produce in India, although some of it was exported to Australia, America and Egypt. The great breakthrough for the new Indian jute industry came only in the 1880s, when 23 mills with a total of 6,000 looms and 48,000 millhands were all set to capture the British market too.

The Calcutta jute mills soon held a world monopoly in the manufacture of cheap gunny bags. Therefore it was tempting to arrange for prices to be fixed by a suitable organisation. The Indian Jute Mill Association (IJMA) was founded in 1884 and maintained stable prices by ordering its members to curtail their working time or by sealing a certain number of looms in each mill, whenever over-production threatened to spoil the prices. The Bombay Millowners Association had been unsuccessful in maintaining this kind of collusive discipline; the IJMA did very well, because it was operating under monopoly conditions, whereas the cotton textile industry had to face worldwide competition. Moreover, the circle of jute millowners was much smaller, they were all located in Calcutta and therefore collusion was much more easily arrived at. However, they were unable to achieve a total control of jute production. There were other jute mills abroad and the export of raw jute could not be controlled to such an extent as to dictate prices to the foreign competitors. In Calcutta, the collusive spirit of the jute millowners worked against the admission of newcomers into their charmed circle. The establishment of new mills was not welcomed and whenever they were built, this was mostly done by one of the old companies. Indian entrepreneurs could therefore enter this field only at a much later stage, and they were generally at odds with the oldtimers.

The collusive spirit of these oldtimers was enhanced by the fact that most jute mills belonged to one or other of the large Scottish managing agencies that controlled the export-oriented economy of Eastern India. More information about the mode of operation of these managing agencies will be provided in the next section of this chapter. At this stage we may just mention that these agencies not only managed jute mills, but also tea estates, coal mines and steamship companies for river transport as well as for overseas trade. Their operations were influenced by the situation of the world market and they were not interested in the Indian home market, as the cotton textile industry was. Accordingly, the pattern of growth of the jute industry was different from that of the cotton textile industry. In terms of the number of spindles, the cotton textile industry grew by about 10 per cent per year from 1879 to 1888. The jute industry experienced initially only a short spurt of growth at about 14 per cent per year around 1879, and in the period from 1884 to 1895 it settled down to a more moderate growth of 5 per cent per year. In the early twentieth century, however, this pattern of growth rate was suddenly reversed. The cotton textile industry grew at only 3 per cent per year, whereas the jute industry had now attained a rate of 10 per cent per year. This was also reflected in terms of the number of workers employed by the two industries. The cotton textile industry had 100,000 millhands by 1879, whereas the jute industry reached this target only ten years later. In 1905, the cotton textile industry had 200,000 millhands, but this time the jute industry reached the same target only five years later. The expansion of the cotton textile industry was accompanied by a rapid growth in the number of mills and by an increasing degree of decentralisation. By 1911 there were altogether 261 cotton textile mills in India, of which only 87 were located in Bombay; at the same time there were only 54 jute mills and they were all in Calcutta.

Although these two major Indian industries grew along parallel lines, they were so different and so distant from each other that there was no mobility of the factors of produciton between them. Neither capital nor labour was ever transferred from the one to the other; they might as well have existed on different continents. Nor did they generate a joint demand for ancillary industries or for the manufacture of textile machinery; they procured whatever they needed separately in Great Britain. The penetration of the Indian market by the forces of the world market thus did not provide a chance for an integrated industrialisation of the country. At the most, some isolated industrial enclaves emerged here and there. Moreover, the concentration on the production of raw materials for export attracted most of the available capital and provided no incentive for the formation of industrial capital. This type of marginal industrialisation in isolated enclaves was particularly noticeable in Eastern India, with its export-oriented economy. Tea-plantation enclaves, coal-mining enclaves and industrial enclaves like that of the Calcutta jute industry were interconnected only by means of the managing agencies that controlled all these activities; otherwise they remained isolated from each other and from their respective hinterland.

The coal mines, which produced the fuel for the industrial centres and for the railways, were a striking example of this enclave economy within a colonial system. Indian coal could be mined for the most part fairly close to the surface and deep shaft mining was started only much later. The first mines were started at Raniganj in Bengal. The Bengal Coal Company, which originally belonged to Dwarkanath Tagore's firm Carr, Tagore & Co., had acquired a zamindari there and had settled miners as tenants. Agriculture and mining were combined in this way. The more important mines in the Jharia field were opened up only at the end of the nineteenth century. For these mines people from the neighbouring Chota Nagpur region were recruited as miners. The rapid expansion of coal mining then necessitated the recruitment of labour from more distant places. From 1905 to 1908 coal production increased from 3.3 million to 7 million tons per year and the number of miners from 40,000 to 70,000. This was an unusually rapid rate of growth under Indian conditions, and it can be compared to a similar spurt of coal production that had occurred in Japan in the decade ending in 1895, when it had risen from 2.6 million to 8 million tons per year.

The rapidly growing number of miners was accommodated in humble quarters scattered all over the Jharia coalfield. The food they required was transported by railway from distant plants and the rural economy of the immediate hinterland of the coalfield remained untouched by this development. The mines were operated in a very primitive way and required only minimal investment; a British mining engineer who was in charge of the boiler and the winches was normally the only permanent employee, everything else was done by Indian raising contractors, who received a certain amount per ton of coal raised by their crew of miners, among whom there were also many women and children, who were paid very meagre wages by these contractors. The low cost at which the coal was produced did not necessarily benefit the industries that consumed this fuel. The railways procured coal for their own use at low prices, but charged high freight rates for the transport of coal to the industrial centres. In fixing these rates, they seem to have taken into consideration the landed cost of British coal in Indian ports as the upper limit of what the market could take. In Bombay, however, British coal was still cheaper than Indian coal until the First World War interrupted maritime trade.

Managing agencies that controlled both coal mines and jute mills did not take advantage of this combination to provide cheap fuel for their mills as one might think; on the contrary, they usually supplied coal to their mills at fixed prices well above the current market rate. In this way they had a captive market for their coal and could make a profit on such transactions at the expense of the shareholders of the mills. The managing agencies made the transition from pioneering industrial development to parasitical profiteering very quickly. Those who owned such agencies were no longer interested in technological innovation and bold investment; they concentrated on financial wizardry and made the best of existing possibilities rather than sponsoring new industries. This is quite understandable, if one considers the general scarcity of industrial capital in India. Under such conditions, it was prudent to get as much leverage as possible out of the capital at hand rather than trying to generate more capital.

5.4 THE SCARCITY OF INDUSTRIAL CAPITAL

India's industrial capital was very modest at the beginning of the twentieth century, when compared with rural capital and merchant capital. In 1913, total rural indebtedness amounted to 5 billion rupees and the total value of agricultural land was rated at 40 billion rupees. At the same time, only 300 million rupees were invested in industrial enterprises. There were altogether about 2,700 joint-stock companies with a total capital of 760 million rupees; 500 of these 2,700 firms were industrial enterprises. The average investment in the non-industrial firms was 0.2 million rupees per unit and in the industrial firms 0.6 million rupees per unit. This average investment per unit is not just a statistical figure; it corresponds quite accurately to the normal investment required for a medium-scale cotton textile mill. Large investments of a single firm, like that of the Tata steel mill, which required 23 million rupees, were very unusual indeed. It is even more surprising that the Tatas could raise this enormous amount within three weeks in 1907. There were altogether 8,000 shareholders who contributed to this initial capital of the Tata Iron and Steel Company (TISCO). Many of them were capitalists from

Bombay, but there were also 15 Maharajas among them, who together contributed 3 million rupees and thus matched the contribution of the four members of the Tata family, who were the main sponsors of this venture.

The Tatas had selected an extremely auspicious moment for raising this large amount of capital. The year 1907 was one of exceptional economic growth; at the same time the Swadeshi agitation, which arose after the partition of Bengal in 1905, had fired the imagination of all patriotic Indians, many of whom actively boycotted imported British goods. The Tatas appealed to this patriotism and provided an opportunity for rich men to show their patriotism without running the risk of indulging in anti-British demonstrations. There were such patriots also among the Maharajas and they had to be very cautious in showing their patriotic feelings, as they were utterly dependent on the British Indian government, which could easily remove them under some pretext.

Swadeshi, the indigenous production of all essential commodities, was a powerful watchword at that time. Many small industrial firms were also founded so as to fulfil this programme, but most of them went bankrupt, as they lacked the necessary technical knowledge. The Tatas, however, had a proven track record and had also a good deal of capital of their own; thus they were able to raise the huge amount required for their steel project so easily. This example shows that under favourable conditions large amounts of industrial capital could be raised in India, but the conditions were almost always unfavourable. The small entrepreneur who wished to start a new venture could not hope to raise capital as the Tatas did. He depended on a suitable institutional framework that would provide industrial credit. In Japan the finance minister, Prince Matsukata, had established such a framework in the late nineteenth century. His programme culminated in the establishment of the Industrial Bank of Japan in 1900. In addition to a differentiated banking sytem, there was also a system of deposit bureaux of the finance ministry, which helped to gather small savings and to channel them into the mainstream of the national economy of Japan. By 1914 there were 12 million depositors who had entrusted their savings to the government in this way. In India, however, anybody who had any savings at all deposited them rather on his wife's neck in the shape of a golden necklace. Only in severe distress would he think of asking her to part with this ornament to save the family from starvation or to hold on to the land when the moneylender foreclosed the mortgage. Thus the savings of small people were never available for large-scale investment.

The scarcity of industrial capital in India was, however, not only due to the lack of an adequate financial infrastructure; it was also related to an even more fundamental problem: the enormous appreciation of the value of land. Between 1860 and 1913, the price of land rose by about 4 per cent per year, while other prices increased only at a rate of about 1.5 per cent. This unjustified appreciation of the value of land led to the strange situation that this value, which made up a quarter of national wealth in 1860, amounted to one-half of it in 1913. This pernicious type of appreciation, which was in contrast to the experience of all industrial countries, was a much more serious obstacle for the accumulation of industrial capital than the hoarding of precious metals, which is usually mentioned by those who try to explain India's retarded industrialisation. While this appreciation prevailed, it was impossible to channel rural capital into industrial investment. The appreciation itself indicated that there was plenty of money in the countryside, but it was chasing around for land and could not be syphoned off. The Japanese combination of land mortgage banks, deposit bureaux and an industrial credit bank could have helped to attract some rural money and to convert it into industrial capital. Such instruments were not available in India under colonial rule, however. The British Indian administration was only interested in collecting the land revenue and this task was facilitated by rural moneylending; no further innovations were required for this purpose. The primacy of a colonial policy of taxation and budgeting with the main aim of meeting the Home Charges stifled India's financial development, and it also contributed to that disproportionate appreciation of the value of land, which was not at all related to any increase in its productivity.

The managing agencies played a special role within this hidebound colonial system. They offered a package deal for everything that was in short supply in India — industrial capital, technical knowledge, modern management, international commercial intelligence, etc. Initially, a managing agent was just an executive who helped an entrepreneur to establish and to run a plantation, a coal mine or a factory. Such an entrepreneur was often not familiar with local conditions and also did not want to hire managers on his own, but gladly turned to an already established team with a proven record of managerial skills. Such managing agencies were compensated by getting 10 per cent of total turnover as a commission. This provided them with an incentive to do their best for the enterprise. Soon these agencies were managing many different firms simultaneously.

When the development of this system of management reached a certain stage, there was a reversal of the roles of managing agent and entrepreneur. Success, experience and creditworthiness enabled the managing agencies to float new companies themselves. Often these companies consisted only of a letter-head, but they did have shareholders, who were totally at the mercy of the managing agency. The agency itself would retain only a small amount of the shares of such a company under its management, as it controlled it anyhow. Under such conditions, the managing agencies were tempted to play financial games with the shares of such letter-head companies. The market was tight and the investors gullible; thus some window-dressing and a high dividend could help to sell shares at a profit. A managing agent could shift profit and loss from one company under his control to another and thus inflate the balance sheet of the one whose shares he wanted to sell. Once the deal was concluded, he could repeat the performance with another company under his control. Such financial wizardry was much more profitable than the 10 per cent commission with which the managing agents had to be satisfied in the initial stages of their business. Now they took the commission and added to it the profit they could make by acting as unofficial investment bankers and brokers. In the absence of genuine investment banking, they had a field day in conducting this type of business.

This strategy, which had been adopted to some extent already by Dwarkanath Tagore, proved to be so attractive that it did not remain restricted to Calcutta, but was also copied by the Bombay textile magnates. The dangers inherent in this game were that the managing agents made a speculative virtue out of the necessity imposed upon them by the scarcity of industrial capital in India. Moreover, managing agents tended to stick to 'business as usual' rather than taking risks in promoting technological innovation. They used their brains for designing financial transactions rather than for planning industrial progress. The large British managing agencies in Calcutta became veritable giants in the field of export-oriented industries, and through the shipping companies, which usually also belonged to their industrial and trading empires, they even controlled the lines of maritime transport. They had branch offices in London and in Asian ports and had all the commercial intelligence of the world at their fingertips. They used this, however, for restrictive practices in order to dovetail supply and demand, rather than for the exploration of new avenues of economic growth. Independent companies that did not belong to one of these great managing-agency empires could not survive and had to come to terms with them. This was shown by the example of the old Bengal Coal Company, which was one of the largest coal producers in India and sold its coal in the free market. In 1908, it surrendered its independence under the pressure of its own shareholders and entrusted its management to the agency of Andrew Yule, who controlled one of the largest trading empires and saw to it that from now on the Bengal Coal Company would neatly fit into the pattern of restrictive market manipulation.

Rising land prices without any increase in agricultural productivity and restrictive market manipulation with very limited industrial investment by the large managing agencies — these are the two main features of Indian underdevelopment that emerged in the nineteenth century. Both are symptoms of the same disease: financial paralysis under colonial rule. Capital, the most mobile factor of production, got stuck to land, the immobile factor of production. The rapid appreciation of the value of land meant that the land itself, rather than any improvement in its productivity, which would also have given employment to agricultural labour, attracted almost all the available capital. Since there was hardly any capital investment that generated income in terms of wages, there was not much demand for industrial consumer goods. In this way industry was starved of capital and demand, and fell into the clutches of managing agents who indulged in restrictive practices and financial speculation in order to make the most of a situation that they accepted and that they did not try to change. This whole pattern had congealed in the nineteenth century and even major shocks of different kinds such as the First World War, the Great Depression and the Second World War could not change it. These shocks affected the world market and the colonial system much more than the Indian economy, which continued to suffer from the chronic disease of colonial paralysis. Only after India attained political independence could some progress be made in overcoming this paralysis, but the colonial heritage remained a burden for a very long time.

The Indian market, which developed in the course of the nineteenth century, was a fragmented one. Regional isolation, which was due to high costs of transport, was overcome by the expansion of infrastructure such as the railway network. But at the same time the pressure of rent and revenue, of rural indebtedness and population increase had influenced the structure of the demand for different kinds of commodities. There was a small top stratum of salaried employees, traders and moneylenders who had benefited from colonial rule. They could afford to buy a variety of commodities beyond the bare necessities of life, but they bought imported goods to a large extent. The poor masses had not much buying power; at the most they would be able to buy a limited quantity of coarse grey cotton cloth. The export of agricultural produce was stepped up under colonial rule, but there was little scope for indigenous processing of such export commodities. Industrialisation was in this way restricted to a few lines of production, which remained isolated from each other and did not have linkage effects. The formation of industrial capital was very limited under such conditions, and the expansion of the market was static and not dynamic. Even major events, which should have led to dynamic change, did not make a lasting impact. The First World War was such an event; it had important economic consequences, but it did not change the course of India's fate to any considerable extent — except perhaps for its long-term effects, as it was the beginning of the end of colonial rule.

6

The Impact of the First World War

6.1 WARTIME PROFIT AND THE REDISTRIBUTION OF INCOME

The First World War made an impact on the Indian economy in several ways: the prices of agricultural produce increased considerably, the silver currency appreciated by leaps and bounds, the industrialists benefited from windfall profits to such an extent that they were overcome by a veritable euphoria of investment once the war ended and investment goods could be imported again. The living standard of the poor declined, however, because there was a redistribution of income in favour of the rich. The polarisation that was later on enhanced by the Great Depression and the Second World War began during those years of the First World War. Wartime inflation operated as a regressive tax, which hit the poor more than the rich. This inflation was accentuated by the special features of the Indian currency system. At the same time, this development fostered the accumulation of capital and a new drive for investment, which of course had to be postponed as long as the war prevented the import of machinery.

The high profits of the industrialists in India were mainly due to the full utilisation of capacities installed before the war and the general rise in the price of all commodities. The fragmentary nature of India's industrialisation could not be changed during the war; this fact became obvious to everybody concerned, as a demand emerged that could not be satisified, whereas in earlier years Indian industry had always suffered from a lack of demand, which had discouraged investment. The main impact of the war was thus a revolution of rising expectations. Most of these expectations were disappointed in the inter-war period. This problem will be discussed in the next chapter. In the present chapter, we shall deal with the wartime experience of Indian industry and agriculture, and with the vagaries of the Indian currency. In the final section, we shall deal with the problem of stagnating per-capita income — a phenomenon that was in striking contrast with the accumulation of wartime profits.

6.2 INDIAN INDUSTRY AND THE WAR

For India's largest industry, the cotton textile industry, the war meant a boon of indirect protection, as the connections of maritime trade with Europe were interrupted. Imports from America and Japan increased in this period, but they were still of marginal significance. Textile imports receded from a pre-war annual average of 2.1 billion yards in 1906–8 to a war-time average of 1.4 billion yards in 1916–18. The Indian textile mills stepped up their production from 0.6 billion to 1.3 billion yards in this period. This industrial progress was partly compensated by a decrease in the production of hand-loom weavers, whose output was reduced from 1.1 billion to 0.7 billion yards. This meant that per-capita availability of cloth receded from 13 to 10 yards per year and this helped to push up prices.

Industrial production was stepped up by hiring more workers and working more shifts. The number of millhands increased from 260,000 in 1913 to 293,000 in 1918 (c.12 per cent), whereas the number of spindles actually decreased from 6.8 million to 6.6 million and the number of looms increased only slightly, from 104,000 to 118,000. Net profits after depreciation and after deducting the commission of the managing agents amounted to about 60 per cent per year in the period of greatest wartime profits. In Bombay, this boom led to a major structural change in the organisation of the industry. There was a noticeable concentration of ownership, family enterprises disappeared and companies with limited liability whose shares were traded at the stock exchange increased.

The jute industry, being an export industry, was at first badly hit by the war, but it soon received new orders — for sand bags to be used in many theatres of war. With this development and the general rise in prices, the value of exports increased once more. At the same time, there was a remarkable structural change in the pattern of production. Before the war, exports had consisted of about 50/50 raw jute and jute textiles. During the war, the value of the raw jute exported receded to about 20 per cent of total jute exports. This was, of course, also due to the fact that the price of raw jute remained fairly low, whereas jute textiles became more expensive. The jute industry achieved its expansion of production just like the cotton textile industry, by means of a better utilisation of installed capacity. This was much easier in this case, as many looms had been sealed by IJMA in the pre-war years in order to restrict production in the interest of stable prices. The number of spindles and looms increased only slightly from 1914 to 1918 (spindles increased from 800,000 to 840,000; looms from 38,000 to 40,000), whereas the number of workers increased from 238,000 to 275,000 (c.12 per cent). The profits of the jute industrialists were made at about the same rate as those of the cotton textile millowners. Thus both major Indian industries did very well in the course of the war.

Coal mining in India also benefited from the war. Whereas 500,000 tons of coal had been imported in 1914, this import dwindled to an insignificant amount in 1916. At the same time coal exports, which had stood at about the same level as imports in 1914, increased to 1 million tons in 1916. After this date exports receded, as the internal Indian demand for coal had to be met. Before the war the Indian west coast had been provided with British coal, whereas Bengal coal was exported to the East; during the war years, however, Indian coal captured the entire Indian home market. Annual average production of coal increased from 11 million tons in 1906–10 to c.20 million tons by the end of the war. In spite of increased production, the price of coal rose from 3.80 rupees per ton at the beginning of the war to 4.60 rupees at the end. Even government control of coal prices could not stop this price rise. Increased production at higher prices meant windfall profits for the mineowners, that is, the British managing agencies of Calcutta, which also owned most of the jute mills.

The two older industries, jute and cotton textiles, as well as the coal mines, merely derived windfall profits from the war boom, but for the Indian steel industry this boom was of decisive importance, as it probably would not have survived otherwise. The British had given no chance to this infant industry. Indeed, the British head of the Indian railways had scornfully made a bet that he would eat Tata's rails, if they ever reached the market at all. During the war, however, the British gladly bought 1,500 miles of such rails for Mesopotamia, where British strategic interests were at stake. Dorab Tata, who remembered that bet, in 1916 said that the haughty gentleman would certainly have suffered from indigestion, if he had stuck to his promise. Except for rails and construction steel, the Tatas could not produce much else during the war. Steel sheets and other more sophisticated products had still to be imported. Nevertheless the Tatas managed to increase their steel production from 31,000 tons in 1913 to 181,000 tons in 1918. Steel imports decreased drastically in this period, from about 1 million tons in 1913 to 165,000 tons in 1917. Tata supplied about half of the steel consumed in India in 1917, but of course this consumption had been greatly curtailed by the war. Encouraged by this trend, the Tatas planned a large-scale extension of their steel mill in 1917. This could be implemented only some years after the end of the war, and at that time TISCO was facing a crisis and could not enjoy the fruits of this bold investment programme. But if it had not been for the war, the Indian steel industry would never have reached its take-off stage at all. There were still some problems with regard to self-sustained growth under colonial rule, as we shall see in the next chapter; nevertheless, TISCO had come to stay and Jamshed Tata's dreams had come true.

Another industry that owed its start to the war was the cement industry. By 1918, there were three factories, together producing 84,000 tons cement. The capital for this new industry was mostly raised in Bombay, whose cotton textile industry had also helped to produce a major part of the capital for the steel industry. The cement industry had started so late because in India cheaper building materials were used for the most part. Just before the war there had been a boom of urban construction in Bombay and this had encouraged the capitalists there to raise 2 million rupees for the first cement factory. During the war the chances for further investment were limited, due to the scarcity of imported investment goods — once more, new investment had to wait until the war was over.

Although the industrialists enjoyed their windfall profits during the war, the real wages of labour stagnated and even fell at the time of the steep increase of food-grain prices in 1918. There was a great deal of labour unrest in that year. The war had hardly stimulated Indian agriculture and the demand for food could not be met by it in times of bad harvests.

6.3 THE CONSTRAINTS OF AGRICULTURAL PRODUCTION

The area under food grains remained more or less the same in India throughout the war, with the exception of the disastrous drought of 1918, when this area was reduced by about 15 per cent (see Table 6.1). In the four years before 1918 an annual average of 56 million

Table 6.1: Cultivated area and grain production, 1912–19

	Total cultivated area (million hectares)	Area under food grain (million hectares)	Grain produced (million tons)	Total area under cash crops (million hectares)	Area under cotton (million hectares)	Area under jute (million hectares)
1912	78	63	52	15	5.6	1.2
1913	76	61	47	15	6.3	1.1
1914	81	65	52	16	6	1.3
1915	78	65	56	13	4.5	0.9
1916	81	66	58	15	5.4	1
1917	81	66	57	15	6.1	1.1
1918	70	57	39	13	5.6	0.9
1919	79	64	55	15	6	1.1

Source: G. Blyn, cf. Bibliography, Section 6.3.

Table 6.2: Food grain prices (1900 = 100)

	1913	1915	1917	1919
Rice	149	144	125	208
Wheat	100	129	116	193
Jowar	91	97	93	211

Source: M. McAlpin, cf. Bibliography, Section 6.3.

tons of food grain had been produced, whereas in 1918 there were only 39 million tons. Very little food grain was either exported or imported in those years. A reduction of food grain availability by 17 million tons (c.30 per cent) was a big blow. It is typical of the conditions of colonial agriculture that cash crops such as cotton and jute did not show such a decline, even in a year like 1918, because the best land was set aside for them. The humble cash crops such as oilseeds registered a steep decline in the area of cultivation and shared the fate of the food grains in this respect.

The steep rise of agricultural prices during the war can be attributed almost exclusively to the fateful drought of 1918. The outbreak of the war had not caused a price rise and in the two years with good harvests (1916 and 1917) the prices had even fallen in the midst of the war (see Table 6.2). The sudden rise in prices in 1918 was not merely caused by the bad harvest; the rapid appreciation of the Indian currency also contributed to it and the fact that the prices thereafter remained at this artificially high level must also be attributed to similar factors and not merely to the seasonal vagaries of agricultural production.

6.4 INFLATION AND THE INDIAN SILVER CURRENCY

Since the mints had been closed to the free coinage of silver rupees in 1893, the rupee was a token currency manipulated by the Secretary of State for India. The rupee was based on a so-called gold exchange standard, and the Secretary of State had two reserves at his disposal with which he could support his monetary policy: the gold reserve and the paper currency reserve. The first served as a general backing for the Indian currency and the second was established in order to back the circulation of bank notes, which still remained rather marginal when compared to the massive amount of silver coins.

The instruments the Secretary of State could use in order to pursue his monetary policy were the 'council drafts' and the 'reverse council drafts'. The former were bills of exchange to be redeemed in rupees in India by the British Indian government, whereas the latter were bills to be honoured by the exchange banks in London on behalf of the Secretary of State. The council drafts were, of course, much more frequently used. They enabled the Secretary of State to transfer the 'Home Charges' and facilitated the payment of invoices, which British businessmen had to effect in India for commodities they had bought there. The Secretary of State could also use these instruments in order to build up his reserves in London. He could do this very easily because India always had an export surplus in those days. Businessmen gladly bought such council drafts from the exchange banks, as this instrument of remittance was of course much cheaper than the transfer of bullion to India. By issuing more or less of such drafts, the Secretary of State could influence the flow of money and thus regulate the exchange rate of the rupee to some extent. If the exchange rate threatened to drop below 1s 4d, he could issue reverse council drafts (that is, buy rupees in London, instead of releasing rupees by means of council drafts). He could have intervened in this way by spending his entire reserves and he could even have raised credit in the London money market for this purpose. This necessity did not arise, however, and marginal interventions were sufficient in order to keep the rate stable at 1s 4d.

In the first years after the closing of the mints, the Secretary of State had to adopt a deflationary policy in order to stabilise the exchange rate. This was done by curtailing the minting of silver rupees. With the expansion of economic activity in the early twentieth century, he could reflate the currency by coining more rupees once again. The intrinsic value of these rupees was now well below their face value. During the war, however, the price of silver suddenly rose and the intrinsic value of the rupee threatened to exceed the nominal value. If the Secretary of State had allowed this to happen, the entire silver currency would have been suddenly withdrawn and thrown into the melting pot to emerge again as bullion to be sold at a higher price. Therefore he had to permit an appreciation of the rupee in keeping with the rise in its intrinsic value.

Moreover, owing to the increasing economic activity in the war years, more rupees had to be coined because the circulation of the paper currency was still rather limited, as people were not familiar with it and therefore did not trust it. This additional demand for silver helped push up the silver price even more. In one year, India managed to absorb twice the amount of the total annual world production of silver in this way.

For India's national economy this process was doubly unfortunate. India absorbed silver at a great cost and only a few years later much of this silver was demonetised and sold at a much lower price, after the wartime boom had subsided. Even worse than this, the inflated silver currency prevented the readjustment of prices after the war. An inflated paper currency could have been brought under control by means of a currency reform and a corresponding devaluation. An inflation backed by a silver currency, however, could only be combated by a slow process of deflation, by melting down old coins returned to the government after being worn out by a long life in constant circulation. At the beginning of the war there were about 1.8 billion silver rupees and 0.5 billion rupees in bank notes in circulation; by 1919 there were 2.9 billion silver rupees and 1.7 billion rupees in bank notes. The total currency in circulation had thus doubled in the course of the war. This expansion had mainly taken place in the brief span of time from 1916 to 1918, when the total currency in coins and notes increased from 2.6 billion to 4 billion rupees. As this happened to coincide with the drought of 1918, there was a sudden rise in prices caused by the double effect of scarcity and inflation.

For the industrialists, this curious development of the currency, which combined inflation and appreciation, had an altogether different effect than for the poor workers, who suddenly saw their real wages dwindle. The high exchange rate of the rupee at the end of the war made imported investment goods comparatively cheap and this contributed significantly to the investment euphoria of the industrialists, who were just waiting for a chance to utilise their enormous wartime savings.

6.5 THE STAGNATION OF PER-CAPITA INCOME

While the small group of Indian industrialists and businessmen had a field day, great masses of the population suffered from a decline of their standard of living. Not only did the urban workers face a decline of their real wages; the peasants also did not do well, as the internal terms of trade for agriculture deteriorated during the war, whereas they had steadily improved in the pre-war years. The share of agriculture in the net domestic product declined, although the

Table 6.3: Net domestic product and the terms of trade for agriculture, 1891–1921

	Net domestic product (billion rupees)	Share of agriculture in NDP	Population (millions)	Per capita income (rupees)	Terms of trade for agriculture (1873 = 100)
1891	36.7	18.6 = 51%	280	131	128
1901	40.6	19.4 = 48%	284	143	146
1911	47.3	22.7 = 48%	303	156	153
1921	48.0	22.1 = 46%	306	158	124

Source: A. Heston, cf. Bibliography, Section 6.5.

number of people working in agriculture remained more or less the same. As the net domestic product stagnated, the per-capita income also stagnated, whereas it had increased in the pre-war years. The fact that the per-capita income stagnated and did not decline was due only to an extremely low rate of population growth (see Table 6.3).

Although the impact of the war did raise the expectations of Indian industry, it only bestowed the doubtful blessings of artificially high prices on Indian agriculture. Industry contributed only 3 per cent of the net domestic product, whereas agriculture and animal husbandry still accounted for 68 per cent; cottage industry, etc. for about 10 per cent; and the tertiary (service) sector for about 19 per cent. The masses of the people did not experience a revolution of rising expectations, but only noticed an inflationary rise of all prices. This led to a general discontent, which soon found an expression in terms of a rising tide of Indian nationalism. During the war political articulation had been curtailed by the Defence of India Act. The frustrations of the post-war years and a repressive regime led to political unrest, which also spread to the business classes, whose rising expectations were deeply disappointed by British economic policy in the early 1920s.

7

Economic Conflicts in the Post-War Period

7.1 MANIPULATION OF THE CURRENCY AND THE ILLUSION OF INDIAN FISCAL AUTONOMY

The assurance of fiscal autonomy, which was contained in the new British Indian constitution of 1920, was in striking contrast with the blatant manipulation of the Indian currency by the Secretary of State in the immediate post-war years. Many Indian nationalists interpreted the actions of the Secretary of State in terms of a conspiracy theory, accusing him of deliberately thwarting this fiscal autonomy in order to assert British interests. In fact much of what the Secretary of State did could be attributed to his helplessness in dealing with a situation that was no longer amenable to the usual measures for controlling the stability of the Indian currency.

Until 1916 the Secretary of State had been able to maintain a stable exchange rate at 1s 4d. This ratio later on appeared to be something of a 'natural' rate, which should be restored. As pointed out above, the Secretary of State had managed to maintain this rate by means of his reserves and the issuing of council drafts or reverse council drafts. Only twice in earlier years — once during the brief economic crisis of 1907–8 and again at the beginning of the war — had the Secretary of State resorted to the buying of rupees by means of reverse council drafts. In the first instance, buying rupees worth £8 million sterling had been enough to shore up the exchange rate. The sudden rise in the price of silver had then necessitated a gradual adjustment of the rate to the intrinsic value of the rupee. By April 1918, the rate had reached 1s 6d. At this point there were some fluctuations and the Secretary of State had issued reverse council drafts worth £5 billion sterling in order to stabilise the exchange rate. But in May 1919 another upward trend of the silver price required further adjustments of the rate. The Babington Smith Committee, which was appointed at that time in order to make recommendations for a proper exchange rate, asked John Maynard Keynes for his advice. Ever since the publication of his book on *Indian Currency and Finance* in 1913, Keynes was considered to be the greatest authority on this subject. He told the committee in July 1919 that the exchange rate should be fixed at 2s 0d, although the actual rate was 1s 8d at that time. He defended his recommendation with the argument that stability could be achieved at that level and India would also be shielded against further internal price rises, which he considered to be undesirable for political as well as for economic reasons. He also stated that the rate of 2s 0d could be maintained, even if the intrinsic value of the coins rose above it; some coins might go into the melting pot then, but once they reappeared in the market as bullion they would depress the silver price and thus prevent the melting down of further coins.

With the silver price rising even faster in subsequent months, the Secretary of State did not want to risk the experiment Keynes had suggested and adjusted the exchange rate month by month, until it had reached 2s 4d in December 1919. When the report of the Babington Smith Committee was published, the 2s 0d ratio that it had recommended in accordance with Keynes's verdict was already outdated. The British Indian government, however, considered it to be a long-term goal to stabilise the rupee at that rate, even though the only Indian member of the Babington Smith Committee, D.M. Dalal, had protested against such a high exchange rate. Dalal had also pointed out that the government had contributed to the rising exchange rate by prohibiting the export of silver from India and raising the rate of council drafts. Dalal did not say so, but those believing in the conspiracy theory could have alleged that the Secretary of State, Edwin Montagu, who belonged to a famous family of London silver traders, would be happy with a development of this kind. India acted as a silver trap and thus supported the world market price for silver very effectively.

Montagu faced even more criticism when the trend was suddenly reversed. The prices of all commodities, including silver, fell in the world market and the high exchange rate of the rupee came under pressure too. In the meantime a Currency Act had been passed, which stipulated that the exchange rate should be maintained at 2s 0d. Accordingly, Montagu was obliged to support the rupee at that level by issuing reverse council drafts. But even after buying up rupees worth £55 million sterling in 1920–1 — an altogether unprecedented intervention — he could not prevent the exchange rate from falling to 1s 3d (or 1s 0d in terms of the value of the rupee in gold). This massive, but ineffective intervention was not criticised as an ill-advised measure, but was attributed to British pressure groups. The high exchange rate acted as an import bonus for British goods and thus not only harmed Indian industries, which produced for the home market, but also affected Indian exporters, as it made Indian commodities more expensive abroad. That this was no false alarm is shown by the foreign trade statistics: in 1920 and 1921, India imported goods worth a total of 4 billion rupees from Great Britain and only exported goods worth 1 billion rupees to Great Britain.

After the steep decline of the exchange rate in 1921/2, the British Indian government followed a long-term policy of deflation in order to support the exchange rate. The reverse council drafts had failed as an instrument for this monetary policy so the alternative course of contracting the Indian currency had to be pursued systematically. There was no new coinage after 1922 and old coins returned to the government were put into the melting pot and sold as bullion in the world market. This even helped the government to improve its budgetary position. The coins that had been taken out of circulation were not replaced by bank notes either. From 1919 to 1929, a total amount of coins worth 1 billion rupees was taken out of circulation, while the amount of bank notes was kept more or less constant. This policy was successful; by 1923 the exchange had once more reached 1s 4d and by 1924 it had risen to 1s 6d.

In 1925, sterling had once more been placed on the firm foundation of a gold standard and the rupee was supposed to share this blessing. A new currency commission (the Hilton Young Commission) was appointed and it recommended to fix the rupee once and for all at 1s 6d, as the 2s 0d rate had proved to be unrealistic. It was pointed out by the commission that this new rate would correspond with the level of prices and wages prevailing in India. Again, there was the dissenting voice of an Indian member; Sir Purushottamdas Thakurdas, who represented the interests of the cotton textile industry, alleged that the British had deliberately missed the chance of fixing the rupee at 1s 4d, which corresponded to the pre-war level. He prudently did not refer to the interests of Indian industry, but argued that a higher exchange rate would be unfair to the indebted Indian peasant, whose debts had been incurred at the old rate and would be increased by 12 per cent, if the rate of 1s 6d was fixed once and for all. He added that the indebted peasant would be even worse off, if prices should fall; prophetic words, indeed, in

Table 7.1: Price index, 1900–40 (1873 = 100)

	Agricultural produce	Non-agricultural products	Export commodities	Import commodities
1900	147	96	134	96
1905	135	108	116	96
1910	148	116	127	109
1915	201	130	155	146
1917	198	164	170	262
1918	210	210	190	289
1919	322	239	277	274
1920	319	266	281	280
1921	293	205	239	228
1922	287	223	245	201
1923	241	222	224	193
1924	246	218	222	217
1925	281	219	233	211
1926	283	193	225	195
1927	263	170	209	185
1928	267	182	212	171
1929	252	182	216	170
1930	206	154	177	157
1935	142	113	128	122
1940	147	111	164	181

Source: M. McAlpin, cf. Bibliography, Section 7.1.

view of the subsequent course of events during the Great Depression.

In the 1920s, prices remained high in India, in spite of the deflationary policy of the government, because world market prices were also high. The prices had reached their highest level in 1920 and after that there had been a downward correction. But if we take prices of agricultural and non-agricultural commodities separately, and also make a distinction between import prices and export prices, we see rather different patterns of price trends from the pre-war period to 1929 (see Table 7.1). The prices for agricultural produce as well as for exports (which consisted mainly of such produce) were fairly high, even before the war. The prices for non-agricultural commodities and for imports were linked in a similar way. During the war, import prices rose first and surpassed the other prices in this way until 1918. In that year, there occurred a sudden increase in agricultural prices, which has been explained above. Non-agricultural commodities showed only a slight increase after 1918 and there was a definite correction under the impact of falling world market prices in 1921, which affected the import prices. From 1924, there was once more a very close correspondence between non-agricultural and import prices such as had existed in the pre-war years. The agricultural prices, however, continued to remain fairly high, in spite of the deflationary policy of the British Indian government. A small deviation from this trend could be noticed only in 1923 and 1924. The export prices, which were earlier quite closely correlated with the agricultural prices, were now significantly lower than the latter. This was obviously due to the fact that cash crops grown for export reflected the world market price, whereas the prices of grain for internal consumption were no longer as closely tied to the world market price as they had been before the war.

The problem of high agricultural prices will be discussed in detail in the next section of this chapter. As far as the other price trends are concerned, we may state that Keynes's advice that a high exchange rate would protect India against price rises due to high world market prices proved to be irrelevant, as the world market prices were declining after 1920. On the other hand, a high exchange rate helped to lower the prices of non-agricultural imported goods in the Indian market, a fact that upset the Indian industrialists, who were therefore clamouring for protective tariffs. This demand was now viewed much more sympathetically by the British, as the import bonus of a high exchange rate did not only benefit them, but also their European and Japanese competitors. A system of 'discriminating protection' with preferential tariffs for British goods would benefit both British and Indian interests. At the same time, such a system could be defined as part and parcel of India's fiscal autonomy, which had been violated in such a flagrant manner by the manipulation of the exchange rate.

There was a definite change in the structure of India's foreign trade in the 1920s (see Table 7.2). In the two years 1920 and 1921 together, goods worth 6.5 billion rupees were imported, whereas goods worth only 5.4 billion rupees were exported. In subsequent years, exports once more surpassed imports. From 1923 to 1929, India exported on an annual average goods worth 3.5 billion rupees and imported goods worth only 2.5 billion rupees. There was throughout a negative balance of trade with Great Britain, which had to be compensated for by export surpluses elsewhere (see Table 7.3). Imports from Great Britain declined steadily, and from 1925 to 1929 India imported on an annual average goods worth only 1.2 billion rupees from Great Britain, although for the same period the sum of imports from Germany, Japan and the United States amounted to 0.5 billion rupees and with these three countries India always had a positive balance of trade.

In the 1920s, the British were not greatly alarmed about rising foreign competition; the policy of supporting a high Indian exchange

Table 7.2: Major export commodities (million rupees)

Annual average for each decade	Raw cotton	Cotton textiles	Raw jute	Jute products	Opium	Rice	Tea
1910–9 (57%)	349	136	184	330	53	217	161
1920–9 (63%)	692	116	255	493	20	309	260
1930–9 (66%)	327	46	133	274	—	215	214

Table 7.3: Indian exports and imports and trade between India and Great Britain, 1890–1939 (billion rupees)

Total for each decade	Export	Import	Export surplus	Import from GB	Export to GB	India's balance of trade with GB
1890–9	10.5	7.4	3.1	0.6	0.3	−0.3
1900–9	15.9	11.4	4.5	0.9	0.5	−0.4
1910–9	24.9	17.6	7.3	1.1	0.7	−0.4
1920–9	33.5	27.0	6.5	1.4	0.7	−0.7
1930–9	18.1	15.2	2.9	0.5	0.5	—

Source: K.N. Chaudhuri, cf. Bibliography, Section 7.1.

rate still benefited British exporters. The instrument of 'discriminating protection', which has been mentioned above, was therefore applied exclusively to steel in the 1920s and was extended to other commodities only during the Great Depression. As this instrument had been tried in the 1920s, it was readily available as a convenient precedent in the days of the depression. In fact, the British managed to weather the storm of the Great Depression in India by using the three main instruments employed in the 1920s: a high exchange rate, a deflationary monetary policy and discriminating protection. In this way they damaged the Indian economy and enhanced and prolonged the impact of the depression, but they retained their control over India as a debtor nation. The Indian peasants were most severely affected by this policy: they experienced only the adverse effects of the course of events, whereas others derived their profit from it.

7.2 AGRICULTURE: STAGNATION AT HIGH PRICE LEVELS

The high prices of the 1920s did not make any impact on agricultural production: wheat and rice yields per acre remained as low as ever. Rice production was more dependent on the vagaries of the monsoon than wheat production, because a great deal of wheat was grown in the canal colonies of the Punjab. On average, 12 million hectares were under wheat with a yield of 0.75 tons per hectare. The area under rice fluctuated according to the rainfall but was between 32 million and 33 million hectares (that is, whenever the monsoon failed, about 1 million hectares of rice land had to remain fallow). Yields varied from 1.3 tons per hectare in bad years and 1.6 tons per hectare in good ones.

In general, two consecutive good years were required in order to depress the price level; similarly, more than one bad harvest was required in order to raise the price level. Regional variations in prices hardly existed in the 1920s; the traders tended to stabilise the price level so as to make their transactions predictable. In 1921 there was a very good rice harvest, and the 1922 monsoon brought a great deal of rain and thus that year's harvest was even better. At the same time, the deflationary measures discussed above did show some results, and therefore the prices showed a significant fall early in 1923. But the harvest of 1923 was a bad one, the subsequent two were moderate and in 1926 and 1927 there were bad harvests again. Accordingly, the prices rose and in 1925 and 1926 they reached the same high level as in 1922.

Whereas the output of food grains stagnated, cash crops showed a different trend. Their output was affected by world market prices rather than by the vagaries of the monsoon, and those prices were still fairly high at that time. The production of raw cotton, which was slightly reduced in 1920 and 1921, was at a fairly steady level of 1 million tons per year from 1922 to 1929. A great deal of cotton was exported, and these exports were worth about 0.7 billion rupees per year. This exceeded the value of raw jute exports (0.3 billion rupees per year) and even that of the export of jute products (0.5 billion rupees). In addition to the traditional cash crops, there was a rapid expansion of the production of groundnuts, which had stood at about 0.5 million tons in earlier years, but was stepped up to 0.7 million tons in 1924 and 1.6 million tons in 1927. This was almost entirely a South Indian phenomenon. In the Madras Presidency, groundnut cultivation was extended from 0.8 million hectares in 1924 to 1.5 million hectares in 1928. In that year, the total area under groundnuts in British India amounted to 1.9 million hectares.

Cash crops like cotton and groundnuts were sold by the peasants in a fairly free market; they were no longer tied so closely to the merchants and moneylenders. After getting used to good prices in the 1920s, the peasants were hit even more by the depression of the 1930s. But the freedom of the market place was as yet not universally assured to India's small peasants. Those who lived in a main area of cultivation, where they had access to marketing co-operatives and where transport was no problem, could get better prices than those who lived in remote areas, where they had to depend on a series of middlemen. In general, the cotton market in Western India was fairly free, whereas the jute market of Eastern India was restricted by a tight network, which tied the local buyers to the wholesale merchants of Calcutta.

In addition to a better access to the market and high prices, the peasants benefited from a relatively low rate of land revenue. Revision settlements were usually due after a period of 30 years and thus most districts still enjoyed low pre-war rates. Those who came up for revision settlement in the 1920s, however, were faced with steep increases of the revenue demand. This happened, for instance, in the Bardoli *taluk* of Surat District in Gujarat in 1925, where the settlement officer recommended an enhancement of 29 per cent. When the peasants protested, the government of the Bombay Presidency reduced the enhancement to 22 per cent. But then Vallabhbhai Patel organised a no-tax campaign in Bardoli in 1928 on behalf of the Indian National Congress. The peasants showed an amazing solidarity in this non-violent campaign, and finally the government had to relent and accept an independent inquiry, after which the enhancement had to be reduced to 6 per cent. Even more important, however, the inquiry revealed that the standards of assessment were highly arbitrary. The Bombay government wanted to remedy this by introducing new revenue legislation, but this took a great deal of time and meanwhile no further revision settlements were attempted. The British had always been afraid of widespread peasant unrest in India and Bardoli scared them. The fact that in each presidency at the most one district would come up for revision settlement every year prevented the emergence of large-scale campaigns. From the point of view of the revenue authorities, Bardoli had set a very bad example and had severely damaged their reputation.

While peasants who paid revenue to the government benefited from this state of affairs, tenants who paid rent to landlords also gained from rising prices, since the landlords were prevented by tenancy laws from enhancing the rent by more than about 1 per cent per year, as mentioned above. Thus the landlords could not participate in the profits from high prices and had to think of other means to get at the cash of their tenants. Since occupancy tenancies fetched high prices in the land market and the sales of tenants' rights were usually subject to the approval of the landlord, he could ask for a handsome fee, called *salami*, whenever he approved of such a transaction. Wherever tenants had only a lifetime tenure, the landlord could exact a fee when the tenant wanted to pass on his land to his sons or relatives. As long as the going was good, no conflicts arose in this way, but a decline in the income of the peasants was bound to lead to nasty confrontations.

Peasant indebtedness also increased in this period of high prices, when the peasants were very creditworthy and could easily pay high rates of interest. Whereas revenue and rent were fixed for long periods of time, interest rates could be quickly adjusted to the prevailing conditions. Moneylenders anyhow charged very high nominal interest rates, which were designed to keep the debtor in debt for ever. The effective interest rates varied with the ability of the debtor to pay his dues. The moneylenders were flexible in this respect; they also did not want to starve their debtors, as they lived on their work. The good times of the 1920s witnessed a rapid expansion of rural credit as well as rising land prices, which always rose much more than the prices of produce, as was mentioned above. While not stimulating production, the period of high prices contributed to the further expansion of the superstructure of indebtedness and high land prices, which was precariously perched on a rather shaky foundation. In fact, this superstructure was stabilised by the stagnation of agricultural production, because a dynamic increase of production would have brought prices down and precipitated the collapse of that superstructure. Under conditions of stagnant production, Indian agriculture nevertheless experienced at first a period of high prices, and subsequently a severe and prolonged depression; the superstructure expanded like a bubble which then burst, causing widespread misery in the Indian countryside.

The monetary policy, which has been mentioned above, contributed to a large extent to these violent fluctuations. This policy served British interests and was bound to transmit external disturbances to India rather than to shield it against them. Indian agriculture was subjected to the forces of the world market without really participating in it. The most volatile forces of the world market that transcend space and time very easily, namely the fluctuations of credit and prices, swept through India and reached the remotest village without changing the modes of peasant production. Because of the relationship of the rupee to the pound, which was governed by exchange rates that were arbitrarily fixed by the British, there were intimate connections between London as a financial centre and the remotest village of India. This financial centre no longer had the enormous weight that it used to have before the First World War, when Great Britain had a balance of payments that permitted it to act as lender of last resort to the whole world. Therefore London was unable to stem the tide of the Great Depression, which hit rural India with a vengeance. This will be discussed in the next chapter; the subsequent sections of the present chapter will be devoted to a survey of the most important branches of India's industry in the 1920s.

7.3 THE COTTON TEXTILE INDUSTRY: UNDERUTILISED CAPACITIES AND LABOUR TROUBLE

The Indian textile magnates had invested their wartime profits in new machinery, which was imported in a big way in the early 1920s. In Bombay, imports of textile machinery worth 30 million rupees were recorded in 1920; these imports increased to 60 million rupees per year during the two subsequent years, and then receded to 45 million rupees in 1923. Thus textile machinery worth nearly 200 million rupees was imported during those four years and the number of looms had almost doubled in this way. It soon became obvious, however, that these newly installed capacities could not be fully utilised. This utilisation had to wait for more than a decade, when import substitution in the field of cotton textiles made some progress under the regime of 'discriminating protection' introduced by the British.

If one looks at the long-term trend of Indian cotton textile production (mills only), one perceives a straight line which ascends from about 0.4 billion yards in 1900 to 2.4 billion yards in 1930. At times the actual production oscillated around that trend line. In the years before the First World War, the actual production figures corresponded to the trend line; in the first year of the war there was a momentary shortfall of production, but owing to wartime demand production soon overshot the trend line. From 1916 to 1923, there was a more or less constant output of 1.6 billion yards per year. This, of course, implies that in 1923 actual production was below the trend line, which was reached once more only in 1924, when output rose to 1.9 billion yards. The years of large-scale investment in the early 1920s were therefore years of stagnant production. From 1925 to 1927, production rose high above the trend line and peaked at 2.4 billion yards. In 1928, the year of the great strike, which will be discussed below, production dropped to 1.8 billion yards, but in 1929 it rose again to the peak figure of 1927. The late 1920s were thus a time of particularly violent oscillations around the trend line.

The history of the Indian cotton textile industry was marked by important structural changes in the first three decades of the twentieth century, which are not revealed by this analysis of the trend of production. Before the First World War, the Indian cotton textile industry was not only working for import substitution, but was also an export industry. Exports came mostly from Bombay, whereas the upcountry mills produced for the home market. After the war, India lost this export market mainly owing to Japanese competition. The upcountry mills, which mostly produced cheap coarse cloth for the home market, were not hit by this loss of the export market. The Bombay mills, however, faced competition on two fronts: Japanese competition as well as that of the upcountry mills, which were closer to their respective markets and mostly paid lower wages. Bombay tried to meet this challenge by moving up-market, i.e. by producing finer cloth so as to push ahead import substitution in this field. In this sphere, however, Bombay faced both British and Japanese competition.

Bombay was still the major textile centre of India, but by 1920 it had only about half of all looms and spindles installed in India and the expansion of upcountry mills continued in the 1920s, whereas Bombay's position declined. Moreover, the Bombay millowners had to face a steep drop in their profits. In 1920 gross profits had peaked at 102 million rupees and in 1921 they were still 82 million rupees; by 1924, however, profits had dwindled to 2 million rupees, and in 1925 the Bombay millowners were in the red. They had to reduce their costs and this also meant cutting wages, which were relatively high in this city, because of the higher expenditure on food and rent. This explains why labour trouble remained confined to Bombay, whereas the smaller upcountry mills had very little of it. It also explains why the Bombay millowners were clamouring most vigorously for protective tariffs, although they certainly could not claim protection for an 'infant' industry. These millowners were prepared to share the market with the British, if they would only keep the Japanese at bay. The Bombay millowners also showed sympathy for the hand-loom weavers, because those weavers competed at the most with the upcountry mills, but not with Bombay.

The Bombay millowners showed less sympathy for their own millhands. There was a head-on collision in the late 1920s, which was precipitated by the peculiarities of labour recruitment, mentioned above. As long as the industry expanded, the moccadam who took a commission both from the millowners and from the labourers whom he recruited did not meet with any resistance. He performed a useful function, which was worth its pay. But when the industry stopped expanding, the moccadam turned into a parasite. As no new recruits were required, he had to get his fees from those who were already employed. He did this by threatening them that they would be fired, if they did not pay him. In this way the go-between fomented labour trouble. The peculiar system of recruitment also implied a rather erratic wage structure. There was no standard rate, and wages differed even among mills run by the same managing agency. Under such chaotic conditions, it was hopeless endeavour to enforce a general wage-cut, as the Bombay Millowners Association tried to do in 1925. All wages were supposed to be cut by 11.5 per cent. Communist trade unionists organised the millhands against this measure. This led to the first big strike in September 1925. About 250,000 millhands participated in this strike and 12.5 million man-days were lost. Three years later, even more millhands joined another major strike: 500,000 struck work and 31.6 million man-days were lost, and another 12.2 million man-days in 1929.

Left-wing intellectuals like Subhas Chandra Bose and Jawaharlal Nehru thought that the class struggle had started in earnest in India, and that political and social emancipation could be achieved simultaneously. The Great Depression changed this situation very radically, however, and in any case the number of industrial workers in India was still very small. The hope that the Indian working class would spearhead the movement for political and social emancipation was premature, and in fact this situation did not change very much in subsequent decades.

7.4 THE SEVEN PROSPEROUS YEARS OF THE JUTE INDUSTRY, 1922-8

In striking contrast with the cotton textile industry in Bombay, which faced major problems in the 1920s, the jute industry of Calcutta witnessed its proverbial fat years from 1922 to 1928. By 1922 this industry had 47,000 looms, to which 5,000 more were added over the next six years. In 1922 the industry employed 320,000 workers, and by 1928 the number had increased to 350,000. The most important fact, however, was the increasing utilisation of installed capacity and the rising export prices of jute products. In 1922 jute products worth 400 million rupees were exported; the peak was reached in 1925, with exports worth 600 million rupees, although by 1928 exports still totalled 550 million rupees. The Great Depression soon put an end to this boom, and more than seven lean years were in store for the jute industry.

One prosperous industry, however, was hardly sufficient for supporting a general tide of industrial progress. This is clearly shown by the production of Indian coal, which was by now the major source of energy for Indian industry. The peak of coal production of 28 million tons in 1919 was never reached again in the 1920s. In 1920 only 18 million tons were produced, and from 1921 to 1927 there was an annual average of 20 million tons. In 1928 production reached 23 million tons and the following year 24 million tons.

The coal mines belonged to the same managing agencies that controlled the jute mills. The position of these agencies had been strengthened by the economic trend of the 1920s, but the agencies had not been able to prevent Indian 'outsiders' from entering the ranks of the millowners. Birla and Hukamchand started their jute mills in Calcutta in 1921 and 1922, respectively, and competed with the established British firms. As long as the going was good, there was not much friction, but when the Great Depression affected the jute mills, the 'outsiders'' activities was deeply resented, because they did not want to participate in the very restrictive crisis management of the British firms.

7.5 THE STEEL INDUSTRY: THE BEGINNINGS OF 'DISCRIMINATING PROTECTION'

The Indian steel industry, which was an import-substituting industry just as the cotton textile industry, faced the same problems of limited demand in the Indian home market, which was saturated with cheap imports. Just like Bombay's millowners, the Tatas, India's only steel-makers, clamoured for protective tariffs. The Tatas had invested their wartime profits in a large-scale expansion of their steel mil and they had even raised £2 million sterling in the British capital market for this purpose. The old mill had a capacity of 125,000 tons per year, whereas the new one, which started production in 1924, had an annual capacity of 420,000 tons. Only 248,000 tons were produced in 1924, however, and 320,000 tons in 1925.

The cost of running the steel mill was initially quite high, since engineers had to be recruited from abroad. In the world market, steel prices declined in the 1920s, and the high exchange rate of the rupee meant that India was an attractive market for German and Belgian steel exporters. The Tatas could have gone bankrupt, owing to their optimistic expansion in the face of such adverse circumstances. Under normal conditions, the British would have turned a deaf ear to the call for protection: they would have referred to the doctrine of free trade and would have witnessed the demise of the Indian steel industry without batting an eyelid. In fact, the Tatas had been competitors of the British steel industry and their disappearance would have been welcomed by that industry. British steel, however, was much too expensive in the 1920s and the British steel industry faced similar problems to the Tatas — though for different reasons. Therefore it was in the interest of the British steel-makers to join the Tatas in an attempt to ward off German and Belgian competition. Of course, this could not be stated openly, and therefore it was necessary to invent a new doctrine, which would help to justify protectionism and market sharing.

This new doctrine was called 'discriminating protection': it specified that in fields of production where India had a natural advantage (e.g. coal and ore resources), it was in India's interest to protect the respective industries. There should be no general protection of Indian industry, as this would be repugnant to the principle of free trade, but protection should be granted after careful discrimination between industries that met the test of 'natural advantage' and those that did not satisfy this test. This 'discriminating protection' would lend itself to the simultaneous introduction of 'imperial preferences'. In this way, foreign competitors could be kept out and the market could be shared between British and Indian producers. As the British were in charge of 'discriminating protection', the Indian producers had to accept 'imperial preferences' or forget about protection.

The combination of 'discriminating protection' with 'imperial preferences' was a bad strategy from an economic point of view. Protectionism always imposes a burden on the consumer, who is prepared to put up with this, if it results in general economic growth from which he will benefit. This general growth, however, can only come about under conditions of general protectionism, which helps all infant industries and leads to the emergence of linkage effects. If protection is granted only to some individual industries, this leads to fragmented development, which was in any case the bane of India's industrial growth. If this protection is, in addition, punctured by 'imperial preferences', it produces a special kind of division of labour: for example, India was to produce cheap steel such as rails, etc., leaving the production of quality steel once and for all to the more powerful partner, whose access to the market was assured by preferential tariffs.

The first step in this direction was the Steel Protection Act of 1924, which did not contain any preferential arrangements for British steel. The greatest buyers of British steel in India were in any case the state-owned railways, and they were obliged to buy only 'tested steel' (that is, steel made according to British specifications at home, which supposedly justified its high price). In actual fact British steel prices were much higher than the production of steel of this particular specification justified. The British had priced themselves out of the world market and were therefore very keen to preserve their access to the India market. When the tariff legislation was revised in 1927, British steel was specifically mentioned and preferences were granted to it. This was a flagrant violation of free trade principles and required some special pleading. The British argued that they could have introduced a tariff graded in terms of various qualities of steel, but as the customs officer could not be expected to test the quality of steel, the British product had to be named as such.

The preferences were quite substantial: there was a basic tariff for all steel, to which 50 per cent was added for non-British products, and for non-British rolled steel even 70–80 per cent was added. British interests were well protected in this way, but the Tatas were also happy; their share of the Indian steel market rose from 17 per cent to 30 per cent after the Steel Protection Act was passed in 1924. This protection, however, encouraged no other Indian company to enter the field of steel production. The demand was too limited and after the Tatas and the British had shared the market between themselves, there was no room for others. However, it must be said in favour of the Tatas that they did not rest on their protected laurels, but continuously strove to modernise their steel plant and to add other metal works to it (a foundry, a tin-plate factory, etc.).

The cotton textile industry had to wait for 'discriminating protection' until 1930, when the British decided to keep the Japanese at bay and to share the market with the Indian millowners in a similar way to that in which they had shared the steel market with the Tatas. The procedure adopted in the case of steel served as a useful precedent.

7.6 GANDHI'S 'SUBSTANCE OF INDEPENDENCE' AND THE ARTICULATION OF NATIONAL ECONOMIC INTERESTS

When Mahatma Gandhi formulated his 'Eleven Point Programme', which he called the 'Substance of Independence', in the beginning of 1930, he summarised several of the grievances of the Indian masses as well as of the business community that had been highlighted every so often during the 1920s. Calling these points the 'Substance of Independence' was supposed to mean that, if the British made the respective concessions, this would practically amount to Indian independence. Gandhi was, of course, quite sure that the British would not make these concessions; he formulated these points in order to establish a platform on which all Indian interests could unite and support the freedom struggle.

The Indian business community had shown some interest in Gandhi's campaigns, even at the time of the non-co-operation movement of 1920. The post-war slump and the British manipulation of the currency had induced many businessmen who had earlier been anxious to be in the good books of the British Indian government to look to Gandhi's leadership and to invest in nationalism. Magnates with a national vision like G.D. Birla and Purushottamdas

Thakurdas saw to it that the National Congress received liberal financial support. Gandhi was in constant correspondence with them. He did not write much on economic matters, because he was aware of his lack of knowledge in this field, but he kept himself very well informed as a result of these contacts.

An economic nationalism had existed in India even earlier. In the nineteenth century, men like Dadabhai Naoroji, Mahadev Govind Ranade and Gopal Krishna Gokhale had vigorously criticised British economic policy in India in their speeches and writings, but these remained intellectual debates in which the Indian business community showed hardly any interest. There was a definite change in this atmosphere after 1920, when the contacts of Indian business-men among themselves and with the National Congress increased very quickly. The founding of the Federation of Indian Chambers of Commerce and Industry (FICCI) in 1927 was a major event in this respect. This organisation was the national opposition to the British-dominated Associated Chambers of Commerce, whose weightiest member was the Bengal Chamber of Commerce in Calcutta, the stronghold of Scottish magnates who controlled the large managing agencies of Eastern India.

Several of Gandhi's eleven points were identical with the demands made by FICCI and its eloquent spokesman, G.D. Birla. In particular, Point 2, the devaluation of the rupee by 11 per cent from 1s 6d to 1s 4d, and Point 7, the protection of the Indian cotton textile industry, were directly copied from FICCI resolutions. Other points as Point 3, the reduction of the land revenue by 50 per cent, or Point 4, the abolition of the salt tax, were not directly related to the interests of the business community, but they would have been welcomed by them, as they would have increased the purchasing power of the Indian masses. At any rate, there was no point in this programme that went against the interests of the businessmen, who wholeheartedly supported Gandhi's campaign of 'civil disobedience' and contributed generously to the funds of the National Congress. The Congress needed these funds in order to maintain large numbers of volunteers, who had given up their careers and joined the freedom movement. Gandhi was a great fund-raiser and he also knew how to keep accounts; the businessmen respected him for that. More-over, he could do what they had never been able to achieve; they could pass resolutions, but they could not forge the sanctions that would make the British listen to them. Astute leaders of the business community like G.D. Birla realised that and were glad to spend their days *In the Shadow of the Mahatma*, as Birla entitled his autobiography. This did not prevent Birla from stepping out of that shadow once in a while to lobby for Indian business interests in London. These contacts between the business community and the National Congress had been established in the 1920s, and they were intensified during the years of the Great Depression.

8

The Consequences of the Great Depression

8.1 THE DILEMMA OF THE RURAL ECONOMY: FALLING PRICES AND THE BURDEN OF DEBT

The Great Depression was born in the United States of America, where three factors, which were initially unrelated to each other, contributed to its sudden impact on the world economy: an over-production of wheat, the incompetent management of the American credit system, and an uncontrolled stock market overwhelmed by a speculative frenzy. Mechanised wheat production had been stepped up in the vast plains of the American Mid-West. For some time, prices could be stabilised by storing surplus wheat. For this, credit was required and it would be granted as long as prices remained fairly stable. If the cost of credit increased and/or the wheat price threatened to fall, this delicate balance would be upset and every-body who had stored wheat would try to sell it as quickly as possible, thus contributing to an avalanche, which would depress wheat prices all over the world.

The cost of credit was raised at that time for reasons entirely unconnected with the storage of wheat. The Federal Reserve Board of the United States had looked askance at the tide of uncontrolled speculation in the stock market. There was at that time little legislative regulation of the stock market and the speculative euphoria was way ahead of all fundamentals such as real assets and productive prospects of the companies concerned. In fact, holding companies were created out of thin air just in order to throw more shares into the market, where they sold like hot cakes. The conservative bankers who were on the Federal Reserve Board thought that they could put an end to this game only by means of a deflationary monetary policy. However, this measure affected only the banks and not the stock market, where the speculative boom continued unabated. In the meantime the raising of the cost of credit inhibited further industrial investment and made the continuation of wheat storage more and more expensive. The crash of the stock market in October 1929 destroyed the confidence in the entire credit network. There was a run on banks, many of which went bankrupt. Deprived of further credit, the wheat storehouses opened their gates and the inevitable avalanche swept across the world market. The Federal Reserve Board did not intervene; its conservative members were fully convinced that speculators and imprudent bankers were getting their well-deserved punishment and that this was required in order to restore sanity to the economic system.

Deflation, crash and bankruptcies in the United States sent signals all over the world and a severe credit contraction ensued. Everybody was interested in liquidity now and nobody wished to give credit. London, which had once been the financial centre of the world, could not counteract this worldwide catastrophe, but was caught in it as well. Before the First World War, London could have acted as a lender of last resort, because the enormous resources of Great Britain's positive balance of payments were at its disposal. These resources had dwindled after the war, and London was banking mainly on short-term deposits from all over the world. Such deposits gave London a good deal of financial leverage as long as the going was good, but they could be withdrawn immediately in times of crisis. This happened when the repercussions of the events in America reached Europe. When London was in trouble, negative signals soon reached all places where British banks were active all over the world. In this way, these signals also travelled to the remotest Indian village.

It has sometimes been argued that India had a split credit market: one for transactions in the modern sector at fairly reasonable interest rates, and a rural credit market totally unrelated to the first and dominated by high interest rates. In fact, the credit market was not split, but interconnected by re-financing arrangements. The discrepancies in the cost of credit were due to the large number of intermediaries involved and the nature of the small-scale operations of the local moneylender, who closely supervised a limited number of clients. Once the big banks in the Indian ports refused to give further credit to the small banks in district towns for the buying and storing of grain, the wholesale merchant (*arhatia*), who used to obtain credit by mortgaging his full godown to the local bank, had no funds to finance the buying up of the current harvest in the villages. The village moneylender-cum-trader, who normally exploited his debtor by buying up his produce after the harvest at a very cheap rate and deducting the interest due to him from this amount, was then forced to push his operations into reverse gear. As the arhatia would not take the grain off his hands, he did not want to take it from his debtor and rather asked him to pay back the amount that he had originally given to him as a loan. Normally this would have been the last thing he would have done, because he wanted to extract a high interest payment from his debtor rather than recover the small amount of capital he had originally invested in establishing this profitable relationship.

This sudden reversal of the credit and storage practices broke the ratchet, which had so far prevented the fall of agrarian prices in India after they had attained a high level during the First World War. The wheat price was the first to fall, in spite of the fact that the pattern of supply and demand had not changed within India. Hardly any wheat was exported or imported in this period, and Indian wheat was produced only for the home market. The harvest of 1929 had been a good one, but if the usual mechanism had supported the price level, nothing would have happened. However, the world market price was bound to affect India immediately, as cheap Australian wheat was readily available in Bombay and filtered into the home market from there. The British were always concerned about the Punjab, the main recruiting ground for the Indian army and the major wheat-producing province of India. In order to keep the Punjab quiet, they deviated from their free trade principles and imposed a wheat import duty, which kept the Australian wheat out. By the summer of 1931, the Indian wheat price had fallen to about 50 per cent of the price prevailing in the spring of 1929. After the imposition of the import duty, the wheat price recovered somewhat and in 1933 it once more reached the 1930 price level. In 1934, the combined effect of a good harvest and of an extension of the area under wheat, which had been encouraged by the protective duty, depressed the price level once more. In subsequent years, wheat prices rose only very slowly until the Second World War created a new situation.

The humble millet, which had never entered the world market, was caught in the same downward trend. Wheat could rarely be substituted for them as far as cultivation was concerned, but consumers would, of course, have shifted to wheat, if the price level of millet had not been immediately adjusted to a price level somewhat below that of wheat. Rice, however, maintained a high

Figure 8.1: Rice and wheat prices, 1929–36

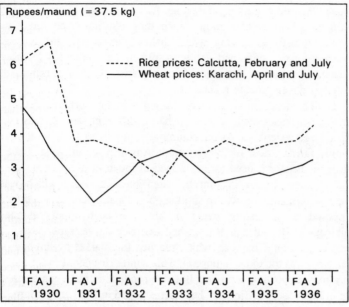

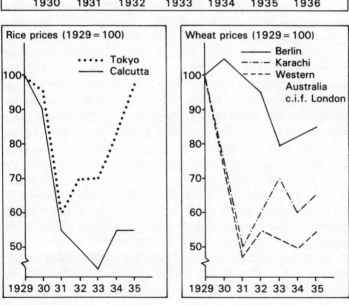

Source of data: D. Rothermund, cf. Bibliography, Section 8.1.

price for some time after the wheat price had fallen. In fact, the Indian rice price rose in the summer of 1930, when the wheat price was in the midst of its rapid decline. Rice eaters would not normally shift to wheat consumption, since they did not even have the implements for preparing wheat dishes; this is why the internal demand for rice remained stable, in spite of the availability of cheap wheat. The Indian rice price fell only after the repercussions of external developments reached India.

Unlike wheat, of which there was a glut in the world market, due to the American avalanche, rice had a different fate. It was still to a large extent an Asian commodity produced in innumerable family farms. Most of the rice trade was also within Asia. Indian rice, for instance, used to be shipped to Japan in order to stabilise the Japanese prices in March, when Japanese rice, which was harvested in autumn, was in short supply. Japan's temperate climate imposed a harvesting cycle of the European type, whereas subtropical Bengal and Burma had two rice harvests per year, of which the winter harvest, which reached the market by the end of January, was the more important. This winter rice could reach Japan at a most opportune moment. But rice production had been stepped up in Japan, self-sufficiency had been attained in 1928 and an import embargo had been imposed on Indian rice. Since the quantities involved were not of great consequence, this did not affect the Indian rice price level. In October 1930, a plentiful harvest reached the Japanese market and prices fell by about one third. This could have remained a purely internal matter, but in a world market that was already apprehensive of falling price trends, the news of the price fall in Japan had an immediate impact on the London rice market, where the price of Indian rice fell drastically in November 1930. There was no immediate reaction to this in India; it was only when the winter rice harvest reached the market in January 1931 that the Indian rice price fell very steeply. The reversal of the usual pattern of credit and trade, which has been described above, must have happened in this case too. In fact, the extremely steep and sudden fall would indicate that such a reversal took place, as any other kind of adjustment would have been of a more gradual type. The volume of Indian rice exports remained more or less the same before and after this event. Thus the fall was not due to a sudden glut in the Indian market caused by a decline of exports, nor was any cheap rice imported into India at this stage. There were no shipments that would have played the role of those of Australian wheat, which forced down the Indian wheat price. Such shipments arrived only later on and they consisted mostly of broken rice, which had earlier been used only as a raw material for the manufacture of starch, but which was now eaten by the poor people of India. When this happened, the rice-producing provinces of India raised a hue and cry and asked for a rice import duty, citing the precedent of the wheat import duty. The British Indian government at first did not give in to this demand, the more so as there was still a rice export duty and it was a bit difficult for the authorities concerned to think of imposing an export and an import duty at the same time. Therefore something happened that was unprecedented in the history of agrarian prices: the price of rice sank well below the price of wheat in the summer of 1933. The clamour for a rice import duty became stronger, but it took the government a long time to do something about it, and finally a duty on broken rice only was introduced in 1935.

A striking phenomenon of the early years of the Great Depression in India was the reappearance of remarkable seasonal and regional variations in the price levels; these had been noticed in the nineteenth century, before the extension of the railways and the steady rise of prices had greatly reduced these variations. Once the ratchet was broken, which had so far prevented a fall in prices, the earlier pattern of seasonal fluctuations reasserted itself. Nevertheless, this does not explain why regional variations also appeared once more, and even adjacent districts showed drastic deviations in the price levels of the staple crop of the respective region. Probably the sudden reversal of the pattern of credit and storage led to panic sales of all stocks, so that even the slightest variations in the local harvest would be immediately reflected by the current price. In subsequent years, these fluctuations and regional variations were once more reduced and prices stabilised at the pre-war level. The phenomenon described here was therefore typical only for the time when the immediate impact of the depression was felt, and the local traders and moneylenders were completely flabbergasted and did not know how to manage the market any longer.

All these dramatic events should, of course, have left subsistence agriculture untouched. A peasant who worked mostly in order to feed his family with what he produced could have remained indifferent to price fluctuations. If he needed some articles which he had to buy from local artisans, he would not feel much of a pinch either, because they would adjust their prices quickly to the new price level, as their food and raw materials were also available at very cheap rates. But most Indian peasants were in a very different position, even if they were mainly subsistence agriculturists. They were faced with revenue or rent demands and with a rate of debt service which had all been pitched at a higher level in the 1920s, when prices were high. Neither the revenue authorities, nor the landlords and moneylenders, were willing to reduce their claims, as they had also been hit by the Great Depression. The revenue authorities argued that the revenue settlement presented a long-term average and could not be adjusted to short-term price fluctuations — and it took some time for everybody concerned to realise that this was not a short-term fluctuation. The landlords pointed out that the legal restrictions on rent enhancement had prevented them from getting their fair share at a time of high prices and that they did not see why they should now forgo what was due to them. Most of them were also in the clutches of moneylenders and could not afford to be lenient. The moneylenders were alarmed because their business was totally disrupted: most of them were also traders and had probably stored some grain, so they had experienced a sudden devaluation of whatever they had stored. They frantically insisted on getting their pound of flesh now, as they saw that their future prospects were dim.

The discrepancy between the depressed price level and the high level of revenue, rent and debt service explains why there was peasant unrest in many parts of India in those years. In fact, it is surprising that this widespread unrest did not lead to the kind of general peasant rebellion that the British colonial rulers had always feared. This general rebellion did not come about because of the many regional differences in revenue administration and agrarian relations. Moreover, the peasants were afraid to go in for radical action, which could lead to a forfeiture of their land. A moderate protest such as that articulated by Mahatma Gandhi was more appropriate than a violent revolt in this case. This is why the peasants flocked to the National Congress in those years and provided a social base for this organisation that proved to be very stable for many years to come.

Mahatma Gandhi had started his famous Salt March in the spring of 1930, before the Great Depression had made any impact on India. His campaign was related to the constitutional conflict concerning the grant of Dominion Status to India. He had picked the salt tax as a target for his campaign because this was an issue that implied a straightforward confrontation with the British Indian government and did not involve matters in which Indian interests would be divided. Moreover, the technical breach of the government's salt laws was easily accomplished everywhere by just picking up salt near the sea or evaporating some saltish water. Many people all over India did this and were promptly imprisoned. After some time this campaign lost its attraction and it was at that point that the fall of the wheat price created peasant unrest in Northern India, which was utilised for giving a fresh lease of life to the Congress campaign by radical leaders like Jawaharlal Nehru. Other leaders who were less radical than Nehru also kept in touch with the equally disgruntled landlords and moneylenders. The Congress recommended itself to all who blamed the British Indian government for the predicament in which they were because of the Great Depression. This caused some internal contradictions in the ranks of the Congress, but as long as agitational unity was the main issue, these contradictions did not become a major problem.

In March 1931, when peasant unrest in the wheat-growing provinces was at its height and when the fall of the rice price threatened to cause similar unrest in Eastern and Southern India, the Viceroy, Lord Irwin, managed to get Gandhi involved in a pact that did not embody major British concessions, but obliged Gandhi to suspend his campaign of civil disobedience and to attend the next Round Table Conference in London. Nehru was furious about this and said that the Gandhi–Irwin pact was a betrayal of the cause of the peasantry. Gandhi faced a great deal of criticism for arriving at this pact with Irwin. There were several reasons that must have prompted him to take this step. First of all, he still remembered the rather unfortunate end to his non-co-operation campaign in 1922, when he had to terminate it because of an outbreak of violence. A pact with the viceroy seemed to be a better end for a campaign that was bound to peter out or turn into violence in the near future. There were also the liberal politicians who had returned from the first Round Table Conference in London with a rather optimistic assessment of the future course of action. The Congress had boycotted this conference and if it also boycotted the next one without being able to show any startling success of its campaign in India, it was bound to be outflanked by others. Then there was the Bombay magnate, Sir Purushottamdas Thakurdas, who paid Gandhi a visit shortly before the Gandhi–Irwin pact was concluded. Bombay had supported Gandhi's campaign financially, but now the severe credit contraction of the winter of 1930–1 made such support much more difficult and Thakurdas must have explained this to Gandhi in detail. At the same time he must have talked about his experience in London at the Round Table Conference too. Thus Gandhi was convinced that a pact with the viceroy was the best option available to him. He did

101

not want to go to the Round Table Conference in order to get involved in endless debates; he just wanted to present the national demand there, and this he could do only as long as the campaign and its successful conclusion in terms of such a pact provided him with the necessary legitimacy for such a step.

Lord Irwin could later on tell his Tory friends in England who had disliked this pact that he had, in fact, forestalled a general peasant uprising in India in this way. At the same time, he had involved Gandhi in the future process of British Indian constitution-making by getting him to attend the Round Table Conference. The Indian peasants, however, were undoubtedly left in the lurch. In North India, they faced the wrath of the landlords as soon as the Congress campaign was suspended. But in political terms, the landlords were very shortsighted. In 1937, the peasants voted for the Congress and not for the National Agriculturists Party, sponsored by the British and the landlords. When extending the franchise under the new Government of India Act of 1935, the British had taken care to include the substantial peasants in the electoral roll, since their occupancy right and regulated rent had been secured by British tenancy legislation. They thought that these peasants would support loyalist parties, as they had good reasons to be grateful to the British. However, the Great Depression changed all that and made the peasants turn against the government. The peasants voted for the Congress, but so did many of the landlords and moneylenders, who also blamed the government for whatever the Great Depression had done to them. Of course, the British were quite innocent in this respect; nevertheless, they had done nothing to shield India from the impact of the depression, as a national government would have tried to do.

8.2 THE BUDGET, THE EXCHANGE RATE AND THE EXPORT OF GOLD: BRITISH INDIAN FINANCIAL POLICY DURING THE DEPRESSION

A national government of India would have probably risen to the challenge of the depression by devaluating the currency, emphasising public works (road building, irrigation, etc.), and following a policy of stabilising prices and securing credit. The Swedish example shows how the depression could be kept out of the country by a judicious application of such policies. The Swedish currency was devalued; no deflationary policy was adopted, but prices were stabilised by providing for a constant money supply; the central bank supported banks so as to prevent their going bankrupt; and the general confidence in the national credit system was thus preserved.

In India, none of these instruments were at the disposal of the British Indian government. The currency was controlled by the Secretary of State for India in London; at that time there was no central bank in India that could have supported the stability of a national credit network. In fact, the final authority with regard to Indian finance and currency was the Governor of the Bank of England, Sir Montagu Norman, whose advice no Secretary of State could have dared to ignore. Norman thought in terms of the interests of Great Britain as a creditor nation under rather adverse circumstances and was not willing to make any concessions to India that might upset the delicate balance of imperial finance. Sir George Schuster, the Finance Member of the Government of India, was prepared to solve India's problems with a view to India's interests. He was heartily disliked in London for that, but he could not do anything against the imperial interest. The main issue at stake at that time was the maintenance of the exchange rate of the rupee at 1s 6d. The rupee was clearly overvalued at that rate and the old argument that had been advanced in 1927, that the rate was in accordance with the prevailing price level, would now have sounded ridiculous in view of recent events. Similarly, Keynes' argument of 1919, that a high exchange rate would serve the purpose of shielding India against a sudden price rise, would have appeared to be a cynicism now. Accordingly, nothing was heard of such arguments, and instead it was stated that the rate must be maintained in order to prevent a 'flight from the rupee' at any cost. Schuster was ordered to follow a deflationary policy so that the contraction of the currency would help to support the exchange rate.

The Labour Secretary of State, Wedgwood Benn, who passed on these orders to Schuster at the behest of Montagu Norman, did not feel at ease in doing so and he noted that as the British government had forced this exchange rate upon India, it should foot the bill and support India with a generous amount of credit. Norman retorted that without the maintenance of the high exchange rate, no credit would be forthcoming. Accordingly, Schuster had to do the needful and pursue his deflationary measures. There were two ways of doing this: the government could continue to melt down silver rupees and curtail the circulation of paper currency, and secondly, the government could enter the Indian money market and mop up large amounts by issuing treasury bills — in this way the money supply available to the public was reduced and interest rates were pushed up. This latter method was followed to an increasing extent in those years. In addition, the British Indian government also bought up a good deal of gold.

Schuster pursued this policy unwillingly. Moreover, he also had to cut government expenditure in order to present a balanced budget. The income from duties and taxes had dwindled and it was difficult to make both ends meet. The high interest rate that prevailed as a result of the very measures of the government created additional problems, because Schuster had to pay the interest on the treasury bills after all. He was well aware of the fact that his policy led to a further depression of prices in India. Except for orders to pursue this course and to send as much gold as possible to London, he received no information about the future aims of British financial policy. When the cabinet in London decided that Great Britain should go off the gold standard and let the pound float freely, the British Indian government had no prior information and got the news like everybody else around the world. Thereupon Schuster acted quickly: at his request, the Viceroy issued an ordinance which suspended the free convertibility of the rupee so as to stop a run on the currency reserves. He also wanted to let the rupee float just as the pound was being made to float. India's financial autonomy seemed to come into its own at last. But the Secretary of State countermanded the ordinance and ordered that the rupee should be maintained at the rate of 1s 6d. The Viceroy stated that he and his whole council would resign on this issue, but the Secretary of State upbraided him and said that this would be desertion in front of the enemy. The Viceroy relented — and soon the whole episode was forgotten because something happened which made the maintenance of the exchange rate extremely easy: a stream of gold poured out of India and created such an export surplus that an even higher exchange rate could have been supported. Montagu Norman could not even have dreamed of this, but the stream of gold was very welcome to him, as it not only restored India's, but also Great Britain's creditworthiness. Schuster was wonderstruck when he saw the heaps of precious ornaments that piled up in the British Indian currency office. They had been sold for the value of their metal and all the delicate work was lost as they entered the melting pot.

How did this stream of gold arise? The explanation is simple: when Britain went off the gold standard, gold appreciated by 20 per cent and this was a signal for all moneylenders to force their debtors to surrender their gold ornaments. If the only option was to sell land or gold, the peasant chose to part with gold. This gold was rightly called 'distress gold'. The British Indian authorities did nothing to stop this flow of gold, and when questioned about it, they stated that the Indians were selling this gold as they were getting a good price for it and there was no reason to prevent them from doing so or to try to keep the gold in the country. Indian nationalists asked for an embargo on the export of gold, but the British stressed the principles of free trade, the more so as London benefited immensely from this stream of gold. Roosevelt pursued an altogether different course in the United States a few years later: he also went off the gold standard, devalued the dollar, prohibited the export of gold and used the large American gold reserves as a backing for an expanding currency, with which he reflated the economy. The British government was furious about this, but could not prevent Roosevelt from doing what he wanted to do. An independent Indian government might well have pursued the same course of action as Roosevelt did. Such a government would have devalued the rupee, increased the circulation of paper money, and used India's de-hoarded gold as a backing for this currency. In this way the de-hoarding would have benefited the India economy, whereas the stream of gold that left the country only bolstered up the position of London as the financial centre of the new sterling bloc, which emerged as a substitute for an international gold standard.

The export of gold from India amounted to about 3 billion rupees in the period from 1931 to 1936. India's creditworthiness increased very much owing to this and, as interest rates were reduced at the same time, the British Indian government could have easily raised the money for a large-scale development programme. Schuster recommended this, but he was not permitted to go ahead with such a programme. Thus India gained nothing from this creditworthiness. The only task that Schuster could complete successfully and with full support from London was the establishment of the Reserve Bank of India. The creation of such a bank had already been recommended by the Currency Commission of 1927, which had fixed the rupee at 1s 6d, but at that time nothing was done about it because the Secretary of State was not eager to surrender his prerogative of managing the Indian currency according to his own discretion. However, the impending constitutional reform, which implied that an Indian Finance Member would be in a position to insist on India's financial autonomy, was a strong motive for going ahead with the plan for a central bank which would be in safe (British) hands so that Indian nationalists had no chance to tamper with the currency. The

Reserve Bank of India, which was founded in 1934, was a bank owned by private shareholders and its governor was nominated by the Viceroy. The first governor, Sir Osborne Smith, was an experienced conservative banker whom Sir Montagu Norman himself had recommended to the Viceroy. But to the great disappointment of those who had put him in charge of the Reserve Bank, he became a convert to the school of thought that advocated a devaluation of the rupee. Of course, he was not permitted to do anything about it and in October 1936 he resigned and was succeeded by the former Deputy Governor, J.B. Taylor, who had an impeccable conservative record. While serving under Schuster in the Finance Department, he had torpedoed all developmental plans that Schuster had suggested. P.G. Grigg, Schuster's successor as Finance Member, who had clashed with Osborne Smith on the devaluation issue, could be well satisfied with Taylor, who shared his views. Compared to Grigg and Taylor, Sir Henry Strakosch, the financial adviser to the Secretary of State in London, looked like a veritable revolutionary. Strakosch was editor of *The Economist* and an admirer of the Swedish economist Gustav Cassell, whose policy had helped to keep credit and prices stable in Sweden. Nevertheless, Strakosch's advice could not change the course of imperial financial policy, just as Schuster's suggestions could not do so. The interests of Great Britain as a creditor nation prevailed and conservative civil servants like Grigg and Taylor were much more helpful in this respect than intellectuals like Strakosch and Schuster, who were ready to support experiments that would have initiated an economic recovery in India.

The official financial policy of the British Indian government, which emphasised deflation, retrenchment and a balanced budget, was bound to make the depression worse and to perpetuate it. It was typical for the depressive and repressive character of this policy that in the midst of retrenchment the expenditure on the police was the only one that was not cut, the land revenue was collected rigorously in spite of the steep fall in prices, and the salt tax was increased in the teeth of nationalist opposition. Gandhi's Salt March of 1930 proved to be of no avail in this respect. Faced with the option to increase either the salt tax or the income tax, the government preferred to raise the first rather than the latter, which would have touched the pockets of the articulate upper class, whereas the salt tax was a burden for the dumb millions. In 1929–30, income from the salt tax had amounted to 67 million rupees; in 1930–1, the income had increased to 68 million rupees, which clearly showed that Gandhi's campaign had made no impact on the collection of this tax.

The budgetary year 1931–2 started at the time of the Gandhi–Irwin pact, which Gandhi considered to be an achievement, whereas the British authorities interpreted it as a surrender. In that year the salt tax was stepped up to yield 87 million rupees and in the subsequent year 102 million rupees. At this rate, the salt tax provided an income of about one-third of that derived from land revenue, which amounted to 330 million rupees. Land revenue and salt tax together made up about one-third of total revenue, and customs duties also amounted to one-third. The latter had dwindled under the impact of the depression. Moreover, some protective tariffs had been introduced and to the extent that they fulfilled the purpose for which they were imposed, they were bound to yield a low income.

When Gandhi had returned from the Round Table Conference in 1932, he had revived the civil disobedience campaign. But this time the British Indian government immediately introduced a tough ordinance rule, which made all activities like no-rent campaigns or a refusal to pay revenue extremely risky. This was very helpful to the revenue collectors, who were surprised to see how readily the peasants paid up. This atmosphere changed again when Gandhi suspended the campaign once and for all in 1933 and the government withdrew the ordinances. From then on, the government and the Congress started to compete for the rural voters. The Viceroy, Lord Willingdon, invited all provincial governments of British India to an economic conference in 1934. If a bold developmental policy had emerged from this conference, the government could still have recovered some ground, but the deliberations of this conference remained inconclusive and the Congress was able to capture the imagination of the prospective electorate.

India's industrialists and businessmen, who had felt the pinch of the depression in 1931 and had advised Gandhi to suspend his campaign and to try his luck at the Round Table Conference, were also once more taking a radical line. They had been irked by the Ottawa agreement of 1932, which had established a regime of imperial preferences. Under this agreement, ten types of Indian raw materials were given preferential treatment in Great Britain, whereas 162 different types of British products enjoyed preferential access to the Indian market. All protective tariffs that had been granted by the British Indian government were reduced for the British in this way. The preferential treatment of Indian raw materials was regarded as a mere eyewash, as these materials would have been imported by the British in any case. Walchand Hirachand, the president of the Federation of Indian Chambers of Commerce for the year 1933, called the Ottawa agreement a 'tragical farce' in his presidential address. When the elections to the central legislative assembly were held in 1934, the first elections in which the Congress once more participated after three years of agitational campaigns, the Congress candidates were very successful and they were able then to act as spokesmen for a national economic policy. Attacks on imperial preference and the demand of a devaluation of the rupee were constant themes of the debates in the legislative assembly.

8.3 PROTECTIVE TARIFFS AND IMPERIAL PREFERENCES: THE STRATEGY OF MARKET SHARING

Even before the Ottawa conference, the problem of protective and preferential tariffs and the strategy of market sharing had been discussed by British and Indian businessmen. The protective tariff for steel and preferential rates for British steel imported into India, which had been introduced in 1927, could serve as a precedent for similar measures with regard to other products. The cotton textile industry of Bombay had clamoured for a protective tariff for a long time, and the textile magnates were quite prepared to accept a preferential arrangement for British textiles in return for British support for their demand.

The Indian textile industry was approaching an abyss, as the rupee exchange rate was kept at a high level, whereas the Japanese yen was about to be devalued. This meant a combination of an Indian import bonus with a Japanese export bonus. The British Indian government had refused to raise the purely fiscal customs duties of 11 per cent ad valorem. Finally, the government made a small concession and in the spring of 1930 introduced a protective tariff on cotton textiles at the rate of 20 per cent for non-British and 15 per cent for British textiles. After the depression hit India, budgetary considerations compelled the government to enhance the customs duties, and while doing this, the duty on cotton textiles was also raised to 25 and 20 per cent respectively in 1931. The budget of 1932 contained a further enhancement to 31 and 26 per cent respectively.

In the meantime the yen:rupee ratio had undergone some dramatic changes. In August 1931, before the pound and the rupee went off the gold standard, the yen:rupee ratio stood at 1:1.36. The Japanese had adopted the gold standard only recently and decided to stick to it; if they had persisted in that, the ratio of 1:1.79, which prevailed after September 1931, would have silenced all complaints about unfair competition. But in early 1932, they also went off the gold standard and devalued the yen drastically. By July 1932 the ratio was 1:1, and by 1933 it had come down to 1:0.75. At this stage, the British Indian government raised the protective tariff to 50 per cent and a little later to 75 per cent.

The Indian Tariff Board of 1932 had strongly recommended a high protective tariff, but it had also pointed out that imperial preference was incompatible with such a protective tariff and that the Indian cotton textile industry needed protection against British competition just as much as against the Japanese. The British Indian government suppressed the report for this reason. Finally, in 1933, the representatives of the British textile industry and of the Bombay textile industry agreed on a market-sharing arrangement (Mody–Lees pact). On behalf of the Bombay Millowners Association, Sir Homi Mody conceded to the British industrialists that they were entitled to preferential treatment, whereas they agreed to support a 'reasonable' degree of protection for the Indian industry. Indian nationalists bitterly criticised Mody for this 'sell-out', but Mody, who belonged to the dwindling group of Indian Liberals, believed that an understanding with British industrialists would pave the way also for constitutional progress and would make the demand for all kinds of 'safeguards' unnecessary. Among Indian socialists this kind of approach raised the fear of a 'fascist compact' of British and Indian business interests. With the benefit of hindsight, both Mody's hopes and the fears of the socialists appear to be naive, but their contemporaries were deeply agitated by the conclusion of this pact and indulged in acrimonious debates.

At the same time as Mody and Lees had their meetings in India, the British Indian government embarked on trade negotiations with a Japanese delegation that had come to India deeply resenting the measures that had been adopted to keep Japanese textiles out of India. Japan was the chief importer of Indian raw cotton and the Japanese had retaliated against the Indian protective tariff by boycotting Indian cotton. They could not have sustained this boycott, however, unless they were prepared to buy much more expensive cotton elsewhere. For the moment, though, this was a good bargaining counter, as the British Indian government was just as concerned about the fate of the Punjab cotton growers as it had been about the Punjab wheat growers at an earlier stage. A compromise was reached according to which customs duties on Japanese cotton textiles would not go beyond 50 per cent ad valorem; for this the

Japanese accepted a quota of 325 million yards of cotton textiles as a limit on their annual exports to India, and they also agreed to buy 1 million bales of Indian raw cotton per year.

The Indian Tariff (Textile Protection) Amendment Act, 1934 embodied the gist of the Mody-Lees pact as well as the substance of the Indo-Japanese trade negotiations. The British were the main beneficiaries of this act. The preferences granted to them amounted to reductions of the general rate by 20–30 per cent, according to the different categories of goods. As they were not tied to quotas as the Japanese were with regard to textiles, the British actually managed to recover a great deal of ground that they had lost both to Indian and Japanese competition in previous years. They concentrated now on the finer counts and left the production of coarse grey cloth to the Indian industry. Since the depression and the high exchange rate favoured the urban classes and enhanced their buying power with regard to imported goods, this trend favoured the British textile industry even more. Gandhi's campaign, which included the boycott of foreign cloth, proved to be as effective in this respect as with regard to the salt tax that was raised in those years.

The Indian textile magnates complained a great deal about imperial preference, but they nevertheless profited to some extent from the protection granted to them. The trend line of Indian cotton textile production shows a significant break in 1930, and it rises much more steeply after that date. There were, of course, some significant deviations from the general trend. In the initial years (1930–2), there was a rapid advance from 2.4 billion to 3 billion yards, then there was a setback, but in subsequent years the steady upward trend was resumed and by 1938 the Indian industry produced 4.3 billion yards. Of course, perfect protection would have produced even better results, because in 1938 0.6 billion yards were still imported. Nevertheless, the speed of import substitution under conditions of imperfect protection was quite remarkable.

There was, however, a natural limit to the expansion of the Indian textile industry: the reduced buying power of the Indian people. The growth of the Indian textile industry in those years was based entirely on import substitution and on population increase, but not on an expansion of per-capita demand. Only the outbreak of the Second World War, with its enormous demand for Indian textiles, saved the Indian industry from encountering this natural limit. The growth of the industry, however, was not accompanied by increasing investment, a fact that made itself felt during the war. The increase in output in the 1930s was achieved by utilising the full capacity of the machines installed earlier. Between 1929 and 1938, the number of looms increased from 170,000 to 190,000 and the number of spindles from 8.7 million to 9.7 million, but the number of millhands increased from 350,000 to 440,000. This disproportionate increase in the labour force (26 per cent, whereas spindles and looms increased by only 11 per cent) shows that the installed capacity was put to use by working more shifts.

8.4 THE RESTRICTIVE CRISIS MANAGEMENT OF THE JUTE INDUSTRY

The jute industry experienced a completely different course of development in the years of the depression. First of all, there was a remarkable retrenchment of the labour force from 340,000 in 1929 to 260,000 in 1933–4. After this date, there was a slow increase once more and shortly before the Second World War the industry employed 300,000 millhands. The number of looms had increased from 52,000 in 1929 to 62,000 in 1939. The productivity of the millhands was improved by about 40 per cent in this period. Whereas there were 6.5 millhands per loom in 1927, there were only 4.5 a decade later, and whereas in 1927 one worker used to handle 17.1 bales of raw jute, he would handle 23.6 in 1937. Since the fall in agrarian prices had greatly enhanced the real wages of millhands, the nominal wages could be reduced somewhat and the rapid increase in productivity did not lead to a higher wage bill. Low agrarian prices also meant cheap raw jute. Under such conditions the jute industry could survive with a decline in the value of exports from 550 million rupees (annual average for 1926–9) to 220 million rupees (1931–4). By 1936–7 the value of exports had risen once more to 300 million rupees. The jute industry supplied mainly bags, in which agrarian produce was shipped. Since this was worth only half its earlier value, the price of the bags had to be adjusted to that level too.

The quick adaptation to the new conditions actually showed the vitality and flexibility of the jute industry. Some companies, particularly Indian 'outsiders', managed to make a profit even in the midst of the depression. But the old conservative British managing agencies, which had got used to the easy times of the early 1920s, were slow to change their ways and rather opted for a restrictive crisis management. Under their tutelage, the Indian Jute Manufacturers Association (IJMA) tried to implement several measures aimed at reducing production so as to keep prices at a high level. The Bengal government was approached to help with this, as IJMA could not enforce these measures. The main problem was that of disciplining the 'outsiders', who did not belong to IJMA and were not at all willing to follow its restrictive lead. Sir Edward Benthall of Bird & Co., the leading light of IJMA, adduced every conceivable argument in order to persuade the government to lend a helping hand in this matter. He mentioned the rising unemployment of millhands; the sufferings of the poor jute-growing peasants; the imminent danger of a crash of the Calcutta Stock Exchange, if the shares of the jute companies suddenly tumbled. The Bengal government then passed an order whereby periods of work were curtailed and a certain number of looms sealed. However, this regulation was circumvented even by those who had asked for it; clandestine shifts could easily be arranged. Everybody was interested in compensating the loss of income due to falling prices by stepping up production.

When the industry recovered somewhat in 1935, the advocates of government intervention suddenly rediscovered their faith in a policy of *laissez-faire*, the more so as the new Bengal government, constituted after the constitutional reforms of 1935, would perhaps be inclined to other interventions that would go against the interests of the jute industry. The crocodile's tears that the jute managers had shed on behalf of the poor peasants could now attract the attention of the government that would want to improve the lot of the jute growers. These people had indeed suffered a great deal in those years. The industrialists had retained large stocks of raw jute in order to depress its price. The usual option of the jute grower of shifting to rice cultivation when the price of jute was low was also foreclosed, due to the fall in the rice price. Indian experts actually recommended state trading in jute as a remedy against the exploitation of the jute growers by the industrialists. This was, of course, rejected by insisting on the principle of free trade. Nevertheless, these arguments sounded very strange in view of the measures the government took at the same time in order to help the tea industry enforce restrictions of cultivation and to monitor the strict observance of export quotas. The quotas were fixed by the Tea Association, but the customs officers were instructed to aid this association in implementing this scheme. Whereas the restrictive crisis management of the jute industry had been a failure, that of the Tea Association proved to be very effective. This was due to the fact that jute textiles were only used for packing and could easily be replaced by other materials, if they proved to be too expensive, whereas there was no substitute for tea, which was grown in only a few countries that could easily form a cartel. This cartel could also discipline 'outsiders' much more effectively than the IJMA had ever managed to do, as even its own members secretly broke the rules established by that body and sanctioned by the government.

8.5 THE STEEL INDUSTRY: IMPORT SUBSTITUTION AND A SHRINKING DEMAND

The consumption of steel and coal is often taken as an indicator of the stage of development of a national economy. In India in the 1930s, this indicator clearly showed the impact of the depression. In 1929 India had consumed 1.4 million tons of steel; by 1933 this consumption had receded to 0.7 million tons and in the subsequent years (1934–8) it attained an annual average of 1 million tons. Indian coal production, which stood at 24 million tons in 1929, was down to 20 million tons in 1933; it then rose slowly until it amounted to 28 million tons in 1938, thus reaching once more the same point that it had reached twenty years before, immediately after the First World War.

Tata Iron & Steel Co. (TISCO) remained the only Indian steel producer until it was joined by the puny Mysore Iron and Steel Works in 1936. TISCO managed to expand its production gradually, in spite of shrinking demand. In the years from 1929 to 1932, TISCO produced annually about 0.6 million tons of steel; then production was stepped up and amounted to an annual average of 0.9 million tons (1936–8), until it reached 1 million tons in 1939. Import substitution progressed in this way very steadily. In 1929, TISCO could supply only 30 per cent of the steel consumed in India; ten years later it contributed 75 per cent. Just like the cotton textile industry, the steel industry almost reached the limits of growth in terms of import substitution by the end of the 1930s, and similarly the Second World War provided an escape from this trap.

In the war years, India's annual steel production amounted to 1.4 million tons on average. After the war, this level was reached again only in 1950. TISCO had the lion's share of this expansion, as other firms had not dared to enter this market, in spite of continuous 'discriminating protection', because the shrinking demand discouraged investment in the industry. There were only two exceptions: the Mysore Iron and Steel Works and the Steel Corporation of Bengal. Both firms had originally operated ironworks before they had started producing steel in 1936 and 1937 respectively. The Mysore firm owed its existence to the ambitious plans of M. Visveswaraya, the Dewan of Mysore, an engineer who greatly admired the industrial progress of Japan and had projected a ten-year plan for India's economic development. This blueprint had no chance under British rule, but in the princely state of Mysore a small-scale experiment could be made at Bhadravati, where a small ironworks was established in the 1920s, which then began steel production in 1936. The Bengal firm, which started steel production in 1937, was sponsored by the Indian Iron and Steel Company (IISCO), which had been founded in 1918 with this name, but had never ventured into the field of steel production, as steel prices began to fall soon after the ironworks of this company had been established at Barakar. It was only in 1937, when steel prices began to rise once more while protection was still continued, that IISCO launched the Steel Corporation of Bengal, which started producing steel only in 1939. In that year the Mysore firm attained for the first time a production at full capacity, which was only 25,000 tons per year. TISCO had a capacity of 0.8 million tons and the Bengal firm of 0.2 million tons.

Much more important than steel production was the growing production of pig iron in India. From 1930 to 1933, this production stood at 1 million tons per year; in the period from 1936 to 1938 pig-iron production had risen to 1.6 million tons per year. Much of this pig iron was exported — about 0.3 million tons per year in the first period and 0.6 million tons in the second. Great Britain was the main importer of this pig iron, which was one of the commodities for which India had been given preferential access to the British market. The price of pig iron fluctuated a great deal. In 1930 Indian pig iron fetched 39 rupees per ton; from 1932 to 1936, however, it only fetched 22 rupees. Rearmament in Europe helped to raise the price of pig iron and in 1937 it sold at 41 rupees per ton and in the following year at 50 rupees. The steel price rose similarly and this is why steel production became an attractive proposition for the first time in 1937.

8.6 THE METEORIC RISE OF THE SUGAR INDUSTRY

The three industries that have been mentioned so far had all had a somewhat chequered history, even before the Great Depression. During the years of the depression, a fourth industry, which had been rather insignificant previously, became of major importance:

the sugar industry. A great deal of sugar cane was grown in India — in the 1920s, there were on average 1 million hectares under sugar cane — but most of this sugar was converted into *gur* (the village-made brown sugar) instead of being refined in factories. The limited quantities of white refined sugar that were consumed in India (mostly in the urban areas) were imported from Java. Under the impact of the depression, this imported sugar became very cheap. By 1930, India imported 1 million tons at a price of 109 rupees per ton. By 1932, these imports had dwindled to 0.4 million tons and in the same year the British Indian government imposed a prohibitive tariff on imported refined sugar (about 190 per cent ad valorem). This stimulated industrial import substitution as well as an expansion of the area under sugar cane. By 1936 this area had been extended to 1.7 million hectares and yields per unit had increased by one third. In the years from 1932 to 1936, machines for sugar refineries worth 73 million rupees were imported, and 33 million rupees were invested in this way in one year (1933). By 1936 import substitution was almost complete, as only 23,000 tons of sugar were imported in that year.

In 1937 this booming Indian industry would have been able to cross the threshold from import substitution to export production. This would have been of vital importance for this young industry. Unfortunately, however, there was a glut in the world market and an International Sugar Agreement was reached which fixed national quotas and also defined which countries had to be regarded as importers and which as exporters. The countries defined as importers were not permitted to export sugar. As usual, India was represented by British officiers when this agreement was arrived at and these officers had been instructed to get India classified as a sugar-importing nation. This raised a storm of protest in India and the Secretary of State for India would also have liked to support India's case, but his colleague, the Colonial Secretary, pressed him to forget about this. When the protective tariff was imposed in 1932, no imperial interests were at stake, because the sugar that was kept out of India was Javanese sugar; in 1937, however, imperial interests were very much in the limelight, as several British colonies were sugar exporters whose quotas had to be protected at the expense of the Indian sugar industry.

The Indian sugar industry, which had expanded so rapidly — about 100 new refineries had been started in the 1930s — was severely hit by this British decision. The area under sugar cane was reduced from 1.7 million hectares in 1936 to 1.2 million hectares in 1938. The sugar industry tried to manage this crisis by establishing a syndicate, which was supposed to control production so as to maintain the price level. However, the syndicate had even more trouble with 'outsiders' than the jute industry. The governments of the United Provinces and of Bihar therefore decided to help the syndicate by permitting only syndicate members to process sugar cane. Supported by this drastic intervention, the syndicate immediately raised the price of refined sugar. The area under sugar cane promptly expanded to 1.8 million hectares in 1940. This sudden conversion of an expansive new industry into a state-supported cartel created many problems: it subjected the industry to political patronage and clever politicians could get a good deal of leverage out of this business.

8.7 NEW ENTERPRISES IN THE COUNTRYSIDE: OIL PRESSES, RICE MILLS AND MOTOR VEHICLES

In addition to the sugar industry, there were other rural enterprises that prospered in the 1930s. Their growth was less obvious, but it was perhaps even more important in view of future developments. Agrarian credit and the prices of land stagnated in the 1930s. Rich peasants who were not indebted used the opportunity of adding to their landed property in that period, and the polarisation of the rich and the poor became more striking at that time. Among the rural rich, there were entrepreneurs who invested their surplus funds in machinery for the processing of produce such as pressing oil or milling rice, and some of them also bought motor vehicles and organised local transport in competition with the railways, which had hitherto held a monopoly. The import statistics throw some light on this development: from 1930 to 1938, oil presses worth 26 million rupees and rice mills worth 9 million rupees were imported. Compared to the 93 million rupees invested in the machinery for sugar factories in this period these seemed to be modest amounts, but as they speeded up local processing of agricultural produce, they were of seminal importance for rural economic growth.

Local transport also attracted a great deal of investment. From 1930 to 1938, motor vehicles worth 315 million rupees were imported (this included buses worth 100 million rupees). During the same period, the railways imported engines worth 52 million rupees and wagons worth 73 million rupees. Private investment in road transport thus far surpassed state investment in rolling stock. The state's share in the investment in motor vehicles was probably rather limited. Just like the investment in oil presses and rice mills, these investments in motor vehicles were certainly not backed by a few large entrepreneurs, but by a host of small ones. A further indication of this type of investment is the total amount spent on the import of sewing and knitting machines in this period: 50 million rupees. This was almost as much as the 60 million rupees invested in new machinery for the jute industry. Since these small-scale investments are difficult to trace, not much research has been done in this field. The rural/urban distribution of these investments can only be a matter of guesswork. Nevertheless, it seems to be obvious that in this period a kind of rural bourgeoisie grew up outside the big cities, and this bourgeoisie invested at least some money in the means of production instead of going in only for moneylending or for buying more land. The dehoarding of gold and the gains of the middlemen who bought and sold this distress gold may have contributed to this kind of investment. But if we consider the enormous amount of gold exported in this period, which was worth 3.4 billion rupees, and look at the sum total of machinery imports in the same period, which amounted to 901 million rupees (cotton textile industry 166 million, jute machinery 60 million, sugar machinery 93 million, tea industry 15 million, mining machinery 42 million, oil presses and rice mills 35 million, sewing and knitting machines 50 million, motor vehicles 315 million, railway engines and wagons 125 million), and if we take into account that India not only exported gold, but also goods worth 16 billion rupees during this period, we see that the import of investment goods was rather modest. As such goods were not produced in India at that time, the import statistics provide fairly accurate information on the total amount invested.

A final glance at the import statistics will show us an interesting feature, which was very characteristic of the pattern of consumption: 155 million rupees' worth of alcoholic beverages were imported from 1930 to 1938 — almost as much as the amount invested in new cotton textile machinery. These beverages were certainly not consumed by the peasantry, but by British officers and civil servants and the Indian urban classes, which were very well off in the years of the depression. The high exchange rate made imports cheap, the low agrarian prices meant cheap food and low wages for domestic servants. Thus the urban classes and the rural masses had an altogether different impression of the years of the Great Depression. The urban classes had no particular reason for political dissatisfaction at that time and this is why the social base of Indian politics shifted to the rural areas in the 1930s — a fact that was of major importance for the future course of events.

117

9

India's War Profit:
the Debtor turns into a Creditor

9.1 FORCED SAVING, PRINTED MONEY AND THE NATIONAL DEBT

The Second World War initially had the same impact on India as the First World War. Prices rose, industrial equipment was utilised to full capacity, capitalists made enormous profits, and the gap between the rich and the poor widened. This time, however, there was no spurt of economic growth. The First World War had followed a period of worldwide economic expansion, in which India had shared to a modest extent. Industrial capacities installed before the war were then fully utilised, including India's novel steel plant. The Second World War, however, followed a prolonged depression, from which India had suffered more than the industrial nations of the West. In this period, hardly any new industrial equipment had been installed and the renewal of outdated machinery had been postponed. The utilisation of installed capacity soon reached its limits and thus prices increased as wartime demand grew. Moreover, Great Britain claimed a much greater share of Indian production in the course of this war than in the previous one. This will be discussed in detail below; at this point it may suffice to stress the importance of this fact for the acceleration of wartime inflation: purchasing power was created in terms of industrial wages and profits, but at the same time goods that could have absorbed it were exported in order to aid the war effort. The British government bought goods produced in India on credit and subjected India to a regime of forced saving. This amounted to a kind of compulsory investment in government bonds, but it was not necessary to issue such bonds as the government could freely print money. As more and more money was printed, the sterling currency reserves of the Reserve Bank of India deposited with the Bank of England in London increased to the same extent. But these reserves could not be touched by India during the war.

A short survey of the expansion of the Indian currency in the course of the war will demonstrate the effect of this regime of forced saving and of the printing of money. In 1939 there were 3.4 billion rupee coins and 2.6 billion rupee notes in circulation. Ten years earlier there had been 4 billion rupee coins and 1.6 billion rupee notes. During the years of the depression, more and more coins had been replaced by notes. During the war, notes were printed that corresponded to the equivalent of 11 billion rupees in sterling reserves deposited in London. In addition, there was a sum of 4.8 billion rupees, which had been given as credit to Great Britain by the Reserve Bank of India. This made up a total of about 16 billion rupees, which far surpassed India's national debt, which stood at 9.5 billion rupees. Thus India had turned from a debtor into a creditor of Great Britain. This was of major political importance for the process of decolonisation. It is easier to grant independence to a creditor whose account one manages than to a debtor whose liabilities one may have to share. India had to pay for this political advantage in terms of structural deficiencies, which were enhanced by the impact of the war.

Modern industrial economies are often beset with the problem of stagflation. Wages and prices increase, while the profits of capitalists are reduced and the propensity to invest as well as industrial production recedes. The Indian war economy showed similar symptoms for entirely different reasons. Profits were high, real wages declined, but there was no scope for investment, as investment goods could not be manufactured in India at that time and it was almost impossible to import them during the war. Moreover, the raising of industrial capital was impeded by the British, who mopped up all credit in order to finance the war effort. The peculiar effects of a wartime stagflation also made themselves felt in the agrarian sector. Prices rose steeply, but this did not lead to increased production, as the mode of production of innumerable small peasants could not be changed all of a sudden. In the subsequent sections of this chapter we shall first examine the wartime claims on industrial production and then the severe crisis of the food supply.

9.2 BRITISH CLAIMS ON INDIA'S INDUSTRIAL PRODUCTION

It was of great consequence for India's industry that the British government suddenly emerged as its largest customer. In the past, there had been much criticism of the British Indian government's practice of ordering most of its stores from Britain, even though less expensive products were available in India. Before the First World War the Stores Purchase Department of the Government of India had its office only in London. After that war an office had also been established in India, because the war had shown that government would have to rely on Indian products in an emergency. However, the orders of this department in India remained negligible. The government was not interested in encouraging import substitution in India and preferred to 'buy British'. Thus, for instance, in 1926 the department bought goods worth only 39 million rupees in India and imported stores worth 135 million rupees from Great Britain. When the Great Depression affected the British Indian budget, there was a shift towards acquiring cheaper stores in India, but at the same time government expenditure had to be reduced and thus Indian industry could not benefit very much from government orders. This changed very rapidly when the Second World War began. The jute industry had to supply sand bags, which were in great demand in all theatres of war. The cotton textile industry had to manufacture cloth for uniforms, as nearly 3 million Indian soldiers went abroad in the service of the empire and many more uniforms were exported. The products of the Indian steel industry, which had just managed to survive in the inter-war period, were also in great demand now.

Procurement of wartime supplies was managed very adroitly by the respective British departments. Instead of sequestering the respective plants for war production, they left them under private management, but prices were fixed by the departments concerned. These fixed prices applied only to whatever the government procured; everything else could be sold at higher prices in the market. The scarcity of goods and the growing purchasing power of urban consumers enabled the textile industry to sell its goods at very high prices indeed. The government tried to get its due share by either taxing profits or increasing sales taxes. The latter were passed on to the consumers. Although urban consumers did not feel the pinch of this regressive taxation, the rural poor were hit by it very hard. The uniforms that Indian soldiers wore out on distant battlegrounds were compensated for by the reduced consumption of cloth by poor share-croppers and agricultural labourers in India.

The Indian cotton textile industry could not add to the number of its approximately 200,000 looms during wartime, and there was only some addition to the number of spindles, from 10 million to 10.2

million. The limited increase in production from 4,012 million to 4,726 million yards of cotton textiles and from 1,235 million to 1,652 million lb of yarn was made possible by working more shifts and employing more labour. The number of millhands increased from the beginning to the end of the war by 20 per cent, from 442,000 to 512,000. This corresponds to the 20 per cent increase in the production of cotton textiles. The larger increase in the production of yarn (30 per cent) seems to indicate that there was a greater demand for industrial yarn from hand-loom weavers, who could step up their production more easily than the mills.

Whereas the cotton textile industry could benefit from increased exports as well as from internal demand, the export-oriented jute industry was subjected much more to the vagaries of the war. The beginning of the war meant a boom for that industry: in 1939 it produced 1.2 billion jute bags and 1.5 billion yards of jute cloth. The Japanese advances in South-East Asia greatly reduced the industry's export potential: in 1942 only 0.4 billion jute bags and 0.9 billion yards of jute cloth were produced. Nevertheless, increasing prices helped to compensate the millowners for at least some part of this decline in production. The value of the production of 1939 amounted to 478 million rupees and that of 1942 to 258 million; that is, the value had declined by less than half, while the production had been reduced to about one third. Moreover, the relatively low price of raw jute meant that the millowners could still make a handsome profit. Towards the end of the war production increased somewhat, but prices increased even faster. In this way the value of the production rose to 578 million rupees, although the volume was much smaller than in 1939.

The much larger profits of the cotton textile industry of Bombay and Ahmedabad, and the reduced potential of Calcutta's jute industry, indicated the rise of these centres of Western India and the decline of the industrial metropolis of the East. After the war, this discrepancy was further accentuated by the fact that the capitalists of Western India made full use of the sterling reserves for importing investment goods, whereas the British managing agencies that dominated the jute industry and the coal mines of the east sold out their interests and drew on those sterling reserves in order to repatriate their capital.

Whereas the war meant a boost to the cotton textile industry and a blow to the jute industry, it provided a real breakthrough for the steel industry. As explained earlier, Tata Iron and Steel had been the only Indian steel producer for a long time and had managed to survive only by means of discriminating protection and slow import substitution in a period of declining demand. At the same time India had exploited its rich iron-ore deposits in order to export pig iron. There was thus no scarcity of raw material for an expanding steel production, which jumped from 0.8 million tons in 1939 to 1.1 million tons in 1943, that is, by more than one-third in four years. The limited capacities did not permit a further increase in production. Wartime profits also encouraged large-scale investment after the war.

All other Indian industries were of such modest dimensions that it is hardly worth looking at them. Chemical products and cement production made some progress during the war. Ambitious plans for the production of motor cars with American participation, as well as the idea of establishing an aircraft industry, had received no encouragement from the British. The aircraft plant established at Bangalore in the very enterprising princely state of Mysore was used solely for repair work during the war. The first Indian factory for textile machinery, which had been completed just before the war, was sequestered and used for other purposes during the war, although the Indian textile industry was in dire need of textile machinery. The British gladly used the existing capacities of Indian industry during the war, but were not inclined to sponsor the growth of new industries that would compete with them after the war.

Before the war, the British Indian government was wedded to orthodox liberalism. Except for some protective tariffs for the sake of expediency, there was no deviation from liberal principles and interventionist measures were taboo. All this changed rapidly in the course of the war. For the procurement of goods and for handling the food crisis, the government had to create a formidable interventionist machinery. This machinery was geared to solving immediate problems rather than designed in the interest of long-term planning. The learning process was slow and painful for those civil servants who had been brought up on the notion that any interference with the working of the market can only lead to disaster. They were now interfering with the market in a big way, but they still could not think of countervailing measures such as controls of the distributive system. The food crisis, which was not a crisis of food availability, but of the distribution of food and income, put the British Indian administration to a severe test.

9.3 THE FOOD CRISIS: AGRARIAN PRICES AND INCOME DISTRIBUTION

When agrarian prices rose at the beginning of the war, the Viceroy, Lord Linlithgow, wrote to the Governor of the United Provinces of Agra and Oudh that he was confident that the peasants would now have no reason for discontent any longer. This was a great consolation for the British in India, as peasant unrest caused by the decline of prices in the years of the Great Depression had been a major political problem. While being complacent about this new trend of rising prices, the Viceroy did not express any fear of the potential effect of high prices, although the experience of the First World War should have been a warning in this respect. No provisions were made for the control of food distribution in the event of a crisis. In the early years of the war, prices rose steadily, but moderately. The harvests were good, and the market seemed to function smoothly. Suggestions of introducing price controls, which had been made by some officers, were quickly shelved as they seemed to be unnecessary.

In May 1942, when the war was approaching India's shores and Burma, a major rice-producing area, was lost, the Viceroy finally promulgated an ordinance, the Foodgrains Control Order. In the absence of the requisite machinery for implementing this order, nothing happened for quite some time. The fixing of prices by government proved to be utterly useless, since it only helped to establish a black market. The Governor of Madras adopted sterner measures; he prohibited the export of rice beyond provincial boundaries in June 1942 and then made rice trade a state monopoly in September 1942. Figure 9.1, showing the rice price in that province, clearly demonstrates that these measures were very successful. In the meantime the government of India still experimented with the fixing of prices and decided in January 1943 only to buy food grain in surplus provinces and sell it in deficit provinces. By August 1943 1 million tons of grain had been procured in that way. Trusting its new ability of handling the problem in this way, the central government abolished price controls and sanctioned the free trade in rice in Eastern India. However, the limited stocks stored by the government did not suffice to discourage hoarders. Bengal rice traders invaded neighbouring provinces and drove up the prices everywhere. Alarmed by this development, the central government abandoned its experiment in August 1943 and imposed price controls once more: this, of course, could only encourage the

Figure 9.1: Food grain prices in India, March 1937 to March 1944

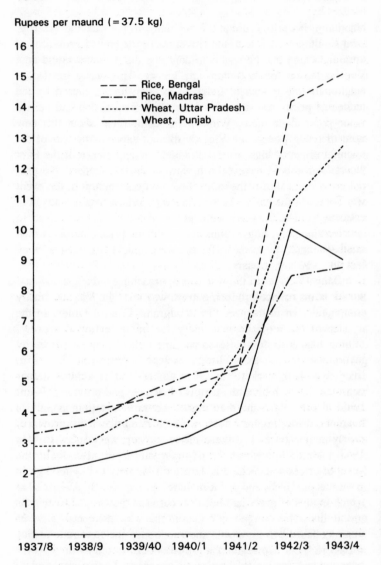

Rupees per maund (= 37.5 kg)

Source of data: H. Knight, *Food Administration in India, 1939–47* (Stanford, 1954).

speculations of hoarders. The Government of Bengal was neither willing nor able to adopt energetic measures as the Governor of Madras had done. In Madras, where the cabinet had resigned at the beginning of the war, the governor could do what he pleased. In Bengal, there was still a democratic government supported by an unstable coalition and thus the hands of the administration were tied. Very soon the Bengal rice price was twice as high as that in the neighbouring Madras Presidency and a terrible famine engulfed the unfortunate province. It is said that this famine claimed 1–3 million victims; the lower figure would account only for those who starved immediately, whereas the higher figure includes those who died owing to subsequent epidemics among the undernourished. The victims were mostly agricultural and industrial labourers who did not grow rice themselves and could not afford to buy it. The crisis was not a crisis of production and supply, but one of distribution or entitlement (that is, of a highly skewed income distribution, which deprived the poor of the essentials of subsistence). That this was a crisis of distribution and not of production is clearly shown by the fact that raw jute prices remained comparatively low. Jute grows in rice fields; therefore a shift in the price the producer got for rice would have resulted in the substitution of rice for jute and a comparable rise in the raw jute price.

The terrible Bengal famine, which claimed its victims in the midst of ample harvests and was only due to hoarding and administrative inefficiency, finally caused the government to intervene more effectively. Rationing was introduced in all major urban centres. Urban consumers who received incomes boosted by wartime inflation could afford to pay high food prices and would thus encourage hoarders; it was therefore necessary to curtail urban consumption by rationing. But whereas Bombay had already started this in May 1943, Calcutta followed suit only in January 1944, after the central government had ordered it against the wishes of the provincial government. By February 1944 there were a total of 104 cities in which food was so rationed; it took the government one more year to introduce this measure in an additional 400 towns and cities. In this way 42 million urban consumers were subjected to rationing by early 1945. An organisation that could store food procured by the government was only able to start its operations by November 1944. All this was a bit late as far as the war was concerned, but it came in handy during the immediate post-war food crisis of 1945–6, when the distribution problem was enhanced by a real shortfall in agricultural production. By early 1947, 900 towns with a total population of 152 million inhabitants received rationed food grains. This was a remarkable achievement, if one considers the total lack of preparedness for such measures which had prevailed until 1943.

The strategy and machinery of state intervention that had emerged owing to wartime needs became of great importance for the further development of the Indian economy. Without these preconditions, all concepts of economic planning would have remained mere pipedreams. The government of independent India inherited this machinery and was able to implement its five-year plans in this way. Even much of the contents of these five-year plans had been conceived during the war, although not by the British Indian government, which indulged in state intervention only for short-term crisis management. A brief survey of the emergence of these concepts of economic planning during the war will conclude the present chapter.

9.4 THE WARTIME ORIGINS OF ECONOMIC PLANNING

The Indian National Congress had toyed with the idea of economic planning even in the 1930s. A concrete beginning was made in 1938, when a planning commission chaired by Jawaharlal Nehru was inaugurated by the Congress and sponsored by the provincial governments wherever Congress ministers had accepted office. The personnel of this planning commission was not restricted to Congress members; it also included independent experts and even representatives of some princely states. The resignation of the Congress ministers in 1939 deprived the commission of its immediate relevance, but Jawaharlal Nehru saw to it that its report was completed nevertheless in 1940. The report was of a purely qualitative nature: it listed priorities of industrial investment without mentioning the sums to be invested or the ways and means of financing such investment. The Congress thereafter stopped planning during the war, as most of its leaders were in prison.

In the meantime two members of the British war cabinet, Bevin and Cripps, drafted an economic plan for India, which they submitted in 1942. Churchill, who obviously wanted to divert Cripps's attention after his unsuccessful mission to India in April 1942, had suggested this idea of a memorandum, which would convince Indians that the British and not the Congress and the Indian capitalists were their true friends. In keeping with this aim, the Cripps–Bevin plan started with the encouragement of Indian agriculture and then proceeded to a scheme of modest industrial growth, jointly sponsored by private capital and the state. The idea of a 'mixed economy' was thus already projected by these two British planners. Their memorandum never saw the light of day, but got lost in the dusty shelves of British and Indian archives. The Viceroy suppressed it, because he feared that instead of scoring a propaganda victory by its publication, he would only attract hostile criticism, as the British had no money to spare to support any kind of planned development and thus this plan would look like a ridiculously futile exercise, even more so as the government was at that time quite helpless in dealing with the food crisis.

When the war turned in favour of the British in 1943 and planning for post-war reconstruction seemed to be justified, a group of Indian industrialists got together and drafted a fifteen-year plan for India, to be implemented from 1947 to 1962. The first part of this so-called 'Bombay Plan' was published in January 1944. In contrast with the earlier plan proposals, this one was not purely qualitative, but mentioned concrete figures. The per-capita income was supposed to be doubled in the course of the plan period. A total investment of 100 billion rupees was to be divided among industry (45), housing (22), agriculture (12) and other sectors (21). This distribution was typical for the trend of thought among Indian nationalists: industry was considered to be the motor of economic growth, whereas agriculture was supposed to be more of a liability than an asset. The second part of the 'Bombay Plan', which was published a year later, was devoted to employment and distribution, problems that had been neglected in the first part. It was stated here that whereas in 1931 the rural sector had employed 72 per cent of the workforce, industry 15 and services 13, these sectors would have 58, 26 and 16 per cent respectively by the end of the plan period in 1962. Unfortunately these targets have not been reached even today. In 1980, the respective percentages were 71, 13 and 16 — not very different from the figures for 1931.

The authors of the 'Bombay Plan' did not only provide concrete figures for their investment programme: they also indicated how they wanted to finance the plan. The amount of 100 billion rupees would be accounted for as follows: 10 billion from sterling reserves, which would be available by the end of the war; 40 billion savings during the plan period; 6 billion export earnings; 3 billion proceeds from the sale of hoarded gold; 7 billion foreign aid or credit; 34 billion deficit spending (i.e. printing money). This last method of financing was openly recommended and it was even stated that this should be possible without generating inflation.

'Mixed economy' was an avowed aim of the 'Bombay Plan'. The state should finance and run the basic industries, whose investment needs were large, whereas profits were bound to be limited. Private capitalists could look after those sectors where investment would promise quick returns. Critics of this plan therefore termed it 'fascist', because it envisaged a symbiosis of the private and the public sector, in which the private sector would reap the profits, whereas the public sector would have to be supported by the tax-payer. As we shall see below, this criticism was prophetic, though, of course, the pure state capitalism advocated by those critics would not necessarily have yielded much better results as far as the taxpayer was concerned.

The 'Bombay Plan' was criticised not only by left-wingers, but also by the orthodox liberal, Dr Gregory, the economic adviser to the Viceroy. Lord Wavell, the new Viceroy, preferred to shelve the withering criticism of the plan by his adviser rather than to make it public. He felt that it was better to take the wind out of the sails of the planners by appointing one of them as Member of Planning and Reconstruction of the Viceroy's Executive Council. The man whom he picked for this assignment was eminently suited for it: Sir Ardeshir Dalal, a former civil servant who had made a brilliant success of a business career as a director with Tatas, whose senior boss, J.R.D. Tata, was also one of the authors of the plan. Dalal was, of course, interested in promoting the interests of Indian industry. In this he was frustrated very soon and he resigned within a year of his appointment. The immediate cause of his resignation was an unsuccessful mission to London, where he had pleaded for British aid to Indian industry. Dalal insisted that such aid should be given only to purely Indian companies and not to British companies operating in India. The British government stated that it was unable to discriminate against British firms that had got themselves registered in India in order to benefit from the protective tariffs granted to India in the 1930s. These firms had seen to it that their rights were enshrined in the Government of India Act of 1935, and thus the government was indeed handicapped in this respect. This proved to the Indian capitalists once more that their only hope was an independent government of India, as the British were pledged to uphold British interests. When Dalal saw that by remaining a member of the Viceroy's council he would only provide an alibi to these British interests without being able to do anything, he decided to quit. The 'Bombay Plan', which he had helped to draft, remained on paper only and was never implemented. Several of the authors of the plan, including the big industrialists Birla and Tata, and John Matthai, who became a finance minister in Jawaharlal Nehru's government, were very influential in independent India. Their advocacy of a 'mixed economy' was crucial as far as future planning was concerned. In this way, most elements of independent India's economic planning emerged in the course of the Second World War — the instruments of state intervention as well as the major concepts of planning — and this proved to be of great importance for India's economic development.

10

India's Dilemma: Dynamic Industrialisation and Static Agriculture

10.1 THE CONSTRAINTS OF ECONOMIC POLICY

Independent India's economic policy was based on the hope that a dynamic industrialisation would help to trigger off an equally dynamic development in the field of agriculture. This economic policy, however, was conditioned by the constraints of the colonial legacy. When India attained independence in 1947, this was not due to a revolution, although there had been a long and ardent freedom struggle. The independent republic took over the colonial administration, the legal and educational systems, and the entire infrastructure as a going concern. The fact that the transfer of power was accompanied by a partition of the country was a burden for the new state, but this partition also reinforced the maintenance of the *status quo*, as any departure from it was thought to be a threat to the integrity of the new republic. The strong position of the central government was emphasised and attempts at creating a new federal order were postponed, as they seemed to violate national unity. After long debates and considerable unrest, the principle of linguistic states was adopted and several new federal units emerged in the late 1950s. At the same time, however, the power of the centre was strengthened by the new process of economic planning. When India started to receive foreign aid in the late 1950s, this also contributed to the leverage of the central government. Moreover, the old imperial practice of reserving the most dynamic sources of taxation for the centre was also continued by the independent government of India. However, the Finance Commissions, which according to the Indian constitution were appointed at regular intervals of five years in order to assess the shares of the central and the state governments in various revenues, etc., did make an impact on federal finance in the long run. Whereas the relationship of central government expenditure to that of all the state governments put together was about 2.6 to 1 in 1950, it changed to 1.6 to 1 by the 1970s. Of course, this strengthening of the financial position of the states was part and parcel of a general increase in the share of government expenditure in the gross national product. By 1975 total expenditure of the central and all the state governments amounted to 28 per cent of GNP, and in 1985 it reached 40 per cent.

The imperial heritage was not only noticeable in what might be termed reluctant federalism, it also conditioned the approach of the Indian government to the large majority of the population in the countryside. The British had tried to win over the rich peasants by restricting the rights of landlords. Where the peasants did not pay rent to a landlord, but revenue to the government, they had benefited from the fact that the land revenue had not been enhanced since the days of the Great Depression, and its impact on the peasantry had been greatly reduced by wartime inflation. The National Congress had adopted the role of a peasant party during the Great Depression and did not want to alienate the peasantry by revising the land revenue after coming to power in independent India. Thus the land revenue was soon only of symbolic significance; in most districts the cost of its collection was higher than the amount collected. Therefore the land revenue could not be used as an instrument of economic policy. At the same time the revenue authorities lost interest in the proper maintenance of revenue records; these were the only substitute for a record of rights, which was conspicuous by its absence in most parts of rural India. Without such a record, most measures of land reform could never be implemented and remained wishful thinking. The only measure that was implemented success-fully was the abolition of the rights of the superior landlords (*zamindars*) of Northern and Eastern India. The rights of these landlords had already been curtailed by British Indian tenancy legislation, and there was not much difficulty in going one step further and abolishing these rights altogether, the more so as the landlords obtained due compensation.

The amount of compensation was graded in such a way that the process of abolition became politically feasible. The few large landlords got comparatively less, as they could not exert much political pressure, whereas the greater numbers of small landlords were much better off. The landlords were also permitted to resume the best acres of land that they had leased out. Subletting was prohibited under the new land reforms, but it was easy to employ

131

share-croppers and call them 'partners', if the authorities concerned were too inquisitive. In this way the former landlords joined the ranks of the rich peasantry, and jointly they emerged as a powerful political force in the countryside, preventing any further reform. The imposition of ceilings on landholdings was easily circumvented by parcelling out land to members of a family or just hiding behind the smokescreen of manipulated land records. A revised revenue assessment with a progressive rate according to the size of the respective holding would have been a better approach to land reforms, but this would have been a serious political challenge to the dominant strata of rural India. The reliance on rural vote banks during elections was incompatible with such a challenge. Moreover, land revenue just as any other direct taxation was out of favour with a government that preferred indirect taxation or even deficit spending and the printing of money to touching the pockets of dominant interests. A look at the revised estimates for the financial year 1985-6, the latest data available at present, shows the results of this emphasis on indirect taxation. Total expenditure of the central and all the state governments amounted to 850 billion rupees. Only 561 billion rupees of this amount were covered by current revenue income, the rest was raised by means of loans, etc., and there was also a sizeable amount of deficit spending. The only item of direct taxation, income and corporate tax, yielded a modest sum of 55 billion rupees; customs amounted to 92 billion rupees; excise duties to 129 billion rupees; and sales tax to 85 billion rupees.

The emphasis on regressive indirect taxation and the neglect of progressive direct taxation for reasons of political expediency encouraged the redistribution of income in favour of the rich. The relatively privileged urban population and the stratum of rich peasants were the major beneficiaries of economic development. The urban population had prospered both during the Great Depression and in the subsequent war. The rich peasants had initially suffered in those earlier periods, but the more lucky or successful among them had been able to consolidate their holdings at the expense of less fortunate neighbours. They were now free to exploit landless labour or dwarfholders, who depended for their survival on being admitted as share-croppers ('partners').

The government could depend for political support both on the urban population and on the rural rich. Conflicts of interest between these two strata could arise only whenever the government tried too hard to keep agricultural prices down in order to satisfy the urban consumers, thus alienating the peasants, or when grain prices rose too quickly so as to generate urban unrest. Since Indian agriculture is still largely dependent on the monsoon, Indian economic policy often centres on this crucial conflict of interests. The need to strike a short-term balance in this field militates against long-term planning. The fact that India has nevertheless succeeded in making some progress in the course of several five-year plans has to be appreciated in this context.

10.2 THE INITIAL THREE FIVE-YEAR PLANS: 1951–66

Jawaharlal Nehru, who had been the chairman of the national planning commission from 1938 to 1940, now continued this tradition as India's Prime Minister. A Planning Commission was established by a cabinet decision in 1950 and the Prime Minister was its *ex-officio* chairman. Therefore this commission attained a prominent political position, although it was actually nothing but an advisory body of experts. The five-year plans produced by that body were guidelines only; they did not have the force of law. But since the Prime Minister was the chairman of the commission, he was, of course, politically committed to their implementation. Nehru combined these two roles of political leader and chief planner more or less harmoniously, but his successors were often caught on the horns of a dilemma, when they had to make concessions for the sake of political expediency that they should have rejected in the interest of long-term planning. Nehru was not plagued by these problems, because the conditions for economic planning were still quite favourable in his time. Moreover, the National Congress controlled both the centre and the federal states. After Nehru's death, both the economic conditions and the political scene changed very rapidly and planning became a much more difficult exercise.

The first five-year plan (1951–6) was a relatively modest venture. It envisaged a total investment of 35 billion rupees: 20 billion rupees in the public and 15 billion in the private sector. By the end of the plan period only 31 billion rupees had been invested, but the target of increasing national income by 11 per cent had been surpassed — there was actually an increase of 18 per cent. The designer of this plan was Professor Mahalanobis, who had adopted the simple two sector model of Soviet planning: investment goods/consumption goods. He gave top priority to investment goods, as they were crucial for further economic growth. The disadvantage of this strategy was capital deepening, that is, the commitment of large amounts of capital to heavy industry, which would yield low returns. At the same time this investment would generate buying power, which could not be absorbed due to the neglect of consumption goods, and this could lead to inflation. However, in this regard the 'mixed economy' proved to be a decisive corrective: the private industrialists invested in the production of consumption goods, which promised quick returns, and they gladly left long-term investment in heavy industry with low profits to the public sector. Private industry benefited from protective tariffs or the total prohibition of imports. This, of course, tempted many industrialists to go in for shoddy products, which could nevertheless be sold at fancy prices and thus yielded enormous returns. The private sector could prosper without facing competition, and there was hardly any need for a cost–benefit analysis, as profits dwarfed costs most of the time. Moreover, windfall profits accumulated during the war gave a head start to the major Indian companies such as the Birlas and the Tatas, who had sponsored the 'Bombay Plan'. Economic development actually followed the trend projected by the 'Bombay Plan', although Nehru and Mahalanobis had certainly not intended that it should do just that. The good feeling generated by the success of the first five-year plan in any case muted all potential criticism.

Encouraged by the success of the first plan, the Planning Commission adopted a much more ambitious second plan. The total investment was to be of the order of 62 billion rupees (public and private sectors), of which only 46 billion rupees were actually invested. This time Mahalanobis had designed a four-sector model. He retained the emphasis on investment goods, but divided the other sector into three subsectors: (a) industrial, (b) agriculture and cottage industry and (c) services, education, health, etc. Only one-third of the total investment should go to the first sector (investment goods), whereas two-thirds should be devoted to the three subsectors mentioned above. Cottage industry, in particular, was singled out as a major potential producer of consumption goods. The fact that cottage industry required little capital and was labour intensive was highlighted. Of course, for this very reason one also could not expect a great deal of savings from cottage industry, which would be required for future economic growth. However, this problem did not worry the planners at this stage. Heavy industry in the public sector was considered to be the major item once more, as it was the very symbol of economic independence and was thought to be crucial for the maintenance of political independence.

The third five-year plan (1961–6) was conceived in a similar spirit. In this plan period, investment in the public sector was stepped up with a vengeance. Originally the plan had mentioned 75 billion rupees as a target for public-sector investment, but by the end of the plan period 86 billion rupees had actually been invested in that sector. This investment was distributed in the following way: industry 17 billion rupees; transport and communications 21 billion; energy 12 billion; agriculture 11 billion; and others 25 billion. The emphasis on transport and communications showed that the planners had become aware of the bottlenecks created by the inadequate infrastructure inherited from the colonial past. The modest role of agriculture in this plan reflected once more the pattern of thought of all Indian planners, from the authors of the 'Bombay Plan' to Nehru and Mahalanobis. They all looked upon industry as the only key to India's economic development.

Public investment in the three plan periods amounted to a total of 163 billion rupees, of which only 19 billion were devoted to agriculture. Of course, agriculture belonged entirely to the private sector and could therefore not expect to receive a major share of public investment. But whereas private industry greatly benefited from protectionism, agriculture did not benefit from it at all, but was rather burdened by it. The terms of trade moved against agriculture. The planners were, in fact, happy about this trend, because they wanted to keep food prices down so as not to impede industrial development by the vicious circle of rising prices and rising wages. Moreover, agriculture was of no use as a source of taxation, as we have seen above. It would not contribute to public investment, thus its neglect by the planners was practically preordained. Nevertheless, they had to pay for this neglect in due course, because the exclusive emphasis on industrial development without regard for its agrarian base is fatal in a country like India. In the early plan periods this problem did not become apparent, because agricultural production did grow to some extent. It was only by the end of the third plan period that a bottleneck was noticed in this respect. In the following two sections, we shall trace this development first with regard to industrial production and then we shall turn to agricultural production.

10.3 INDUSTRIAL PRODUCTION

Stepping up industrial production had always been an aim of Indian nationalists, who had blamed the British for retarding India's industrial growth. The industrial progress of the independent republic was quite remarkable. The index of industrial production (1950 = 100) stood at 200 in 1960 and at 280 in 1964. In subsequent years there was an industrial recession, which will be discussed in the next chapter.

There were marked differences in the progress of various branches of industry. Heavy industry, which was a top priority of public investment, did go ahead in a big way. Steel production, which amounted to 1 million tons per year during the war and stagnated at that level during the immediate post-war period, reached 3 million tons in 1960 and 6 million tons in 1964. Import substitution under a regime of protectionism also benefited from the growth of the investment-goods industry. Machine tools worth 70 million rupees and textile machinery worth 104 million rupees were produced in 1960. This production continued to grow. But in contrast with this development, the largest and oldest Indian industry, the cotton textile industry, stagnated. Its production of about 5 billion yards of cloth remained practically the same throughout, from the war years to 1964. By the end of the war this industry had a total of 200,000 looms and 10 million spindles and employed 500,000 millhands. The production of yarn amounted to 1.6 million lb. Ten years later, there were 207,000 looms, 12 million spindles and 752,000 millhands, but the production still amounted only to 5 billion yards of cotton cloth and 1.6 million lb of yarn. In other words, productivity had declined to an alarming extent.

The stagnation of this major consumption-goods industry was undoubtedly related to the stagnation of per-capita income of the great mass of the population. On average, rural incomes did not grow by more than 0.5 per cent per year. A notable increase in purchasing power was restricted to a large section of the urban population and the rich peasants. Therefore there was an expanding market for more sophisticated goods such as nylon shirts, radios, refrigerators, but no additional demand for plain cotton cloth. Even the production of bicycles, which are of great importance in India, remained rather modest in those early plan periods. In the years of fastest industrial growth, from 1960 to 1964, when the value of the annual production of machine tools rose from 70 million rupees to 258 million, the production of bicycles only increased from 1 million to 1.4 million. In terms of value, this amounted to an increase from 200 million to 280 million rupees. Thus a rapidly expanding investment-goods industry was confronted with a stagnant production of mass consumption goods. There was therefore a growth of installed capacity of investment goods, and a stagnation of purchasing power, and thus of demand, for industrial goods. Two-thirds of the income of the average household continued to be spent on food. If food prices were going to rise, the amount available for the purchase of industrial goods was bound to be reduced.

The great drought of 1965–6 led to a remarkable rise in food prices. The terms of trade shifted in favour of agriculture, but the new rural purchasing power mostly accrued to the rich peasants, who could not be expected to increase their demand for industrial goods immediately. We shall return to this problem in the next chapter, in the context of the 'Green Revolution'. In the following section of the present chapter, we shall examine the 'pre-revolutionary' development of agricultural production.

10.4 AGRICULTURAL PRODUCTION

Compared to the much-advertised spurt of agricultural production of the 'Green Revolution' in the early 1970s, the growth of agricultural production in the 'pre-revolutionary' years was not as negligible as one might think. Until 1958, the index of agricultural production did not deviate very much from that of industrial production. By 1958 agricultural production had attained 140 (1950 = 100), whereas the index of industrial production stood at 160. After 1958 the two trends deviated very radically, as agricultural production stagnated at about 150 in 1960–3. Nevertheless, India did produce 70 million tons of food grains in 1963; this figure consisted of 37 million tons of rice, 10 million tons of wheat, 23 million tons of millet and other varieties of grain, in addition there were 10 million tons of pulses, and 7 million tons of oilseeds. The 'Green Revolution' changed this record only in terms of a rapid growth of wheat.

In contrast with the 'Green Revolution', this 'pre-revolutionary' growth of agricultural production was entirely due to the extension of the area under cultivation, which amounted to about 15 per cent from 1950 to 1964 (i.e. about 1 per cent per year). The yield per acre did not increase very much, because there was no change in the traditional mode of small peasant agriculture. The increase in production by means of an extension of cultivation was bound to reach a natural limit in due course. Most of this increase did not come from the formation of real capital (terracing, amelioration, etc.), but was simply achieved by ploughing land that was fallow. Pastures and forests were also decimated in this way, and the environment deteriorated more and more with disastrous consequences for the future. Although pastures receded, India still maintained about 180 million cattle and 60 million buffaloes. The 'holy cow', which was much maligned by experts in animal husbandry, actually served India very well by producing bullocks, which are essential for ploughing the fields and for rural transport. The resilience of India's half-starved cattle is remarkable; better-bred cattle would not survive under the adverse conditions to which the 'holy cow' is adapted. Even though beef is not eaten by most Hindus, cattle does contribute to feeding the poor, who do not mind eating carrion. There is a kind of 'parallel economy' here, too, which is not reflected in official statistics.

The conversion of pastures into cultivable land and the ploughing of more and more marginal land that was drought-prone greatly increased the vulnerability of Indian agriculture. The great drought of 1965–6 exposed these weaknesses. It had enormous consequences: the budget and agricultural prices, development plans and the behaviour of voters were all affected by this catastrophe. Whereas industrialisation had been pushed ahead vertically, agriculture had been extended horizontally. Deficit spending had been pressed into service for financing this industrial progress. Under conditions of equally vigorous growth in agriculture and industry, the inflationary potential of deficit spending could have been controlled, but now inflation raised its ugly head and scared the government, which tried to put on the brakes and thus also slowed down industrial growth, as we shall see in the next chapter. In the following section, however, we want to examine the role of deficit spending and foreign aid in the early plan periods.

10.5 PRICES, DEFICIT SPENDING AND FOREIGN AID

The government had freely indulged in the printing of money during the war, as we have seen above. The authors of the 'Bombay Plan' had also recommended deficit spending as a major contribution to the financing of their plan. A moderate amount of deficit spending may indeed help to fuel the engine of economic growth, if it leads to an increase in production, full employment and the generation of demand. But if deficit spending goes hand in hand with capital deepening (that is, investment in heavy industry, which does not

138

yield immediate returns), it necessarily leads to inflation.

In the 1950s, this dangerous trend did not show up. Immediately before the first plan period, India had experienced an imported inflation due to the Korean war boom, which pushed up raw-material prices in the world market. This was soon corrected, as world market prices fell, good harvests prevailed in India and plan expenditure was modest until 1956. In the last two years of the first plan, deficit spending amounted to only 4 billion rupees. Nevertheless, this was already close to the point where the inflationary effect of deficit spending would no longer be neutralised by economic growth. However, the planners went ahead with a much more ambitious second plan and money supply surged. During the first plan period money supply M1 (currency with the public and demand deposits) amounted to about 20 billion rupees, during the second period it increased to 24 billion rupees, and by 1960 it had reached 27 billion. Inflation was kept at bay for some time by a general increase in industrial production and good harvests. Agricultural prices rose from 1955 to 1957; this trend was checked by two good harvests and then reasserted itself in 1959. Even two very good harvests in 1960 and 1961 could no longer stop the inflationary trend. A bad harvest in 1962 and the border war with China, which made India step up defence expenditure, fuelled the inflation. Investment in defence production is particularly counterproductive in this respect, as consumers normally do not buy arms when their purchasing power increases. Thus even in the year before the great drought, the level of prices was 50 per cent above that of 1954. As prices rose, nominal wages also increased, but real wages stagnated and employment did not grow sufficiently. In order to show some progress in this respect, most public-sector firms were overstaffed, and inefficiency and the cost of production were enhanced in this way.

The planners were primarily concerned with the effect of rising prices on the financing of their industrial projects. Therefore they welcomed the import of American wheat; this was made available to India under Public Law 480, which permitted payment in rupees and thus did not cost India any foreign currency. After having exhausted the sterling reserves in 1956, India was worried about the balance of payments and had to shop around for foreign aid. The American wheat loan, as it was called, was therefore accepted with a sigh of relief. During the first plan period India imported 12 million tons of grain, during the second 17 million tons, and during the third 25 million tons (that is, a total of 54 million tons in fifteen years). The effect of the wheat loan has been a subject of heated debates. It may be argued that if India had not been able to import this wheat, agricultural prices would have risen steeply much earlier and would have forced the government to adjust its economic policy, before the drought hit the country and upset all plans for quite some time.

A more positive role was played by foreign capital aid, which greatly contributed to the financing of the plans after 1957. During the first plan period the total amount of foreign aid (loans, grants and others) was $ US 428 million, during the second plan period it rose to $ US 3.2 billion, and in the third it reached $ US 5.5 billion. The official exchange rate was $ US 1 = 4.75 rupees at that time, and thus the amounts quoted above would correspond to 2 billion, 15 billion and 16 billion rupees respectively. The foreign aid component of public investment thus amounted to 10 per cent during the first plan and about 30 per cent in the second as well as the third plan. This shows that foreign aid was of vital importace for the ambitious programme of industrial growth, which would have had to be very much reduced, or financed by an intolerable amount of deficit spending, if this aid had not been forthcoming. The dwindling of foreign aid in subsequent years contributed to the industrial recession which characterised the period after 1965.

With the benefit of hindsight, forced industrial growth that was financed by foreign aid and deficit spending, only to end up in a prolonged period of recession in which the installed capacities could not even be fully utilised, seems to be of rather doubtful value. Jawaharlal Nehru's 'take-off' optimism was obviously premature. Nehru died in May 1964, a year before the drought hit India and ruined all the plans; thus he was spared the pains of disappointment, which his successors had to endure. The planning process was scrapped for some time and only initiated once more after the 'Green Revolution' had raised some hopes of further progress. It seemed as if the tide had turned and as if from then on a dynamic agriculture could breathe new life into a stagnant industry. This did not happen for quite some time, however, and it became obvious that the industrial recession was not just due to the constraints of agricultural growth, but had some other reasons, too. Large-scale poverty and a highly skewed income distribution appeared to be one of these reasons, and this called for a populist political programme. Indira Gandhi ran her famous election campaign of 1971 with the slogan *'Gharibi hatao'* (Vanquish poverty); she won the election, but not the battle against poverty, which proved to be a hardy perennial and neither decreased nor increased, but just stayed put.

11

The 'Green Revolution' and the Industrial Recession

11.1 THE POLITICAL CONTEXT OF THE GREAT DROUGHT, 1965–7

The decisive break in the trend of India's economic growth that occurred in 1965 was due to several factors, the great drought being only one of them. The Pakistani attack of September 1965 was also of great importance. It led to a further commitment to defence expenditure and reduced the flow of foreign aid.

Moreover, political leadership was weak after Nehru's death. Lal Bahadur Shastri, his immediate successor, was perceived to be weak, although he showed his mettle when he stood up to the combined provocation of Pakistan and China. His sudden death in Tashkent removed him from the political scene just at the moment when he had gained some stature. Indira Gandhi was perceived to be a weak compromise candidate, who emerged from the contest for the succession only because the Congress caucus did not like to accept the stern tutelage of Morarji Desai. She was immediately faced with the second year of the great drought, and on top of all this she succumbed to the pressure of the World Bank and drastically devalued the rupee. This measure will be discussed in detail below. At this stage it may suffice to indicate that the positive effects of such a devaluation could not show up immediately, whereas its adverse consequences made themselves felt in a big way. The drought pushed up prices and the devaluation accelerated this trend even more. Planning was suspended in 1966, as deficit spending would have been suicidal in the face of galloping inflation, and foreign aid had dried up too.

Under such inauspicious circumstances, Indira Gandhi had to face a general election in 1967. Since at that time the elections for the Lok Sabha (central parliament) and the legislative assemblies of the federal states were still held jointly, a great deal of local discontent queered the pitch of national politics. The strength of the Congress in the Lok Sabha was greatly reduced and in most parts of Northern India heterogeneous coalitions displaced the Congress governments. Central economic planning seemed to have no future under such conditions and the propensity to invest also declined, both in the public and in the private sector. Only the rich peasants were bound to be optimistic, as they benefited from the steep rise of agricultural prices. They could now invest in various inputs in order to step up their production. Thus the 'Green Revolution' blazed a new trail in the Indian countryside.

11.2 THE ACHIEVEMENTS AND DRAWBACKS OF THE 'GREEN REVOLUTION'

The recovery of Indian agricultural production after the great drought was only partly due to the 'Green Revolution'. In order to arrive at an accurate estimate of the impact of the 'Green Revolution', we have to consider the irregular sequences of good and bad harvests under the influence of the monsoon. Two good harvests had immediately preceded the two years of the great drought, and it was followed by good harvests once more. For a balanced assessment, we shall take into consideration the quinquennial averages of 1961–5 and 1966–70. In this way we include the first year of the drought in the first set and the second one in the second set, so as to establish more or less equal series of good and bad harvests. The result is reflected in the following figures (in million tons): rice 35 and 38, wheat 11 and 18, jowar 9 and 9, bajra 4 and 5, maize 5 and 6, pulses 11 and 11, oilseeds 8 and 8. The only remarkable difference can be noticed in the case of wheat (a 60 per cent increase), whereas rice production increased by only 8 per cent. The millets (jowar and bajra) as well as pulses and oilseeds stagnated. These trends become even more obvious when we examine the quinquennial averages (in million tons) for the subsequent period, from 1971 to 1975: rice 43, wheat 25, jowar 9, bajra 5, maize 6, pulses 11, oilseeds 8. Rice showed an increase of 13 per cent and wheat of 36 per cent, but all the others stagnated. The quinquennial averages for the period from 1980 to 1984 were the following: rice 54, wheat 41, other cereals (jowar, bajra and maize) 30.4, pulses 11.4. This shows a slight change of the trend. Rice production increased at about the same

Table 11.1: Agricultural production, cultivated area and yield per hectare

	Rice	Wheat	Jowar	Bajra	Pulses
Cultivated area (million hectares)					
1955	31	12	17	11	23
1960	34	13	18	11	23
1975	39	20	16	11	23
1980	40	22	15	11	23
1985	41	23	16	11	24
Yield (kg/hectare)					
1955	874	708	387	302	476
1960	1013	851	533	286	539
1975	1235	1410	591	540	533
1980	1388	1648	673	466	493
1985	1568	2032	641	345	544
Production (million tons)					
1955	29	9	7	3	12
1960	35	11	10	3	13
1975	49	29	10	6	13
1980	53	36	11	5	11
1985	64	47	10	3	13

Source: *Economic Survey*, cf. Bibliography, Section 11.2.

steady, but moderate rate; wheat production still expanded at a more 'revolutionary' rate. The other cereals, which had stagnated earlier, made some progress in the second decade of the 'Green Revolution', but pulses continued to stagnate. The major difference between the pre-revolutionary period and the 'Green Revolution' is the fact that production no longer increased through an extension of the area under cultivation, but through an increase in yield. This reduces the kind of vulnerability associated with the cultivation of marginal land, but introduces another vulnerability related to the new inputs such as high-yielding varieties, chemical fertilisers and assured irrigation.

The importance of permanent irrigation, which relieves agri-culture from its dependence on the monsoon, is clearly shown by the progress of wheat production. From 1971 to 1978, the area of wheat under permanent irrigation was extended by 35 per cent. Two-thirds of all wheat was now grown in permanently irrigated fields. In the same period, permanently irrigated rice fields only increased their share of total rice cultivation from 37 to 42 per cent. By 1982, permanently irrigated wheat accounted for 72 per cent of the total area under wheat, whereas irrigated rice had not made any further progress. Accordingly, the average yield of rice stagnated, whereas

Figure 11.1: Production of food grain in India (kg per capita) 1950–80

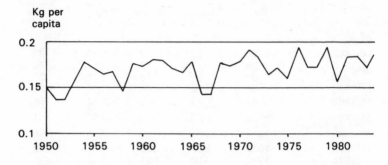

Source of data: World Bank, *World Development Report* (1984).

wheat could register a further improvement in this respect. All other food grains, pulses and oilseeds stagnated. There was a bottleneck in the supply of pulses and oilseeds, and the latter had even to be imported from abroad. Prices increased, but nevertheless the production was not stepped up. One of the major reasons for this shortage is the extreme vulnerability of pulses and oilseeds. They are often decimated by pests and thus their cultivation is very risky. In earlier times they were often grown together with other food grains and were thus not so vulnerable as nowadays, when compact fields of one and the same type of crop provide a veritable field day for rapidly spreading pests.

The regional distribution of the gains from the 'Green Revolution' shows a pattern of striking disparities. Wheat cultivation is concentrated in the Punjab, Haryana and western Uttar Pradesh. Punjab and Haryana jointly produced an annual average of about 7–8 million tons of wheat and 2 million tons of rice in the years from 1973 to 1975. In the period from 1980 to 1984, the quinquennial average of their joint production amounted to 13 million tons of wheat and 5.2 million tons of rice. In West Bengal, rice production stood at 6–7 million tons in 1973–5, and only about 1 million tons of wheat was produced there in those years. The quinquennial average for 1980–4 for rice in West Bengal was 6.8 million tons and for wheat 0.6 million tons — a very dismal record of stagnation indeed. Bihar shows a similar pattern: rice production in 1973–5 stood at 4.5 million tons and wheat production at 2 million tons; the average production of rice in 1980–4 was 6.7 million tons and wheat was 2.5 million tons. The large South Indian state of Andhra Pradesh was not much better off: in 1973–5 rice production amounted to 6 million tons per year, wheat production was negligible, but there was an annual production of about 2.6 million tons of millet. In 1980–4 rice production amounted to 7.6 million tons per year and the production of millet to 2.6 million tons. Millet is also grown in the Punjab and in Haryana, where the annual joint production of millet amounted to 2 million tons in 1973–5 and to 1.4 million tons in 1980–4. The disparities become even more pronounced, if we compare the population statistics of these states. Punjab and Haryana together had a total of about 30 million people (1980–4), whereas Andhra Pradesh, Bihar and West Bengal jointly accounted for about 180 million people. If we sum up the average annual production of food grains for Punjab and Haryana (1980–4), we get about 20 million tons; if we do the same for Andhra Pradesh, Bihar and West Bengal we get about 26 million tons. If we would consider Punjab and Haryana as one isolated unit and the other three states as another isolated unit, we would get a per-capita availability of food grains of 0.67 tons per year in the first and of only 0.15 tons per year in the second. The latter figure corresponds almost exactly to the national average.

We could easily find more indicators of the regional disparities that have shown up under the impact of the 'Green Revolution', but the above-mentioned examples should suffice. Just as regional disparities increased, so did the disparities between poor and rich peasants. These latter disparities are more difficult to analyse, because of a lack of data. The stagnation prevailing in Eastern India seems to indicate that the 'Green Revolution' has more or less bypassed that region, and accordingly there could not have been a progressive polarisation between rich and poor peasants in this area either. In fact, there are pockets in Eastern India, too, where the 'Green Revolution' has made a mark. The delta region of coastal Andhra Pradesh, the districts of Burdwan, Hooghly and Birbhum in West Bengal, and a few spots in the Gangetic plains of Bihar could be mentioned in this context.

Rural income distribution had undoubtedly become more skewed due to the 'Green Revolution'. Nevertheless, India did become self-sufficient as far as food grains were concerned. The quinquennial averages of India's production of food grains amounted to 119 million tons in 1975–9 and 137 million tons in 1980–4. The increase in production clearly surpassed the growth of the population. This is also evident from Figure 11.1, which shows per-capita food grain production for 1950 to 1980. However, this figure also shows that the vagaries of the monsoon still played a major role in this respect. Bad harvests can be observed at intervals of about seven years. Nevertheless, in recent years (1984–6) food grain production has remained remarkably stable, in spite of a sequence of rather disappointing monsoons. This is undoubtedly due to the rapid extension of irrigation. Punjab and Haryana, which are particularly progressive in this respect, have greatly increased their share of the production of rice and wheat in India. Whereas these two states together contributed only 13 per cent to the total output of rice and wheat in 1975, their share had increased to 21 per cent in 1985. The enormous surplus of these two productive states is a major factor in the new pattern of comfortable self-sufficiency in the Indian food grains budget. Food grains stocks held by the government have amounted to about 20 million tons in recent years. In fact, the government is now afraid of a bumper harvest, which would completely upset the present food grain policy.

In spite of the fact that the supply of food grains has been greatly improved, the government has stuck to the by now deeply ingrained practice of procurement at guaranteed prices. The peasants have become used to it. Scrapping this system would mean trouble, and no government wants to alienate the rural voters. Originally the system had been designed in order to cope with bottlenecks in food supply. An independent Agricultural Prices Commission would recommend a procurement price based on a calculation of the cost of production plus an adequate margin of profit. In the period from 1975 to 1981, the government bought about 11 per cent of the total production of food grains each year. This gave a great deal of leverage to the government. For political reasons, the government often paid more to the peasants that the Agricultural Prices Commission had recommended, although everybody concerned knew that this amounted to a subsidy to the rich peasants and would enhance inflation and thus harm the poor. The prices set for certain types of produce could easily distort the market prices, but political expediency overruled the qualms of economists. The days when India's planners had aimed at low agricultural prices for the sake of undisturbed industrial development had been long since forgotten. By now an annual increase in the procurement prices was almost a foregone conclusion, as the peasants expected it. The world energy crisis of 1974, which subjected India to an imported inflation, accentuated these problems. As the prices of inputs increased, the peasants were clamouring for higher procurement prices and fertiliser subsidies. The 'Green Revolution' was nursed by the government in this way.

The impact of the 'Green Revolution' on industrial growth did not make itself felt immediately. After the great drought, a long-term recession had hit India's industrial development. Since this recession was only indirectly related to the performance of Indian agriculture, a recovery of agricultural production would not necessarily lead to industrial progress. We shall explore this complex relationship in the following section.

11.3 THE INDUSTRIAL RECESSION

The direct link between agricultural performance and the beginning of the industrial recession was, of course, provided by the great drought. The impact of this drought was heightened by the fact that agricultural production had been enhanced by extending cultivation to marginal land rather than improving yield. The shock that was caused by this breakdown of the old mode of production led to a suspension of the planning process and a sudden decline in public investment. In particular, the railways, the generation of energy and infrastructure in general suffered from this decline of investment. This undoubtedly deprived industrial growth of a great deal of its earlier dynamics, but there were also the cumulative effects of structural weaknesses in Indian industrial development that caused problems that just happened to coincide with the impact of the great drought. In fact, some of the elements that had encouraged growth up to the mid-1960s showed their negative side later on. The experience with a colonial regime of discriminating protection and imperial preferences had prompted India's planners to adopt a policy of what may be called 'indiscriminate' protection. Import substitution was pursued for its own sake, without regard for any economic considerations such as comparative advantage, the economies of scale, efficiency in factor utilisation, etc. Just as Indian agricultural production was enhanced by the extension of cultivation, industrial growth was based on this kind of indiscriminate import substitution. The law of diminishing returns applied to both types of development, but whereas the great drought terminated the first process and made it clear that an increase in yield rather than an extension of cultivation was now the only option, no similar shock changed the course of industrial development. Instead of a sudden crisis and a qualitative change, there was only a deceleration of growth, which gradually revealed the symptoms of a long-term recession.

One of the structural weaknesses of the Indian industrial economy was the lack of awareness of the growing complexity that required networking and flexible adjustments of supply and demand rather than the rough-and-ready method of setting physical targets, which the Indian planners had adopted in the days when they had to start from scratch. With a large home market and a demand for almost everything, India could afford to forget about export-led growth and could spurn competition as a waste of scarce resources. Initially, all this worked quite well, but in continuing this policy India got locked in a system of high-cost inefficient production, which lacked flexibility, and would not even let 'sick' mills die a natural death. The public sector became notorious for its inefficiency, but even the private sector was paralysed by the prevailing system. An entrepreneur who wanted to close down one line of production, as it had turned out to be a dead end, and start another more promising one would not be allowed to do so by the omnipotent bureaucracy.

Recession is, of course, a relative term. The decline of India's industrial growth rate after the mid-1960s contrasted with its steep rise in earlier years. From 1970 to 1977, industrial production grew by 39 per cent and agricultural production by 33 per cent. This could be taken as a moderate, but well-balanced growth. Western prophets of moderate growth were quick to praise this trend and some Indian experts adopted the same point of view and emphasised that gradual rather than rapid development had also protected India from the undesirable symptoms of dramatic social change. The recession could thus be accepted as a welcome phase of consolidation. However, there were other aspects of such a consolidation too: the cementing of relations of dominance and dependence in the countryside, the spread of concentration rather than innovation in private industry, the growth of inefficiency in the public sector, and the emergence of a 'parallel economy' that evaded fiscal scrutiny.

At the same time there was also a new consolidation of the political power of Indira Gandhi's Congress Party. In 1969, she had split the party in order to escape from the tutelage of the old guard. Although she was not committed to any ideology, she adopted a 'left' profile. The abolition of the privy purses of the Indian princes and the nationalisation of Indian banks provided her with a populist image without costing her too much in political terms. Neither princes nor bankers were powerful pressure groups. By detaching the national elections from the state elections in 1971, she turned the national elections into a kind of plebiscite from which she emerged with flying colours. The liberation of Bangladesh in the same year added to her prestige. She was at the zenith of her political career at that time. Bad harvests, the oil price hike and a major strike of the railway workers in 1974 went against her. In 1975, she proclaimed an emergency and ruled with almost dictatorial powers for more than a year. The economy was geared up at that time, as no strikes were allowed and discipline was maintained through a general fear of quick reprisals. Most leaders of the opposition languished in jail. The announcement of a snap election in 1977 was supposed to catch them unawares. After being released from prison, they had hardly any time to organise an election campaign. However, the emergency had unified the opposition and thus Indira Gandhi lost the elections and was succeeded by Morarji Desai, who had always thought of himself as the best Prime Minister India could have. He was a man of great integrity and administrative ability, but he did not have much of a political base of his own and lacked diplomatic finesse. Unable to cope with the tensions in his heterogeneous government, he had to resign in 1979 and was succeeded by his erstwhile deputy, Charan Singh, who headed a powerless caretaker government until Indira Gandhi emerged once more victorious from the national election of 1980. The death of her son Sanjay, whom she loved and admired, in June 1980 cast a shadow over her new term of office. Her leadership was no longer as bold as it used to be, she lost control of the forces of regional discord and was finally assassinated in October 1984 — a cruel fate, but perhaps pre-ordained, as she herself had felt. At any rate, it saved her from another type of fate: the decay of her political power, which would have come as an anti-climax to her dramatic career.

Although Indira Gandhi liked to project a 'leftish' image, she actually never seriously tried to change the prevailing social order. The pattern of income distribution in India corresponds to that of the United States. Socialist ambitions and a planned economy have not affected the pervasive inequality. After Indira Gandhi had consolidated her power, she revived the planning process, which had been suspended from 1966 to 1969. A fourth five-year plan (1969–74) was inaugurated by her, to be followed by a fifth one; the latter, however, was suspended by Morarji Desai's government, because this new government had other priorities and wanted to put a greater emphasis on agriculture rather than industry. The political vagaries of this period and the enormous spurt of inflation in 1974 at the time of the oil price hike greatly upset the planning process. In fact, the five-year plans were reduced to a kind of commentary on the

Table 11.2: Production of cloth in India, 1970–85 (million metres)

	1970	1975	1980	1985
Cotton cloth mills	4,055	3,961	3,434	2,587
Decentralised sector	3,547	4,130	4,934	6,592
Cotton/man-made fibres mills	107	257	730	783
Decentralised sector	63	159	540	554
Man-made fibres mills	2	1	4	6
Decentralised sector	949	879	1,346	1,977
Total mills	4,164	4,219	4,168	3,376
Total decentralised sector	4,559	5,168	6,820	9,122
Total production	8,723	9,387	10,988	12,498

Source: *Economic Survey*, cf. Bibliography, Section 11.3.

economic development that took place regardless of the plans.

A survey of the development of Indian industrial production in the years from 1965 to 1984 shows a pattern of slow growth. The major industries, in particular, which should have been leading the others, were more or less stagnant. The jute textile industry does not show any growth and the output of the cotton textile mills even shows a remarkable decline from 4.4 billion metres in 1965 to 2.6 billion metres in 1984. This is, however, compensated by a quick expansion of the so-called 'decentralised sector', which includes hand-loom weavers as well as small operators of power-looms. In 1965, only 3 billion metres were produced by the decentralised sector, but in 1984 this sector produced 6.4 billion metres. The striking change in the structure of the Indian textile industry is shown in Table 11.2.

The rapid advance of the decentralised sector in the field of man-made fibres demonstrates that this sector is in many ways ahead of the mills. The economies of scale of the mills were nullified by high wages, labour trouble, taxation and bureaucratic controls, whereas the small-scale operators could avoid most of that. The hand-loom weavers had always been singled out for special protection, and they enjoyed substantial tax benefits. The small-scale operators of power-looms often passed off their products as hand-loom products, and thus obtained benefits to which they were not entitled. The introduction of a new textile policy in 1985, which aimed at equalising the chances of mills and decentralised power-looms, led to a great deal of protest.

The pet child of India's planners, the iron and steel industry, has also followed a rather slow path of growth. The production of pig iron has only increased from 7 million to 9 million tons in two decades and that of steel ingots from 6 million to 10 million tons. The expansion of India's steel industry happened to coincide with a decline of steel prices in the world market. Most of the time Indian steel prices were higher than world market prices, but in the domestic context of high industrial prices, they were often kept artificially low by the government. This amounted to an indirect subsidy to the users of steel in the private sector, whose end-products were not subjected to similar price controls. The public-sector steel mills were rarely able to show a profit and thus could not contribute to further public investment. Overstaffing and inefficient management also contributed to this unfortunate state of affairs. As far as technology was concerned, the Indian steel industry was not very innovative and stuck to methods of production that were not suited to Indian conditions. Indian coal has a high ash content, which has adverse effects if one adopts conventional methods of making steel in blast furnaces that require high-quality coking coal. The new process of producing sponge iron with non-coking coal and then converting it into steel in electric arc furnaces has recently been tried in India with good results. It should, however, have been adopted much earlier in a big way, as India has enormous reserves of iron ore as well as of non-coking coal.

The Indian car industry is another example of the perpetuation of outdated technology. Ancient models of European cars have been produced in India in comparatively limited numbers and at high prices. Only recently has there been some progress in this line. The production of passenger cars and commercial vehicles, which stood at about 70,000 in 1965, was stagnant for about a decade, but has risen in recent years so as to register a total of 190,000 in 1984. The project of a cheap 'people's car' called 'Maruti', which was sponsored by Sanjay Gandhi, did not get anywhere; finally a small Japanese car was marketed under that name in India. Indigenisation of the production of this car was supposed to be achieved within five years, but its import contents remained fairly high for quite some time. The Japanese also ensured that ancillary industries set up in India for the production of car parts, etc. would go in for joint ventures with Japanese firms. Specifications for such items could be drawn up so as to make such ventures mandatory. The output of bicycles shows a more encouraging trend: it stood at 1.5 million in 1965, grew only very slowly until 1975, but reached nearly 6 million in 1984. The production of radios, however, stagnated after an

151

Table 11.3: India in international comparison: income distribution

	Lowest 20%	Second 20%	Third 20%	Fourth 20%	Fifth 20%	Highest 10%
India	7	9.2	13.9	20.5	49.5	33.6
USA	4.6	8.9	14.1	22.1	50.3	33.4
France	5.3	11.1	16	21.8	45.8	30.5
Great Britain	7	11.5	17	24.8	39.2	23.4
Japan	8.7	13.2	17.5	23.1	36.8	21.2
FRG	7.9	12.5	17	23.1	39.5	24

Source: World Bank, *World Development Report* (1984) (data for the years 1975–9).

initial spurt from 1965 to 1970 and remained at an average of about 1.6 million sets for the years from 1970 to 1984.

Whereas the major industries mentioned so far have had a rather disappointing record, the production of cement and fertilisers shows a somewhat brighter picture, particularly in the most recent past. After an initial period of slow growth, cement production jumped from 19 million tons in 1980 to 29 million tons in 1984. Nitrogenous fertiliser production, which was of vital importance for the 'Green Revolution', was greatly stepped up after 1965, when it amounted to only 200,000 tons; by 1980 it amounted to 2.2 million tons and by 1984 to 3.9 million tons. Initially the peasants placed too much emphasis on this type of fertiliser and neglected phosphatic fertiliser, which was also in much shorter supply. Production of the latter amounted to only 100,000 tons in 1965, but reached 1.2 million tons in 1984. This growth of domestic production also helped to reduce imports, which had become more and more expensive owing to the oil price hike. Nevertheless, India's planners had some problems with this encouraging growth of fertiliser user: it was heavily subsidised by the government and this became an increasing burden. By 1985 the fertiliser subsidy amounted to 18 billion rupees. Since agriculture is hardly taxed at all, this subsidy and the procurement prices mentioned above amount to a transfer of resources from the urban and industrial sector to the rural sector.

One of the most problematic bottlenecks of India's industrial development has been the insufficient supply of energy. India has enormous reserves of oil and coal, but their utilisation has been unbelievably slow. It is only in recent years that a real breakthrough has been achieved. The great international oil companies were not interested in finding oil in India. They specialised in exploring oil in places where there were no consumers, so as to acquire it cheaply and sell it at a good price elsewhere. It was only with Soviet aid that India did tap its oil resources in the 1960s, but by the time that production could have been stepped up, oil was cheap in the world market. Therefore India neglected both oil exploration and coal mining, and was caught napping by the crisis of 1974 and the second oil price hike of 1979; indigenous production could not be geared up in a short time and India had to pay an enormous import bill. In 1970, oil imports had accounted for 8 per cent of India's total import bill of 16 billion rupees. In 1975, oil imports amounted to 23 per cent of total imports worth 52 billion rupees, and in 1980 to 41 per cent of a total of 125 billion rupees. By 1984, this share had come down to 31 per cent of 170 billion rupees. This change in the 1980s

Table 11.4: Industrial production, 1960–85

	1960	1965	1970	1975	1980	1985
Coal (million tons)	56	70	76	103	119	162
Iron ore* (million tons)	11	18	32	42	41	43
Crude oil (million tons)	0.4	3.5	7	8	10	30
Pig iron (million tons)	4	7	7	8	8	10
Steel ingots (million tons)	3	6	6	8	10	12
Automobiles (thousands)	50	70	90	70	120	209
Bicycles (millions)	1	1.5	2	2.3	4	5.5
Radios (millions)	0.3	0.6	1.8	1.5	1.9	1.1
Nitrogenous fertiliser (million tons)	0.1	0.2	0.8	1.5	2.2	4.3
Phosphatic fertiliser (million tons)	0.05	0.1	0.2	0.3	0.8	1.4
Cement (million tons)	8	11	14	17	19	32
Jute textiles (billion metres)	1.1	1.4	1.1	1.3	1.4	1.3
Cotton textiles (mills) (billion metres)	4.6	4.4	4	4	3.4	2.6
Cotton textiles (decentralised sector) (billion metres)	2	3	3.5	4	5	6.6
Generation of energy Total (billion KWh)	20	37	61	86	119	183
including:						
Hydroelectricity	8	15	25	33	46	50
Thermal power	9	17	28	43	61	114
Nuclear	—	—	2.4	2.6	3	5.0
Non-utility	2.6	4.6	5.2	6.9	8.4	13.3

* The figures for 1960 and 1965 do not include Goa.
Source: *Economic Survey*, cf. Bibliography, Section 11.3.

was due to a significant increase in Indian oil production, from 10 million tons in 1980 to 29 million tons in 1984; the lion's share (20 million tons) was that of offshore production at 'Bombay High'. Similarly, coal production had also been stepped up from 119 million tons in 1980 to 147 million tons in 1984. The generation of electric energy showed a parallel trend. It progressed from 119,000 MW in 1980 to 169,000 MW in 1984. Nuclear energy contributed very little to this progress; it increased only from 3,000 MW to 4,000 MW in this period, and hydroelectric energy advanced only from 43,000 MW to 53,000 MW, whereas thermal energy expanded from 61,000 MW to 99,000 MW. With some time-lag, the world energy crisis has thus induced a major spurt in the indigenous production of coal and oil as well as in energy generation in India.

The contribution of coal mining to this progress in energy supply had been sluggish for some time, due to institutional and infrastructural constraints. Before 1970, a major share of coal mining had been in private hands. Nationalisation had been contemplated for some time. The private coal-mine owners, who had in any case run their mines with as little investment as possible, naturally had not invested anything in the years preceding nationalisation, which had been imminent for some time. Although the mines were nationalised in 1971, this merely constituted a change of ownership rather than a change in the rather antediluvian methods of running the mines; it took more than a decade to gear up production. The shortage of railway wagons for the transport of coal proved to be a perennial bottleneck throughout this time. From 1976 to 1980, coal transported by the railway stagnated at about 65 million tons per year, but then there was a sudden rise within the next few years. By 1984, 91 million tons of coal were transported by the railways, but there were still complaints about the shortage of wagons.

The railways had been badly neglected for quite some time. Their network still reflected the colonial legacy, with its emphasis on connecting the interior of the country with the major ports. Interior class-connections were few and far between. This was not only a problem for the transport of coal, but also for the transport of food grains. When American wheat was pouring into the country via the major ports, the old type of network was well suited to it. But when surplus production from the strongholds of the 'Green Revolution' had to be transferred to food deficit areas, the railway faced an entirely new task. Food-grain haulage increased from 15 billion to 24 billion tons/km from 1975 to 1980, and to 32 billion tons/km in 1985. The Indian railways have a total network of 62,000 km, of which only 6,000 km are electrified. They haul 248 million tons of freight and transport 3.5 billion passengers per year (quinquennial averages, 1980–84). Freight rates as well as passenger fares have been increased to a great extent in recent years. From 1960 to 1980, freight rates increased by 170 per cent and passenger fares by 130 per cent. The inflationary spurt of the early 1970s greatly contributed to this increase; from 1970 to 1975, freight rates increased by 50 per cent and passenger fares by 40 per cent. This inflation, which made a deep impact on the Indian economy, will be discussed in the following section of this chapter.

11.4 DEVALUATION, INFLATION, FOREIGN TRADE AND THE BALANCE OF PAYMENTS

Inflationary tendencies had affected the Indian economy even in the early period of planned development, as we have seen. Deficit spending without corresponding growth rates was mainly responsible for this problem. The black-market rate of the Indian rupee deviated to a large extent from the official exchange rate. India's export was hampered by this development and had to be subsidised by the government, which urgently needed foreign exchange in order to import capital goods required for India's industrialisation. Exporters were tempted to manipulate their invoices with the connivance of their foreign partners in order to get higher subsidies or compensatory import licences. A drastic devaluation seemed to be the only measure that would help to cut this Gordian knot of black-market rates, spurious invoices and rampant corruption. At the same time, one could hope to promote exports and liberalise imports by means of this devaluation.

A devalued rupee would make exports cheaper and more competitive, and imports more expensive, so as to reduce the necessity of protective measures. But there were also weighty arguments that could be adduced against a devaluation. For most Indian export items such as spices, tea, jute products, etc., there was a very restricted elasticity of demand in the world market. India's industrial products were not yet of a sufficient quality to compete in the world market, even if they would be cheaply available after the devaluation. On the other hand, India still depended on the import of capital goods, which would be much more expensive after a devaluation. Moreover, India had a foreign debt, for which the debt service would increase. The World Bank brushed aside all these arguments and forced India to devaluate the rupee by about 50 per cent in June 1966. After this event exports did not grow, but imports became more expensive and contributed to an imported inflation. Since this coincided with the great drought, the price index (general consumer price index for industrial workers: 1960 = 100) climbed from 137 in 1964 to 167 in 1967.

The inflationary spurt of the mid-1960s was still relatively harmless, when compared to the one that occurred as a result of the coincidence of another sequence of bad harvests with the oil price hike. Both 1972 and 1974 were years of bad harvests and the oil price increased steeply in 1974. The above-mentioned price index increased from 218 in 1972 to 307 in 1974; in other words, prices had trebled since 1960. The second oil price hike of 1979 happened to coincide with another bad harvest, and thus in 1980 the price index climbed to 420. In 1982 there was a deficient rice harvest, which once more pushed up the price level. By 1985 the index stood at 615 — a sixfold increase in 25 years.

India's inflationary spurts, which occurred in the midst of industrial recession, showed a peculiar anticyclical pattern. Whereas normally both industrial prices and prime costs follow the ups and downs of boom and slump, in India prime costs (raw materials and wages) tended to rise when they should have gone down. This makes it very difficult to fight inflation in India by the usual methods prescribed in the textbooks. Inflation that is caused by booms and by excess liquidity can be counteracted by means of deflationary measures, but if an inflation is partly an imported one and partly caused by the vagaries of the monsoon, it is difficult to fight it in this way. Deflationary measures would then do more harm than good to the economy. Consequently the growth of money supply was not curtailed in India: M1 increased from 119 billion rupees to 248 billion rupees in 1981 and to 393 billion in 1984, and it stood at 420 billion at the beginning of 1986. (For comparison, in the Federal Republic of Germany M1 amounted to 280 billion marks in 1984, and the currency component was only 36 per cent of this amount; in the United States M1 stood at $ US 548 billion, and the currency component amounted to 29 per cent.) In India the currency component of M1 was always much larger: it amounted to 53 per cent in 1975, 56 per cent in 1982, and 57 per cent in 1984. The printing of money had been stepped up to a great extent. Bank notes in circulation amounted to 65 billion rupees in 1975 and to 230 billion rupees in 1984.

The eminent Indian economist, I.G. Patel, now Director of the

London School of Economics, published articles during his tenure of office as Governor of the Reserve Bank of India in the early 1980s in which he called for greater monetary discipline. In its annual report for 1984–5, the Reserve Bank mentioned that measures had been adopted to curb liquidity growth in the economy, but in the same report it is also admitted that there was still an overhang of liquidity in the system, which contributed to rising prices. Monetary discipline cannot be easily implemented in the Indian context, as the government is pledged to policies of subsidies and price supports, has to resort to deficit spending, and also borrows money in order to make up for deficits in the revenue account. The budget estimates of 1985 envisaged a deficit in the revenue account of 56 billion rupees and projected gross market loans to the tune of 57 billion rupees. This trend continued and even official circles got worried about the large amount of credit that the Reserve Bank of India had to grant to the government, over and above the credit that other banks had provided. In 1986–8 the Reserve Bank credit to the government amounted to 50 billion rupees. This would upset the new policy of monetary targeting, based on the recommendations of the Reserve Bank's committee, which reviewed the working of the monetary system in 1985. That committee highlighted the importance of 'high-powered' money such as the Reserve Bank's credit to the government and pleaded for a reduction of this type of credit, which is so conveniently available, but fuels inflation, as it amounts to the creation of reserve money, which is the base for the expansion of the money supply. However, the alternative recommended by the committee, the issue of government securities at attractive interest rates, which would be readily taken up by the public, would involve the government in an increasing debt service. Therefore the recourse to cheap Reserve Bank credit is inevitable, and that bank cannot refuse it.

When the Reserve Bank of India was established in 1934, Sir George Schuster, the Finance Member of the Government of India, had said that the Governor of that bank was in such a strong position that he could even bring down a government by means of his monetary policy. This may be true, but so far no governor has dared to embark on such a collision course. I.G. Patel was no exception to this rule. After all, he knew the problems of government very well, having served as Finance Secretary of the Government of India before he became Governor of the Reserve Bank. Monetarism as a doctrine is certainly intellectually attractive, but under the economic and political conditions prevailing in India it is not of much practical use.

From 1960 to 1985, M1 increased from 27 billion to about 410 billion rupees (that is, fifteen times), whereas consumer prices increased sixfold. This would indicate that less than half of the growth of money supply was inflationary, whereas the rest was justified by the actual growth of the economy. A steady and moderate rate of inflation is accepted even by Western industrial nations, which pride themselves on their good record of maintaining stability. The trouble with India's inflation, however, was its unpredictable progress by fits and starts, which destabilised the economy whenever they occurred. Since inflation always amounts to a kind of regressive taxation that affects the poor more than the rich, these spurts of inflation that were due to the world market or the monsoon or both also affected the political atmosphere. In India, people invariably tend to blame price fluctuations on the government, whereas they would not immediately notice a creeping inflation. Indian politicians know this very well, but so far there is hardly anything that they can do about it. Being very sensitive to the threat of unpredictable inflation, the Indian government generally tended to curtail investment, thus contributing to industrial recession. Slow growth and unemployment are less resented by people who are used to the moderate 'Hindu rate of growth' (3.5 per cent), as Professor Raj Krishna used to call it, than a sudden price rise. For Indira Gandhi, who had been quite cautious in this respect, it was an irony of fate that soon after she had conducted a resounding election campaign with the slogan *'Gharibi hatao'* (Vanquish poverty) in 1971, she was faced with a major inflationary spurt in 1974. In a way she was lucky that the next major spurt occurred when she was out of office, and that the rate of inflation receded after she had been re-elected. Only an assured growth of agricultural production and a sufficient domestic supply of oil, coal and other sources of energy can shield India against further shocks. Once this is achieved, it will also be possible to keep inflation under control and make it creep rather than jump, in order to avoid political trouble. The experience of the 1980s seems to indicate that some progress has been made in this direction. Inflation has been steady, and there have been no major spurts. Agricultural production has been quite satisfactory and industrial growth seems to have speeded up once more. Although the old index (1970 = 100) shows about 6 per cent industrial growth throughout the 1980s, the new one (1980 = 100) shows about 8 per cent for the mid-1980s. The difference is due to an adjustment of the weightage of various industries, and the new index seems to reflect the rate of growth more accurately.

Table 11.5: India in international comparison: foreign trade

	Commodities ($ US million)		Average annual rate of growth (%)			
	Export 1982	Import 1982	Export 1960–70	Export 1970–82	Import 1960–70	Import 1970–82
India	8	14	4.7	4.7	−0.9	2.6
USA	212	254	6	5.6	9.8	3.8
France	92	115	8.2	6.1	11	6.2
Great Britain	97	99	4.8	6	5	3.5
Japan	138	131	17.2	8.5	13.7	3.5
FRG	176	155	10.1	5.6	10	5.1

Source: World Bank, *World Development Report* (1984).

This analysis shows that India's major concern is domestic economic growth rather than export-led growth, which was praised as a marvellous economic remedy by those who were fascinated by the sudden emergence of the newly industrialised countries in East Asia. Of course, export pessimism has been a self-fulfilling prophecy in India and India's share of worth trade has steadily declined. Scepticism about export-led growth in India should not be equated with this general export pessimism. India needs foreign exchange in order to import essential commodities. Accordingly, India's export potential cannot be neglected. The structure of India's foreign trade has changed a great deal from 1950 to 1980. In 1950, about 80 per cent of Indian exports consisted of such items as tea and raw materials or semi-finished goods such as leather; by 1980, more than 50 per cent consisted of manufactured goods. The composition of imports changed too. In 1950, more than 60 per cent were finished goods; by 1980, this category had receded to 20 per cent. There is, of course, a negative side to this latter development. The import of machinery, which increased from 15 to 30 per cent of total imports from 1950 to 1965, receded to 14 per cent by 1980; this is a reflection of the industrial recession as well as of the rising tide of oil imports, which greatly inflated the figures of raw-material imports.

As we have seen above, oil imports dwarfed all other items after 1974. Whereas the amount of oil imported by India in the 1970s remained at a more or less steady level of 16 million tons per year, the value of these imports increased very steeply. Another type of raw material that India had to import to an increasing extent, owing to the shortfall of domestic production, was vegetable oil. In 1975, the value of these imports amounted to only 142 million rupees; by 1977, this item had increased to 7 billion rupees. This trend continued in subsequent years. The quinquennial average for edible oils imported from 1980 to 1984 was 6 billion rupees.

The structural change of India's foreign trade was also accompanied by major changes in the directions of trade. In the 1970s, the OPEC countries emerged as major trading partners of India for obvious reasons. It is remarkable, though, that India also managed to step up exports to those countries. The remittances of Indians who went to work in those countries were also of great importance, as we shall see below. India's trade relations with Japan were not only expanding steadily, but also showed a harmonious balance of trade, whereas trade with the United States and the West European countries expanded in such a way as to lead to major deficits in India's balance of trade. Of the West European countries, Great Britain and the Federal Republic of Germany were India's major partners. Initially, Great Britain had by far the greater volume of trade with India, but then the FRG caught up with Great Britain and attained about the same volume of trade with India in 1984; however, Indian imports from the FRG surpassed those from Great Britain.

A special role in India's foreign trade was played by Eastern Europe, and primarily by the Soviet Union, which always claimed the lion's share of about 60–70 per cent of India's trade with Eastern Europe. In this trade relation, India's exports usually surpassed imports from that area, but export earnings could not be freely converted into other currencies. Critics claimed that this kind of trade was disadvantageous to India, because it attracted goods that India could have sold for hard currency elsewhere. There were also isolated cases of the re-export of Indian goods by the Soviet Union, which gave grist to the mill of those critics. In general, however, India did have an advantage from gaining access to the Soviet market, which could absorb great quantities of Indian tobacco, cheap footwear and textiles, and even capital goods, which India could not have sold elsewhere. In 1970, the total volume of India's trade with Eastern Europe amounted to 5.5 billion rupees (17 per cent of India's total volume of foreign trade); in 1984, it stood at 40 billion rupees (14 per cent). In general, this trade was fairly well balanced, with the exception of the period from 1980 to 1982 with regard to Indo-Soviet trade. In those three years, India exported to the Soviet Union a total of goods worth 44 billion rupees and only imported goods worth 35 billion rupees, thus accumulating a positive, but non-convertible balance of 9 billion rupees. The Soviet Union has been a major supplier of oil to India, but with the decline of the oil price this item becomes less important for balancing trade. The Soviet Union is also a major supplier of arms to India, and this part of the relationship is not quite amenable to the usual methods of accounting.

India's balance of trade with the rest of the world has been negative for most of the period from 1950 to 1980. In the times of rapid industrialisation before the mid-1960s, import surpluses increased; after the devaluation and the onset of the industrial recession, India achieved an even balance of trade in 1970. The oil price hike upset this balance again, but in 1976 India managed to have a positive balance of trade; however, the next oil price hike of 1979 queered the pitch once more.

Foreign aid was used to bridge this gap; for most donors, this aid was an indirect method of subsidising exports. By the end of the third five-year plan in 1966, India had received a total of 45 billion rupees of foreign aid ($ US 10 billion, according to the old official exchange rate). Only 7.5 per cent of this sum was in the form of grants; the rest consisted of loans. In the seven years after devaluation and the onset of recession, there was less aid: 63 billion rupees ($ US 8.4 billion, according to the new rate of exchange). In the subsequent seven-year period (1973–9), the volume of aid increased once more and India received 97 billion rupees ($ US 13 billion). Most of this aid was again in terms of loans, but because of the mounting debt service, more grants were given in the late 1970s, amounting to about 20 per cent of the annual aid received. At the same time, however, the percentage of loans that were not tied to specific projects also declined. During the initial three five-year plans, loans that were not tied amounted to 40 per cent of the aid received; from 1966 to 1971 this type of aid declined to 20 per cent, but it increased again to about 50 per cent from 1972 to 1976, only to decrease again to 20 per cent subsequently.

India's debt service after the devaluation amounted to 3.3 billion rupees in 1967 (2.1 billion rupees amortisation and 1.2 billion rupees interest). By 1983, debt service had increased to 8.7 billion rupees (5.7 billion amortisation and 3 billion interest). In 1985, total debt service amounted to 13 billion rupees. Compared to the crushing burden of debt service of other Third World countries, India was still much better off and had an excellent credit rating. In this way, India was able to go in for more commercial credit, as the prospects of aid became dim.

In the years of growing foreign debt service, India was able to accumulate foreign exchange reserves in an unprecedented manner, owing to the remittances of Indians working abroad. The manpower export to the oil-exporting countries proved to be very lucrative as far as the Indian balance of payments was concerned. In order to encourage the remittances, Indians working abroad were permitted to open special accounts in Indian banks. The remittances so deposited were freely convertible. In actual fact Indian citizens were prohibited from maintaining accounts in foreign countries after returning home, but this prohibition could be easily circumvented; therefore it was prudent to introduce this new scheme. The net transfer of these remittances increased from 4.1 billion rupees in 1975 to 9.3 billion rupees in 1978. This bonanza continued for some time: by 1980 private net remittances amounted to 21 billion rupees and in 1984 they reached almost 30 billion. In addition to Indians working abroad on temporary contracts, the government also tried to woo non-resident Indians who were permanently living abroad and had mostly done very well in business or in the professions. These non-resident Indians were not only offered free convertibility, but also preferential interest rates. The decline of interest rates elsewhere made this a very attractive proposition. By the end of 1985, non-resident external rupee deposits amounted to 31 billion rupees; in addition, the non-residents had deposited foreign currency worth 18 billion rupees in India. Total non-resident deposits thus were worth 49 billion rupees. The special favours shown to the non-residents were somewhat resented by Indian capitalists at home, but this policy certainly contributed to India's credit rating abroad and to a fairly comfortable position as far as the national balance of payments was concerned.

In contrast with the balance of trade, India's balance of payments was generally positive or only slightly in the red in recent years. The quinquennial average of India's trade deficit for the period from 1980 to 1984 was 57 billion rupees. International debt service amounted to about 10 billion rupees per year in this period. Foreign aid received during that period amounted to 20 billion rupees per year; thus there remained a net inflow of about 10 billion rupees per year. Invisibles on current account contributed an additional net inflow of 33 billion rupees per year. Of these invisibles, the private remittances mentioned above had the lion's share of more than 60 per cent. The remaining deficit could be covered by drawing on the International Monetary Fund and by running down India's foreign currency reserves, which nevertheless amounted to 68 billion rupees in March 1985 at the beginning of the budgetary year 1985–6.

11.5 THE PROSPECTS OF LIBERALISATION

The budget of 1985–6 heralded the beginning of a new phase in India's economic development. Rajiv Gandhi, who had become Prime Minister on the day his mother was assassinated (31 October 1984), had quickly established his democratic legitimacy by a resounding victory in the parliamentary elections of December 1984. His vision of taking India into the twenty-first century included a major emphasis on technological progress, which could only be achieved by liberalising the Indian economy so that it could stand the test of international competition. This was, of course, easier said than done. Sheltered behind protective walls and used to a policy of planning in terms of physical targets that requires piecemeal licensing and monitoring, Indian industry had become more and more fossilised. Research and development had been emphasised almost to the point of encouraging Indian engineers to re-invent the wheel so as to reduce the dependence on foreign technology. Hardly any innovation, however, had emerged from this endeavour, as research and development can only thrive in an atmosphere of free competition. Those who really had something to offer left the country and contributed to research and development elsewhere, rather than just going through the motions at home. Even before Rajiv Gandhi had placed a new emphasis on technological progress, there had been tendencies in India to buy technology rather than capital goods abroad. But without a structural change of the economy, the isolated grafting of imported technology would hardly lead to the desired results. A new approach had to be adopted; physical planning and licensing had to be replaced by instruments of financial and fiscal management of the economy so as to provide a framework for growth, innovation and investment. The budget of 1985–6, which was introduced by Rajiv Gandhi's efficient and honest Finance Minister, Vishwanath Pratap Singh, was supposed to provide such a framework. Tax cuts were designed so as to encourage investment as well as more honesty in tax payments. Critics doubted whether V.P. Singh would really collect more taxes in this way, as he claimed he would be able to do. They also decried his budget as a budget for the rich and against the poor. By firing corrupt tax collectors and raiding some of the key industrialists of India who were suspected of tax evasion or of manipulating invoices, V.P. Singh did step up tax collections significantly and also silenced those critics who had said that he wanted to pamper the rich.

Another important measure of the new dispensation was the publication of the draft of a Long-Term Fiscal Policy, which permitted private entrepreneurs to anticipate the future course of budgeting so as to base their decisions on rational calculations. Earlier, Indian budgets had sometimes been as unpredictable as the monsoon. Taxes would be lowered or raised at random, in keeping with immediate fiscal needs and political expediency. For this reason the budget was always anticipated with keen interest — almost like the outcome of a cricket match. The Long-Term Fiscal Policy not only blazed a trail for more rational decisions in the private sector, it also insisted on the generation of surplus in the public sector as a precondition for the non-inflationary funding of the seventh five-year plan (1984–9). The increase in government borrowing to make up for deficits in revenue income was depreciated in this draft document, but nevertheless the budget of 1985–6 had to resort to this type of borrowing, too, as we saw above when we examined the growth of money supply.

The budget of 1985–6 did lead to an increase in investment and a rapid growth of imports, due to the liberalisation of foreign trade policy and the lowering of tariffs. This was deplored by a host of critics, who felt that India would soon have such an enormous trade deficit that it would become utterly dependent on foreign creditors. They also feared that the high hopes of the government that India's export potential would grow once the Indian economy was exposed to foreign competition would not be fulfilled. The old spectre of export pessimism still haunted Indian economists. These economists were soon joined by critics with vested interests in decrying the new policy. Indian manufacturers of capital goods, who had operated in the prevailing atmosphere of high-cost production of antiquated machinery, were naturally afraid of the new dispensation. If the Indian investment-goods industry, which had been nursed behind the walls of protectionism, was to be exposed to the full blast of competition all of a sudden, it would be wiped out in no time, warned the critics. Imports did, indeed, increase to an amazing extent in 1985, and by the end of the fiscal year in March 1986 total imports worth 197 billion rupees were recorded, whereas exports only remained at 110 billion rupees. The deficit in the balance of trade thus amounted to 87 billion rupees, whereas it had only been

54 billion rupees in the previous years. The major beneficiary of India's liberal import policy was Japan. Imports from that country increased from 12 billion to 18 billion rupees from 1984 to 1985; imports from Great Britain, the USA and West Germany increased by about 3 billion rupees for each country.

The liberal import policy was also quite helpful as far as central government finance was concerned. Customs duties have become an increasingly important item in the budget. Whereas they yielded only 34 billion rupees in 1980, they totalled 92 billion in 1985, and the revised budget estimate for 1986–7 mentions 115 billion rupees. The new budget for 1987–8 shows 128 billion rupees as expected income from customs duties.

The dynamic drive that characterised the first budget of Rajiv Gandhi's government was not continued in subsequent budgets. The second one (1986–7) disappointed those who had hoped for further steps towards liberalisation, and the most prominent feature of the third one (1987–8) was a steep rise of defence expenditure and another hefty sum of deficit spending. This third budget was presented by Rajiv Gandhi himself, as he had assumed the finance portfolio in January 1987, when he had moved his Finance Minister, V.P. Singh, to the defence ministry. However, although the budgets no longer revealed new ideas, there was encouraging news about the implementation of the seventh five-year plan. More than 60 per cent of the plan targets were going to be fulfilled in the first three years of the plan period. India seemed to be poised for a major step ahead. Indeed, India could not afford to miss such a step ahead, as it is estimated that more than a billion people are going to live in India by the year 2000.

12

Population Growth and Economic Development

12.1 DEMOGRAPHIC PERSPECTIVES

The first general census of India was conducted in 1872, but only the second one of 1881 is considered to be sufficiently accurate to be comparable with the subsequent ones, which were conducted at decennial intervals, the most recent of which was in 1981. In 1901 there were 238 million people, in 1911 252 million and in 1921 only 251 million. After this period of intermittent stagnation caused by famines and diseases, there was a steady increase. Initially, the rate of population growth was moderate, but later on it accelerated so that the resultant curve more and more approximated a parabolic ascent. From 1921 to 1941, the growth rate increased from 1.1 to 1.4 per cent. After the partition of India, 381 million people were counted in the new Republic of India in 1951. The growth rate was now 2.2–2.4 per cent. From 1951 to 1984, the population approximately doubled (1981 = 683 million). If this trend continues, the next doubling of the population will take only 22 instead of 33 years (that is, by 2006 India will have a population of 1.3 billion).

This rapid growth is not caused by an abnormally high birth rate, but by a declining death rate. In fact, infant mortality has not declined to such an extent as had been expected. Recent findings have shown that high rates of infant mortality still persists. This also implies that the average life expectancy is still only 48 years for men and 46 years for women. There has been a remarkable improvement, however, in the survival rate of those who have completed their first year of life, because large-scale famines and epidemics have been eliminated in recent decades. Family planning, which has been widely propagated in India, has not yet achieved the desired results. Success in this programme depends on adequate health services in rural areas. Such health care, however, would have to work for the reduction of infant mortality and for better chances for women, who have been neglected so far, and this would mean that no immediate reduction of the population growth rate could be expected. If more infants survive and more women reach their productive age, the population will increase rather than decline, at least initially.

In contrast with most other countries of the world, India has an amazing deficit of the female population, which amounted to 20 million in 1981. This deficit is almost exclusively situated in Northern India, and it can neither be explained in terms of a higher female infant mortality nor by a high death rate of mothers at the time of delivery. Most of the deficit arises in the second decade of life and this is probably related to the still very widespread habit of early marriage. A young daughter-in-law who is not yet a mother can easily be replaced; therefore not much is done for her health care. There may even be the temptation of welcoming her demise, as a second marriage also means a second dowry. This temptation is reduced when the daughter-in-law is expected to inherit a share of her parents' property in due course. Traditionally, Hindu daughters were not entitled to such inheritance and the dowry was considered to be a compensation for that drawback. After the reform of Hindu law, daughters do inherit and the demand for a dowry has been prohibited by law. Nevertheless, it is not easy to distinguish between gifts and a dowry. Such gifts are gladly received, but the right of inheritance is also exercised, and this gives a great deal of leverage to the in-laws rather than to the married woman. The conservative opponents of this reform had predicted this. The structure of rural society, particularly in Northern India, prevents the achievement of more independence by women, and their right of inheritance only enhances the position of the husband's family. At least that may protect those who have something to inherit from the sufferings of the poor, who cannot look forward to any inheritance. Once the married woman becomes a mother, preferably the mother of a son, she is much better off and can safely look forward to the time when she herself graduates to the position of a mother-in-law. The female deficit caused by the social conditions that have been described here acts as a check on population growth. An improvement to these conditions and a disappearance of the deficit would mean an increase in the population of 6 per cent and a substantial increase in the productive potential of that population.

Due to rapid population growth, India is a 'young nation' in the literal sense of the term. Children below the age of 5 years make up 13 per cent of the population, and children aged between 5 and 15 constitute another 25 per cent; thus 38 per cent of the population are of an age at which they normally should still attend school. Unfortunately, however, this attendance is rather limited, particularly in rural areas, where children above the age of 10 are needed for help in the family farm or in other odd jobs. The age-groups that are normally gainfully employed (15–60 years) make up 56 per cent of the population, whereas people older than 60 form only a small percentage of the population — 5.5 per cent. Pensions and old age benefits are thus not a problem in India, since in any case most old people do not receive such benefits.

It is a characteristic feature of the Indian economy that from the beginning of the present century until 1987 only about 10 per cent of the population have been employed in the industrial sector in the strict sense of the term. In absolute numbers this has, of course, meant an enormous expansion of the workforce. However, the stagnant percentage shows that there has been hardly any important shift in the workforce from agriculture to industry. This will be discussed in greater detail in later sections of this chapter, which deal with national income and with urbanisation.

The acreage of cultivated land cannot be extended any more as a great deal of marginal land has been added in recent decades that should rather be released for afforestation. In this context, cultivated land becomes even more valuable and is guarded by those who own it and who can draw upon the growing number of landless labourers. This development need not be a bad one, if the labourers earned a decent wage and productivity increased. But this happens only in a few areas of India, whereas in others the exploitation of labour and the inadequate use of the productive capacity of the soil go hand in hand. He who owns land can sit back and relax, waiting for the labourers supplied by population growth, who will till the soil for him for a meagre wage.

The well-known theory of W. Arthur Lewis, who thought that in developing countries the rural sector would offer an unlimited supply of cheap labour to the industrial sector, which would thus be able to make rapid progress, has been controverted by the Indian experience. It is not the industrial sector, but the landowners who exploit this rural reserve army of labour. These landowners therefore do not need to modernise their operations. It is an irony of fate that India's planners must be grateful for this capacity of the rural sector to retain labour, because the urban industrial sector is unable to absorb it. Population growth thus stabilises the existing social structure and the traditional modes of production rather than subverting them. Seen from this perspective, the praise for India's slow but steady growth is a consolation for the rich, but a harsh verdict for the rural poor, who are condemned to hard labour with hardly any reward. From a demographic point of view, India's future does not look too good. Seen from this perspective the fact that the rate of economic growth stays just a little ahead of population growth assumes a special importance. Slow growth supports the art of survival of the poor, who produce just enough to make it possible, on this modest but broad foundation, for the superstructure of modern Indian industry to be constructed by a minority of the people who have managed to escape from rural poverty.

12.2 NATIONAL INCOME: THE PROBLEMS OF ASSESSMENT

Per-capita national income is accepted as the most general measurement of economic development. It takes into account the effect of population growth and shows to what extent the growth rate of the economy is depressed by the population growth rate. It is, of course, an abstract statistical average and does not tell us anything about income distribution, about the people above and below the poverty line, etc. The assessment of per-capita income is naturally dependent on the quality of the estimate of national income, and those in turn depend on the accuracy of national accounting and the availability of statistical data. This poses daunting problems even for current estimates and plan projections, but the construction of time series for historical analysis is beset with further conceptual and factual problems. Income must be computed in money values and comparison over time requires an assessment at constant prices. For this exercise, even the selection of the appropriate base year may give rise to controversy, let alone all other matters that may have to be taken into consideration.

In an advanced economy with full monetisation, detailed tax records and a high degree of information about financial transactions, national accounting is much easier than in an economy where most of these features are conspicuous by their absence. Even in such advanced economies, there are problems about accounting for services provided without monetary rewards, such as the work of housewives. Such problems are magnified in less developed economies, where subsistence agriculture is still prevalent and much work is done without payment in cash. The economists must then arrive at some methods whereby they can compute the market value of transactions that have never reached the market. Modern systems of national accounting have achieved a high degree of sophistication. Multiple approaches are adopted in order to get at the facts and figures that are entered into the national accounts. For a country like India, this type of detective work is particularly relevant, because two-thirds of the country's activity must be attributed to the so-called 'unorganised sector' of household industries, small enterprises and family farms.

For agriculture, national accounting can at least fall back on the statistics of actual production, but the rural service sector for the most part escapes statistical attention. For instance, the vital contribution of bullock carts to rural transport can only be assessed in terms of more or less informed guesswork. Agricultural production figures are also the backbone of most historical exercises with regard to the assessment of India's national income. The fact that ups and downs of agricultural production affected by the vagaries of the monsoon still determine the variation of per-capital national income can easily be seen from Figure 12.1, which shows per-capita net national product for 1950–85. If we compare this graph with Figure 11.1, showing per-capita production of food grains, we immediately notice a very similar pattern. The same drastic reductions associated with the bad harvest years of 1957–8, 1965–6, 1966–7, 1972–3 and 1979–80 appear in both graphs. Similarly, the gradually rising trend can be noticed in both graphs. If this close correspondence between agricultural production and national income can still be observed today, when the industrial sector is much more important than in earlier times, we may rely on historical work done on national income that was mostly based on agricultural

Table 12.1: Composition of gross domestic product

	Gross product ($ US billion)		Share in gross domestic product					
			Agriculture		Industry		Service sector	
	1960	1982	1960	1982	1960	1982	1960	1982
India	29	150	50	33	20	26	30	41
USA	505	3009	4	3	38	33	58	64
France	60	537	11	4	39	34	50	62
Great Britain	71	473	3	2	43	33	54	65
Japan	44	1061	13	4	45	42	42	54
FRG	72	662	6	2	53	46	41	52

Source: World Bank, *World Development Report* (1984).

171

data. Moreover, the British Indian revenue administration was vitally interested in these data and therefore they have been generated in good measure. Nevertheless, the various historical exercises differ widely with regard to their estimates. This is mostly due to conceptual differences and there have been rather acrimonious debates about such estimates. After all, the issues of colonial exploitation or of the alleged benefits of British rule were at stake.

In the nineteenth century, Indian nationalists found a prominent advocate in the British author, William Digby, who tried to show that India's per-capita income had decreased in the second half of that century. Fred Atkinson, chief statistician of the British Indian government, attacked these findings; according to his calculations, per-capita income had increased. Modern research tends to confirm Atkinson's findings. Per-capita income did increase by about 20 per cent from 1860 to 1900, but most of this increase happened before 1885, whereas the last fifteen years of the nineteenth century were a period of stagnation in this respect. From 1900 to 1920, when population growth stagnated, per-capita income increased again by about 14 per cent. When population growth increased again after 1920, per-capita income stagnated once more until the end of British rule.

In contrast with this record, the independent Republic of India has managed to improve the per-capita income from 1950 to 1980 by about 50 per cent (see Figure 12.1). The annual growth rate amounted to a modest 1.2 to 1.4 per cent, in keeping with an average growth rate of the economy of about 3.5 per cent and a population growth rate of about 2.2 per cent. The growth of per-capita income has been accompanied by an encouraging growth rate of savings, for the most part the savings of households rather than of the expanding public sector of the economy. From 1950 to 1964, the gross savings rate at current prices rose very slowly from 10 per cent to about 14 per cent. The impact of the great drought then seems to have been associated with a sudden increase in the savings rate to about 16 per cent; this level was more or less maintained until 1972. In 1973–4, after another bad harvest year, the savings rate increased to 19 per cent and has gradually increased to 22 per cent in the 1980s. It may be just a coincidence that the savings rate was stepped up significantly in years characterised by spurts of inflation after bad harvests, but perhaps the rise of agricultural prices in those years filled the pockets of those who were able and willing to save whatever they had gained.

Figure 12.1: Net national product per capita at 1970–1 prices

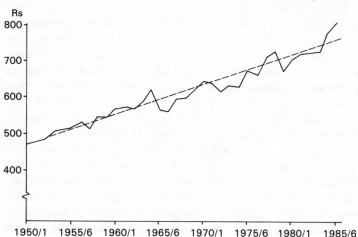

Source: U. Datta Roychaudhuri and M. Mukherjee, cf. Bibliography, Section 12.2.

The encouraging development of household savings, which made up about 85 per cent of all savings, is most probably due to shifts in income distribution. If income distribution had been more equitable, the poor would have consumed more food and others would not have been able to save more money. The rural poor, in particular, have been subjected to a kind of forced saving (that is, to a shortage of means available for buying more food). The contribution of the primary sector to total domestic production has declined from about 60 per cent to 40 per cent from 1950 to 1980, whereas the majority of the Indian workforce (about 75 per cent) still remains tied to that sector. This implies that the rural poor probably have not seen much of the increase of national income. Accurate information on income distribution is difficult to obtain. The experts have to rely on the data on consumer expenditure collected by the National Sample Survey Organisation in this respect. Data for rural India arranged in decile groups have shown that the highest decile group has slightly reduced its share of total household consumer expenditure from 1953–4 to 1973–4 from 26.6 to 23.3 per cent, whereas the lowest five decile groups taken together have edged up from 27.6 to 31.5 per cent. The intermediate four decile groups have more or less retained their shares of 9, 10, 12 and 15 per cent respectively. The decrease in consumer expenditure of the rural rich

173

does not imply a decrease in their income; it most probably indicates a higher rate of saving.

The pattern of distribution of urban consumer expenditure is roughly similar to that of the rural sector, but whereas the rural and the urban sector look very much alike in relative terms in this respect, they do, of course, differ markedly with regard to the absolute figures of income and expenditure. The urban workforce is still rather small when compared to the rural one, but its productivity is much higher. The number of those who work in the public and private sectors in fields other than agriculture has unfortunately not increased very much in recent years. From 1971 to 1980, their number only rose from 16.5 million to 21.6 million. The lion's share of these additional 5 million jobs was created by the public sector (4.5 million). By 1980, this sector employed twice as many people as the private one. In this period, the public sector has enlarged its share of the gross domestic product from 15 to 20 per cent and increased its staff from 11 million to 15.5 million (that is, by 40 per cent).

In the fields of industry, construction and energy, which together generated about 21 per cent of the net domestic product in the period from 1971 to 1980, there were a total of 6.2 million workers in 1971 and 7.7 million in 1980. In these fields the private sector was still dominant, but it expanded much less than the public one. In 1971, the private sector employed 66 per cent of the total workforce in these fields; by 1980, its share had declined to 58 per cent.

In order to demonstrate the great difference between the rural and the urban industrial sector in terms of productivity and output per worker, we shall attempt here a very simple calculation. In 1980, the net domestic product at current prices amounted to 1,000 billion rupees. The contribution of 21 per cent of industry, construction and energy, mentioned above, thus amounted to 210 billion rupees. If we divide this amount by the number of workers — 7.7 million — we arrive at a product per worker of Rs 27,000. This high rate of productivity is achieved only by this particular workforce. If we wish to assess the average product per worker in the large public sector, whose share of the net domestic product amounted to 210 billion rupees too, but which had a total workforce of 15.5 million, we would get only 13,500 rupees. (The public-sector workforce includes all government servants, the army, the railway staff, as well as workers in public-sector industries.) How about the annual product of the peasant or agricultural workers? In order to find out about that we have to arrive at an estimate of the comparable workforce. We should limit this estimate to male workers between the ages of 18 and 58 year. Taking the total number of males between those ages and deducting 20 per cent living in urban areas, we are left with 137 million men. If we deduct from that figure about 25 per cent engaged in rural trades (merchants, moneylenders, carters, artisans) that are not agricultural in the strict sense of the term, we are left with about 100 million peasants and agricultural labourers. The share of the primary sector in the net domestic product amounts to 420 billion rupees; let us deduct one-sixth from this in order to account for primary activities other than agriculture (mining, fishing, forestry, etc.), and we get 350 billion rupees as the total value of the agricultural production for 1980. This is composed of about 120 billion rupees for food grains, 46 billion for oilseeds and pulses, 40 billion for cotton, 40 billion for sugar cane, 20 billion for jute and about 90 billion for animal husbandry, etc. If we divide the total amount of 350 billion by the number of workers — 100 million — we arrive at an annual product per agricultural worker of Rs 3,500. This means that the industrial worker is almost eight times more productive than the agricultural one, and even the average worker in the public sector is nearly four times as productive as the peasant. This is due to the different endowment of urban and rural places of work with the factors of production. With few exceptions, the amount of capital in agriculture is negligible and land is scarce. The total cultivated area of India amounts to $c.$ 150 million hectares; if this is divided by the number of workers mentioned above, it would mean that there are about 1.5 hectares ($c.$ 3 acres) per male agricultural worker. The relatively low yields still prevailing in India imply that not much can be produced on such a plot of land (for example, about 2.5 tons of wheat, or 2 tons of rice or 1 ton of millet). This simple calculation has shown that it should be a top priority to move a large part of the workforce from agriculture to various types of industries. These do not necessarily have to be located in urban areas, but at present they still are and thus the rate of urbanisation would reflect the extent to which the workforce is transferred in this way. The relatively modest rate of urbanisation shows that such transfer is not taking place at a significant rate as yet.

12.3 MIGRATION AND URBANISATION

In most countries, economic development was accompanied by a rising trend of migration from the countryside to the towns and cities. Very often this migration turned into emigration overseas. India also witnessed such a migration to some extent. Under colonial rule, this migration immediately turned into emigration, because of the lack of employment in urban industries. British plantation owners and mine owners in various parts of the empire took advantage of this migration of unskilled labourers after straightforward slavery had been abolished. Indian 'indentured servants' worked in Malaya, South Africa, Mauritius, Fiji and elsewhere.

Independent India no longer had such outlets of overseas migration, with the exception of the recent migration to the Gulf states, which is, however, of a temporary nature only and attracts skilled ·personnel rather than unskilled labourers. Internal migration from the countryside to urban centres was also limited in India. Urbanisation as defined by demographers refers to the exogenous growth of urban areas only and not to the internal reproduction of the urban population; it is measured in terms of the growth of the share of the urban population in the total population. Theoretically, this share could also grow in the absence of migration, if the rate of reproduction of the urban population were much higher than the rural one, but normally the rate of reproduction is higher in rural areas and therefore this theoretical possibility can be safely neglected.

In the first three decades of the twentieth century hardly any urbanisation could be noticed in India. From 1911 to 1931, the share of the urban population in the total population increased only from 11 to 12 per cent. The Second World War brought about a sudden change. In 1941 the share of the urban population amounted to 14 per cent, and in 1951 to 17.3 per cent. Demographers who had thought that economic development would greatly accelerate this trend were very much surprised when the 1961 census only showed an urban share of 18 per cent. In 1971 this share had risen to 20 per cent and in 1981 to 23 per cent. All in all this was a rather modest increase.

Behind this façade of very slow urbanisation, there was hidden a much more dramatic trend of metropolisation (that is, migration from smaller towns and cities to the few large metropolitan centres of India). If we look at Table 12.2 which shows the percentage of cities with a population of over 500,000 inhabitants in the total urban population, we can immediately see that the trend towards metropolisation is very strong in India and is surpassed only by the American rate of metropolisation in the given period. In other countries such as Great Britain and the Federal Republic of Germany, there was a reverse trend in this period.

Table 12.2: India in international comparison: urbanisation

	Share of urban population in total population (%)		Average annual rate of growth (%)		Share of cities above 500,000 in total urban population (%)	
	1960	1982	1960–70	1970–82	1960	1982
India	18	24	3.3	3.9	26	39
USA	70	78	1.8	1.5	61	77
France	62	79	2.4	1.4	34	34
Great Britain	86	91	0.9	0.3	61	55
Japan	63	78	2.4	1.8	35	42
FRG	77	85	1.4	0.5	48	45

Source: World Bank, *World Development Report* (1984).

Metropolisation could be noticed in India at a fairly early stage, and from the very beginning it was concentrated on a few major centres. Even in 1901, 23 per cent of the urban population lived in those major centres. By 1931 this percentage had risen to 27 and by 1951 to 41; it increased further to 56 per cent in 1971 and 60 per cent in 1981. On average, the urban population increased by 34 per cent in India from 1961 to 1971, whereas the total population grew by 24 per cent. It is interesting to note which cities showed an above-average growth rate in this period: Bangalore (70 per cent), Delhi (53 per cent), Hyderabad (44 per cent), Pune (43 per cent), Madras (42 per cent), Bombay (39 per cent). The following cities registered below-average growth: Agra (24 per cent), Allahabad (19 per cent), Calcutta (9 per cent). All cities with above-average growth also had high scores as far as the growth of employment in industry and construction are concerned: Bangalore (67 per cent), Delhi (61 per cent), Hyderabad (85 per cent), Pune (69 per cent), Madras (40 per cent), Bombay (36 per cent). The cities with below-average scores showed deficient growth rates in this respect, too, and Allahabad even registered an absolute decline of such employment.

There are three distinct types of cities in India: those in which workers in industry and construction make up 20 per cent or more of the population (Bombay and Calcutta); those in which such workers constitute about 15 per cent of the population (e.g. Delhi and Madras); and centres of trade and administration in which the share of such workers is less than 10 per cent (e.g. Lakhnau, Allahabad, Patna).

The differentiation of the rates of growth and the trend towards metropolisation implies a shrinkage of the smaller towns and cities

Figure 12.2: India's top-heavy urbanisation (1981)

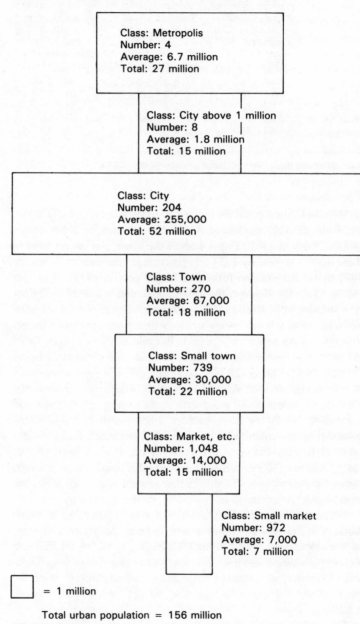

Class: Metropolis
Number: 4
Average: 6.7 million
Total: 27 million

Class: City above 1 million
Number: 8
Average: 1.8 million
Total: 15 million

Class: City
Number: 204
Average: 255,000
Total: 52 million

Class: Town
Number: 270
Average: 67,000
Total: 18 million

Class: Small town
Number: 739
Average: 30,000
Total: 22 million

Class: Market, etc.
Number: 1,048
Average: 14,000
Total: 15 million

Class: Small market
Number: 972
Average: 7,000
Total: 7 million

☐ = 1 million

Total urban population = 156 million

Source of data: *Census of India 1981*.

without industrial potential. Thus urban–urban migration became much more important than rural–urban migration. This has shaped the structure of the urban pyramid in India. Ideally, such a pyramid should look very much like India's population pyramid: broad-based and slowly tapering at the top. The broad base would consist of many small towns and the top would include the few major centres. In fact, India's urban pyramid is topsy-turvy. The 1981 census reveals the following structure of this top-heavy pyramid, which is precariously perched on a rather slender base. At the very top there are four metropolitan centres, which comprise 17 per cent of the entire urban population; beneath them there are eight cities with more than one million inhabitants each, comprising 10 per cent of the urban population. Altogether, these twelve large cities contain 27 per cent of the urban population. Then follow 204 cities, which together make up one-third of the urban population. The twelve largest and these 204 cities (average population of 250,000 inhabitants) encompass 60 per cent of the urban population. The remaining 40 per cent are accounted for by medium and small towns, which hardly offer much productive employment, but are at the most centres of trade and administration (e.g. district headquarters). Rural migrants heading for urban work would not find it there and would go to search for it in the big cities. Moreover, in these big cities the migrants can utilise the infrastructure, even if they do not find more than casual work and do not contribute anything to the maintenance of that infrastructure. Therefore the infrastructure of the big cities is often overburdened and can hardly be maintained properly.

The maintenance of Indian cities is a difficult problem, since municipal finance, and the finance of local government in general, is a much neglected field of public finance in India. A study of this type of finance showed that in 1960–1 the share of municipal expenditure in total government expenditure (central, state and local governments) amounted to 5.5 per cent, but by 1976/7 this share had receded to 4.6 per cent. Rural local government did not fare much better, although *Panchayati Raj* had been proclaimed by India's political leadership with great enthusiasm. In 1960–1 its share in total government expenditure amounted to 4.7 per cent and in 1976–7 to 4 per cent. Municipal and rural local government together thus claimed a share of about 10 per cent in 1960–1 and 8.6 per cent in 1976–7. This shows the very modest role that the institutions of local government are permitted to play in India. A more appropriate relationship is indicated by the example of the Federal Republic of

Germany, where municipal and rural local government claims 24 per cent of total government expenditure, and the rest is equally divided between the federal government and the sum of the expenditure of all state governments.

Indian municipal corporations that have to provide basic services for millions of citizens have to finance their operations by means of an antediluvian system of taxation. Octroi, the taxation of commodities brought into the city, is still the largest source of municipal income. It is also a very flexible source of taxation, unlike the property tax, which should be the mainstay of municipal finance, but which is encumbered with antiquated methods of evaluation, etc. A glance at the Bombay budget shows this very clearly. From 1982–3 to 1983–4, Bombay managed to increase its income from 1.7 billion to 2.3 billion rupees, mainly by changing the method of assessing octroi; instead of collecting piece rates as before, the new charges were ad valorem, and octroi income was stepped up from 1 billion to 1.4 billion rupees in this way. This also enabled the corporation to foot a wage bill that increased from 0.4 billion to 0.5 billion rupees. Octroi is not only a very flexible kind of taxation, it is also collected very cheaply. Whereas the Bombay octroi staff costs only 17 million rupees per year, the property tax staff costs 34 million rupees and collects a much smaller amount (1983–4). Bombay's municipal budget is dwarfed by the enormous sum of the telephone bills of its citizens, which are, of course, collected by an altogether different agency. This shows the stark contrast between municipal poverty and the economic activity of citizens who could easily afford to pay municipal taxes in keeping with the amount they spend on telephone calls. Of course, more municipal expenditure on urban infrastructure, services and amenities would also attract more in-migrants. This municipal poverty could also be seen as an integral part of the defence mechanism against overcrowding. It enforces the 'push-back' effect, which repels the newcomer.

The 'push-back' effect, however, is not just related to municipal poverty. It mainly arises from the fact that the urban population increases by itself and produces many unemployed, who have no place to go outside the city, as they no longer have any rural roots, which most migrants still have. Statistics show that the rate of unemployment is much higher among the settled urban population than among recent in-migrants. This does not imply that in-migrants are more in demand among employers, but that they more readily disappear, if they do not find employment. Behind the placid façade of a limited rural–urban migration and modest rates of urbanisation, there is obviously quite a hectic rural–urban–rural migration, which does not show up in any statistics. The statistics only show in a general way that the Indian population displays an amazing mobility, but this mobility rarely leads to permanent employment in more productive occupations. The census shows that 30 per cent of the population live at places other than their place of birth, but only 3.3 per cent were recorded as living in a state other than the one in which they were born.

The 'push-back' effect is the only automatic defence mechanism that protects the big cities from being totally overwhelmed by unwanted inhabitants. Recent research has shown that whereas there are some economies of scale as small towns grow into big towns, there are diseconomies of scale as far as the big cities are concerned. Although costs per capita decrease up to a point, they increase thereafter. But in spite of such diseconomies and the 'push-back' effect, metropolisation is going to proceed in India more or less at the current rate. From 1971 to 1981, the total urban population increased by 43 per cent, but whereas towns with more than 100,000 inhabitants increased by 54 per cent, smaller towns increased only at the rate of 29 per cent, which is only a little more than the rate of population growth for that decade (24 per cent). If this trend continues, 134 million people will live in towns with more than 100,000 inhabitants by 1991, whereas only 88 million will live in smaller towns. Since the metropolisation rate has always increased much faster than the urbanisation rate in India in recent times, we may assume that even at the time of writing (1987), 134 million people live in towns with more than 100,000 inhabitants. Like all other phenomena of social change in India, metropolisation also shows a great deal of regional differentiation. The regional disparities will be discussed in the next section below.

12.4 REGIONAL DISPARITIES: EAST AND WEST

The Physical Quality of Life Index, which is based on three simple indicators — infant mortality, life expectancy at age one, and literacy — provides a good yardstick for the measurement of regional disparities. If we apply this yardstick to the different regions of India and extend the comparison to the international scene, we arrive at the striking conclusion that Western India has a quality of life comparable to that of Latin America, whereas Eastern India is on a par with the poorest states of Africa. Western India in this case would include all states to the west of a line connecting Delhi with Madras. To the east of this line we find the large populous states of Uttar Pradesh, Bihar, West Bengal, Orissa, Andhra Pradesh and parts of Madhya Pradesh. As mentioned above, Eastern India has been bypassed by the 'Green Revolution' to a great extent, and it is also greatly deficient in the degree of urbanisation and metropolisation. Calcutta, the only metropolis of the east, has a high 'push-back' effect, and the other large cities, of which there are very few in Eastern India (Patna, Allahabad, Varanasi, Lackhnau and Kanpur, the old industrial centre), show below-average growth rates, as employment has not increased in those areas in recent years.

Instead of urbanisation, we can find rural areas with an amazing degree of overpopulation in this region. In 1981, the average population density in India was 220 people per square kilometre. Fertile districts in the rice and wheat zones have about 325–400 people per square kilometre. In east Uttar Pradesh and in adjacent north Bihar, there are a group of districts with 500–600 persons per square kilometre. These districts are situated in a semicircle surrounding Varanasi and Patna. There are altogether about 40 million people in this overpopulated region to the north of the Ganges. The percentage of landless labour is particularly high in this area, but it is not at all outstanding as far as yields per acre and the productivity of labour are concerned. The increase of labour productivity is almost exclusively restricted to Western India; in the east, the exploitation of labour depresses productivity. In earlier times, surplus labour from these overpopulated districts mentioned above would migrate to Calcutta or to Kanpur, but there is no hope of finding work there at present. Furthermore, the public sector is the major employer in Eastern India. As we have seen above, the public sector has employed about 4 million more workers in recent years, but this means hardly any relief for the enormous population of Eastern India, which encompasses about 350 million people in the boundaries outlined above.

In striking contrast with Eastern India stands coastal Western India, with Bombay as a dynamic metropolis flanked by two major industrial centres, Ahmedabad in Gujarat and Pune in Maharashtra. Other urban centres have recently expanded in this area: for example, Thane, a new municipal corporation in Maharashtra immediately adjacent to Bombay with about 3 million people, or Surat and Vadodara (Baroda) in Gujarat. In this entire region, the private sector is the dominant employer. There is a highly differentiated hierarchy of qualified jobs in this region, and therefore the number of unemployed college graduates is far lower here than in Eastern India. In this highly industrialised region only every sixth graduate is employed by the public sector, whereas every second graduate is so employed elsewhere in India. It is remarkable that this region not only leads India in terms of industrial concentration, but also in terms of the frequency of smaller industrial centres. This is particularly true of Gujarat, which also excels in terms of the productivity of agricultural labour.

Tamil Nadu, in the extreme south, which is also part of Western India according to our definition, is another region with striking characteristics. Population growth has been curtailed to a considerable extent, urbanisation has made significant progress and agriculture shows increases in yields per acre as well as in labour productivity. Industrialisation is well distributed; Madras, the regional metropolis, is flanked by a considerable number of large cities whose importance is hardly recognised outside the region (population in millions, in 1981): Coimbatore 0.9, Madurai 0.9, Tiruchirappalli 0.6 and Salem 0.5. They are followed by a number of cities with a population of 200,000 or more: Vellore, Erode, Thanjavur, Tiruppur, Tirunelveli and Tuticorin. There are nine more cities with 100,000 people or more. The strata of smaller towns (50,000–90,000) is also very well represented in Tamil Nadu, with 37 such towns encompassing a total small-town population of 2.5 million. In contrast with the pattern prevailing in India as a whole, Tamil Nadu thus shows a very well-balanced urban pyramid.

A similar structure can be found in another well-developed area of Western India, the fertile Punjab. Yields per acre and labour productivity in agriculture are very high here, but medium and small-scale industry has also made much progress. The pattern of urbanisation reflects this very well. Of course, the regional metropolis, Delhi, is outside the Punjab, but it is mostly inhabited by Punjabis. In the Punjab itself, there is only the medium level and infrastructure of urbanisation, but that is quite respectable. Punjab had a population of 17 million in 1981 and contained the following major cities (population in millions): Ludhiana 0.6, Amritsar 0.6 and Jalandhar 0.4. In addition, there are four cities with populations over 100,000 and eight smaller towns. Ludhiana and Jalandhar, which are only 50 km apart, are jointly considered to be one of India's most important industrial centres.

Western India also contains, of course, some backward regions with hardly any industry, low urbanisation and poor performance in agriculture. But these are almost all very dry areas with a low population density. The only rural area with an extremely high population density in Western India is to be found in Kerala, where there are three districts with between 800 and 1,200 people per square kilometre. However, in these districts rice yields per acre are also unusually high. The rate of population growth has receded in Kerala more or less in the same way as in neighbouring Tamil Nadu. In recent years, Kerala has profited to a surprising extent from the migration of labour to the Gulf states; indeed, construction work financed by remittances has driven up the wages of labour to such an extent that the wage level provides a major obstacle to further industrialisation. This is certainly a unique phenomenon in India's economic history.

The migration to the Gulf states has benefited almost exclusively the people of Western India, particularly those from the coastal areas, whereas the overpopulated districts of Eastern India have hardly participated in it. This is also due to the fact that it is mostly a migration of skilled labour, and of clerks, accountants, and engineers, rather than of unskilled landless labourers. The regional disparity between Eastern and Western India has been accentuated even more by this development.

The striking differences between Western and Eastern India have not suddenly emerged in recent years. We have seen that under British colonial rule, Eastern India had been the major source of agricultural exports and that the export-oriented industry of Calcutta had been firmly in British hands, whereas in Bombay and Ahmedabad another type of industry had grown up which was basically geared to the home market and was led by Indians. During the Great Depression and the Second World War Calcutta declined, whereas Bombay made rapid strides ahead. The government of independent India could hardly reverse this trend. Moreover, Calcutta had lost a large part of its hinterland by the partition of the country and was swamped by refugees from East Pakistan, who had no basic skills, as they had only learned to live on the rents paid by their tenants. Bombay also received some refugees, but these were mostly clever Sindhi merchants who opened their shops on the pavement and soon did very well in business. The Marwari and Gujarati businessmen who had migrated to Calcutta and had bought up the enterprises of the parting British were also not inclined to extend their investment in the East, but rather transferred their profits to Western India.

The new public-sector industrial centres in Eastern India such as

Durgapur, Rourkela, Bhilai and Bokaro, which grew up near the rich coal and ore resources of that region, did not do much for its general economic growth. They remained isolated enclaves, their personnel was mostly imported from elsewhere — very often from Western India — their products also did not enter the local economy. As far as urbanisation was concerned, the impact of the steel towns was minimal: they offered only a restricted number of special jobs, and unauthorised migrants were kept out of these towns, whose municipal government was usually a department of the company concerned. The 'push-back' effect was perfect under such conditions. The stark contrast between modern industry and backward agriculture can be witnessed here, where even hunters with bow and arrow are still to be found close to the modern steel mills.

12.5 TASKS OF THE FUTURE AND THE POLITICAL SYSTEM

India faces some daunting tasks in the immediate future. Regional disparities have to be reduced, income distribution must be made more equitable, urbanisation should be channelled to prevent undue metropolisation, industry must provide more jobs and agriculture more food — because by the year 2,000 more than a billion Indians will have to be fed. In tackling these problems, due attention must be paid to the ecological aspects of economic development. It is not a privilege of the rich nations to worry about environmental degradation. India is threatened by total deforestation, India's great rivers are polluted. Remedial action should nevertheless be easier in India where, for instance, deforestation is not caused by continental air pollution, but by indiscriminate cutting of trees. Poor forest guards are bribed by unscrupulous entrepreneurs who take whole truckloads to the sawmills. Firewood is getting more and more scarce and the burning of cow-dung also has its limits. About half of India's fuel consumption takes places in innumerable kitchens, most of which are equipped with incredibly inefficient ovens that utilise about 5 per cent of the energy of the fuel consumed. Fuel has become more expensive than the food cooked in those kitchens.

According to India's planners, about 30 per cent of India's soil should be covered by forests; official statistics show that only about 20 per cent actually exist, but satellite photographs seem to indicate that only 10 per cent can still be traced. The forests are rapidly disappearing and re-afforestation takes a long time. Landless families could be put in charge of raising and guarding trees. Some experiments in 'social forestry' have already been conducted in various parts of India; they deserve further encouragement. The dwindling of forests causes changes in India's climate, because forests retain water and as they disappear the dependence on the vagaries of the monsoon becomes even greater.

New approaches to the harnessing of India's water resources are also urgently required. Initially, too much emphasis was given to huge barrages, which were supposed to generate cheap electricity and help to irrigate vast areas. Ecological conditions were often neglected in designing the barrages. Many of them are silting up rapidly, as erosion has increased when trees were cut in the valleys around the barrages. The irrigation potential of such barrages was often not adequately used, because peasants did not accept the water or fell back on it only whenever the monsoon failed. Local small-scale irrigation projects were also of little use; they often got stuck in a mire of petty corruption. What was really missing was large-scale public support for the digging of private wells. There is still the ancient institution of *takavi*, which enables the peasant to borrow money from the revenue authorities for improving his land or digging a well. The amounts authorised, however, are calculated in terms of multiples of the land revenue demand, and as that has dwindled, the loans obtainable in this way are negligible. On the other hand, the risk of digging a well and finding no water is too much for the small peasant. In most areas of India, reliable data about groundwater resources are missing and the digging of wells is an unpredictable gamble. The government has responded to this challenge at a fairly late date. A new organisation, the Groundwater Survey of India, has been established only in recent years and it will take time to complete its enormous task. If public authorities could finance the digging of wells and then charge a suitable water rate wherever the digging has been successful, yields could be increased in such a way as to dwarf all achievements of the 'Green Revolution'. Such water supply would also be fully utilised by the beneficiaries, as the example of the Punjab has shown, where peasants have largely financed their own wells. The size of land owned or operated is, of course, a crucial variable in this context. Large-scale irrigation schemes by means of barrages are never utilised to the same extent as private wells. Recent reports seem to indicate that only 6–7 million hectares of the 13 million hectares of land for which irrigation from barrages is supposed to be available have actually been irrigated. A study of institutional constraints to technological change in Bengal has shown that the lack of water control is a major impediment to agricultural growth. Even modern tubewells are not utilised properly. 'Waterlords' emerge who monopolise the access to irrigation. Envious neighbours then take revenge by damaging wells etc. This study included both West Bengal and Bangladesh and it was found that the contrast in political regimes made no difference as far as the deficiencies in water control are concerned.

The harnessing of water resources also includes adequate drainage. The ancient builders of Harappa and Mohenjo Daro must have been great masters of that art. Their well-drained cities would lead one to the conclusion that the art of drainage was also applied to the fields, which were inundated by the Indus. In later times, particularly under British rule, canal irrigation was sometimes pushed ahead without adequate drainage of the irrigated fields and this then led to waterlogging and salinity. It should be easy for Indian experts today to remedy the mistakes of the recent past and to rival those who created the Indus civilisation. A decent treatment of India's rivers is another important task of water-resources management. The Ganges may well have had some mysterious ways and means by which it constantly purified itself, but these self-regulatory devices have succumbed in recent times to indiscriminate industrial and municipal pollution.

All the tasks mentioned here require energetic political action. This raises questions about the nature of the political system prevalent in India. In the preceding chapters, we have again and again discussed the political conditions of economic development as well as the economic constraints of political action. We have analysed such occurrences as man-made famines, spurts of inflation which destabilised politics, and the constant problems of consolidating political power under averse circumstances. Plebiscitarian populism proved to be the only means of getting majorities, which enabled the executive to stay in power until the next crisis required another electoral plebiscite. The short-lived experiment of running the country in an 'emergency' with dictatorial powers showed that this was not a viable alternative. Discipline was instilled at the expense of open communication and this isolated the leadership so completely from the people that it lost all sense of reality. The Indian people tend to look up to *sarkar*, the omnipotent government, but they are quick to turn against those who are blinded by the illusion of omnipotence. The government of India, on the other hand, likes to play the role of 'big government', and indeed the share of the national economy controlled by the government has increased considerably in recent years, as we have seen. The budget has expanded, public-sector enterprises have attained an enormous weight, the government employs the largest share of the workforce. The Indian Administrative Service, an elite corps of officers controlled by the central government, mans all the top positions not only in New Delhi, but also in the state capitals and district head-quarters, as well as many managerial posts in the public sector. This service inherited the traditions of the 'steel frame' of British India. It has also set the style for all subordinate services. The attempt to build up an idealist cadre of rural community development officers has failed: the Block Development Officer nowadays tries to emulate the Collector or Deputy Commissioner at district headquarters, and the Village-Level Worker (*Gram Sevak*) in turn adopts the style of his boss, the Block Development Officer.

Both the rural sector and the industrial sector have been penetrated by this style of government as represented by civil servants. This has not promoted economic progress, because by his very nature the civil servant must be a preserver of law and order and not an innovator who generates economic growth. He is trained to maintain the *status quo*, he cannot be expected to break new ground. Even a rigorous application of the rules known to him may get him into trouble, let along any daring initiative of his own. Posted as manager of a public-sector enterprise, he cannot suddenly change his approach and become an enterpreneur who gladly takes risks. In a 'mixed economy', this predominance of the civil servant is more or less inevitable. In India, where the British built up a bureaucracy that was in many respects ahead of the bureaucracies of contemporary Europe, this predominance was bound to be even stronger than elsewhere.

The illusion of omnipotence, which has been mentioned before, can be enhanced by the existence of a powerful bureacracy. But the web of illusion can easily be torn by outside forces, such as the vagaries of the world market or of the monsoon, and also by internal turbulence. The 'mandate of heaven' can be lost all of a sudden. But whereas this may affect individual leaders, the political system as such will survive, if it is legitimised by new leaders. Gunnar Myrdal has criticised the Indian political system by calling it a 'soft state'. This may be true, if the system is judged in terms of developmental efficiency. But if it is assessed in terms of political resilience, the verdict may be different. A tough dictatorship, be it of the 'white' or the 'red' revolution type, would soon be at the end of its tether in a vast and complex country like India. It could be maintained only by fierce repression, and that would be incompatible with economic development, which does require the participation of the people. Elementary freedom is a precondition of development; this may not be the freedom of liberal orthodoxy, but the freedom of open communication, which acts as a check on the illusions of omnipotence of the leaders.

The message of Gandhi may still find a place in India's resilient political system. So far Gandhi has been worshipped as the 'Father of the Nation', but his message has been forgotten. Throughout his life he was never in a position of official authority, there was no bureaucracy to support him, only bands of volunteers who followed his call. His political actions were creatively designed by him so as to find a response among the people. Some of his symbolic actions, such as his devotion to the spinning wheel, were not quite understood and simply repeated by his followers as a token of respect. The message of the spinning wheel was supposed to be self-reliance by self-employment. Instead of just preaching this message, Gandhi took up the wheel and started to work in order to set an active example. Unfortunately the symbol remained, but the message was lost: perhaps India's young generation may rediscover it.

Annotated Bibliography

The sequence of these notes follows that of the chapters of the book. Only the first entry of a book cited will provide full details; further references will be in terms of short titles. Contributions to the *Cambridge Economic History of India* are quoted by referring to the name of the contributor and an abbreviation *CEHI 1* and *CEHI 2* (i.e. vol. I, edited by Tapankumar Raychaudhuri and Irfan Habib, Cambridge, 1982; Vol. II, edited by Dharma Kumar and Meghnad Desai, Cambridge, 1983). Since no alphabetical list will be provided here, the names of the authors of the books cited have been included in the index.

1 THE STRUCTURE OF THE TRADITIONAL ECONOMY

1.1. For a survey of technology, cf. Habib, *CEHI 1*, pp. 48 ff.; for the activities and the wealth of Indian maritime traders, cf. Ashin Das Gupta, *Indian Merchants and the Decline of Surat* (Wiesbaden, 1978).

Medieval agrarian relations are discussed by Stein, *CEHI 1*, pp. 23 ff., and by R.S. Sharma, *Indian Feudalism* (Calcutta, 1965); see also B. Stein, *Peasant State and Society in Medieval South India* (New Delhi, 1980).

1.2. For the Mughal period, cf. I. Habib, *The Agrarian System of Mughal India* (Bombay, 1963); for Maratha economic history, cf. A.R. Kulkarni, *Maharashtra in the Age of Shivaji* (Bombay, 1969); see also Fukazawa, *CEHI 1*, pp. 193 ff., pp. 249 ff., for Vijayanagar and the late medieval kingdoms of the South, cf. Stein, *CEHI 1*, pp. 102 ff., pp. 452 ff.

1.3. For the cost of transporation and the handicaps of long-distance trade, cf. Raychaudhuri, *CEHI 1*, pp. 336 f., and his reference to the financing of long-distance trade, pp. 346 ff.; for maritime trade, cf. Das Gupta, *CEHI 1*, pp. 407 ff.

1.4. On coinage and the increase in the circulation of silver rupees, cf. Habib, *CEHI 1*, p. 361 ff.; for the increase in population, cf. Habib, *CEHI 1*, pp. 153–71. The Spanish price revolution is discussed by R. Pieper, *Die Preisrevolution in Spanien, 1500–1640* (Wiesbaden, 1985). She presents a critical assessment of E.J. Hamilton's earlier work in the light of recent research. The flow of precious metals from Europe to Asia is discussed by several contributors to W. Fischer *et al.* (eds.), *The Emergence of a World Economy, 1500–1914*, 2 vols. (Wiesbaden, 1986) (especially the contributions of D.O. Flynn, K.N. Chaudhuri, Om Prakash, F.S. Gaastra and A. Attman to Vol. I).

The land revenue problem is discussed by Habib, *CEHI 1*, pp. 235 ff. as well as in Habib, *Agrarian System*; the proliferation of high-level mansabdars is analysed by M. Athar Ali, *The Mughal Nobility under Aurangzeb* (Calcutta, 1966).

2 THE DEVELOPMENT OF MARITIME TRADE AND THE BEGINNINGS OF COLONIAL RULE

2.1. The transition from pre-emporia trade to emporia trade is mentioned by K.N. Chaudhuri, *Trade and Civilization in the Indian Ocean* (Cambridge, 1985); for the activity of merchant guilds in the Chola empire, cf. M. Abraham, *Two Medieval South Indian Merchant Guilds* (New Delhi, 1988); for the developments in China in the eleventh century, cf. J. Gernet, *A History of Chinese Civilization* (Cambridge, 1985).

2.2. For medieval Indian maritime trade, cf. Digby, *CEHI 1*, pp. 235 ff.; he cites the example of the Sultan of Honavar. The connections between Mediterranean trade and Indian Ocean trade are discussed by S. Labib, *Handelsgeschichte Ägyptens im Spätmittelalter, 1171–1517* (Wiesbaden, 1965). A detailed account of the economic history of the Portuguese maritime empire is provided by M. Magalhaes-Godinho, *L'Economie de l'Empire Portugais aux XV et XVI Siècles* (Paris, 1969); the interaction of the Portuguese with Indian coastal rulers is analysed by M.N. Pearson, *Merchants and Rulers in Gujarat. The Response to the Portuguese in the Sixteenth Century* (Berkeley, Ca, 1976).

2.3. A full survey of the European maritime empires is given by H. Furber, *Rival Empires of Trade in the Orient, 1600–1800* (Minneapolis, Mn, 1978); for the Dutch, cf. K. Glamann, *Dutch Asiatic Trade, 1620–1740* (Copenhagen, 1958), and T. Raychaudhuri, *Jan Company in Coromandel, 1605–1680* (The Hague, 1962).

2.4. The major work in this field is K.N. Chaudhuri, *The Trading World of Asia and the East Indian Company, 1660–1760* (Cambridge, 1978); cf. also K.N. Chaudhuri, *CEHI 1*, pp. 382 ff.; for British trade with Bengal, cf. S. Chaudhuri, *Trade and*

Commercial Organisation in Bengal, 1650–1720 (Calcutta, 1975). For a special study of the impact of the Dutch company on Bengal, cf. Om Prakash, *The Dutch East India Company and the Economy of Bengal, 1630–1720* (Princeton, NJ, 1985).

2.5. For a typology of the development of European bridgeheads in Asia and the beginnings of colonial rule, cf. D. Rothermund, *Asian Trade and European Expansion in the Age of Mercantilism* (New Delhi, 1981) (this book contains a detailed annotated bibliography with references to many books that have not been specifically mentioned here).

3 THE AGRARIAN STATE AND THE COMPANY: PARASITISM AND PARALYSIS

3.1. For a discussion of the 'commercialisation of power', cf. C.A. Bayly, *Rulers, Townsmen and Bazaars* (Cambridge, 1983). The agrarian history of Eastern India and the origins of the Permanent Settlement are described by B. Chaudhuri, *CEHI 2*, pp. 86 ff.; for references to the shortage of money supply see B. Chaudhuri, *CEHI 2*, pp. 331 ff.; Divekar, *CEHI 2*, pp. 344 ff.; Kumar, *CEHI 2*, p. 360. For the fate of the weavers of Southern India, cf. K. Specker, *Weber im Wettbewerb, Das Schicksal der südindischen Textilhandwerker im 19. Jahrhundert* (Wiesbaden, 1984).

For the Bengal famine of 1770, cf. B. Chaudhuri, *CEHI 2*, p. 94 and Bhattacharya, *CEHI 2*, pp. 299 ff. The rural migrations caused by the famine are discussed by A. Nagchaudhuri-Zilly, *The Vagrant Peasant. Agrarian Distress and Desertion in Bengal, 1770–1830* (Wiesbaden, 1982).

For Tipu Sultan's revenue settlement, cf. Kumar, *CEHI 2*, p. 225; for the political compulsions which forced Tipu Sultan to gear up his administration, cf. B. Sheik Ali, *Tipu Sultan* (Mysore, 1982).

For North India, cf. Bayly, *Rulers*, pp. 74 ff.; revenue assessment on the Bombay Deccan is described by Fukazawa, *CEHI 2*, pp. 182 ff.; for the revenue settlement of the Sikhs in the Punjab, cf. I. Banga, *Agrarian System of the Sikhs* (New Delhi, 1978).

3.2. The agency houses are discussed by Bhattacharya, *CEHI 2*, pp. 293 ff., 316; see also B. Kling, *Partner in Empire. Dwarkananth Tagore and the Age of Enterprise in Eastern India* (Berkeley, Ca, 1976).

The analysis of foreign trade and the table presented are based on K. Chaudhuri, *CEHI 2*, pp. 826 ff.; for the cultivation of opium, cf.

Bhattacharya, *CEHI 2* pp. 312 ff.; see also B.B. Chowdhury, *The Growth of Commercial Agriculture in Bengal, 1759–1900* (Calcutta, 1964); for the increase in value of landed estates, cf. B. Chaudhuri, *CEHI 2*, pp. 101 ff.; for Dwarkanath Tagore, cf. Kling, *Partner in Empire*.

3.3. For the economic crisis of 1847 and the price rise in the 1850s, cf. Bhattacharya, *CEHI 2*, p. 332; for the Crimean War and the rise in the demand for Indian jute, cf. p. 325. For the beginning of the Indian cotton textile industry, cf. Morris, *CEHI 2*, p. 575.

4 THE EVOLUTION OF AN INDIAN MARKET IN THE NINETEENTH CENTURY

4.1. For a survey of the political history of India, cf. H. Kulke and D. Rothermund, *A History of India* (Beckenham, Kent 1986; New Delhi, 1987); the evolution of the banking system is discussed by D.N. Ghosh, *Banking Policy in India* (Bombay, 1979). For the evolution of state finance in India under the British crown, cf. S. Bhattacharya, *Financial Foundations of the British Raj, 1858–1872* (Simla, 1971). The general background of economic policy is provided by S. Ambirajan, *Political Economy and British Policy in India* (Cambridge, 1978).

4.2. For the expansion of the railway network, cf. Hurd, *CEHI 2*, pp. 737 ff.; the reference to prices before and after the railway reached certain districts in Bengal is based on an article by M. Mukherjee, 'Railways and the impact on Bengal's economy', in *Indian Economic and Social History Review* No. 2 (1980); the relevance of freight rates is discussed by Hurd, *CEHI 2*, pp. 752 ff.

4.3. For the 'Home Charges' and the transfer problem, cf. K. Chaudhuri, *CEHI 2*, pp. 873 ff.; see also N. Charlesworth, *British Rule and the Indian Economy* (London, 1982), pp. 48 ff. The attitude of the British textile industry towards India and the role of British textile exports are discussed by W.G. Hynes, *The Economics of Empire* (London, 1979).

The tables presented in this section are based on the data of K. Chaudhuri, *CEHI 2*, pp. 844 f.; the table showing the export data of different ports is taken from the article by A.K. Bagchi, 'Reflections on patterns of regional growth in India during the period of British rule', in *Bengal Past and Present*, Vol. 95 (1976).

4.4. For a more detailed discussion, cf. D. Rothermund, 'India's silver currency. An aspect of the monetary policy of British

Imperialism', in *Indian Economic and Social History Review*, No. 2 (1970). The monetary policy after the closing of the mints is analysed by J.M. Keynes, *Indian Currency and Finance* (London, 1913); see also S. Ambirajan, *Political Economy and Monetary Management. India 1766–1914* (Madras, 1984).

4.5. The migration of the Marwaris is mentioned by C.A. Bayly, *Rulers*, pp. 249, 279; see also T. Timberg, *The Marwaris — From Traders to Industrialists* (Calcutta, 1978). The role of the Bombay cotton traders is analysed by M. Vicziany, 'Bombay merchants and structural changes in the export community, 1850 to 1880', in K.N. Chaudhuri and C. Dewey (eds.), *Economy and Society. Essays in Indian Economic and Social History* (New Delhi, 1979). British tenancy legislation and the relief of peasant indebtedness are discussed by D. Rothermund, *Government, Landlord and Peasant in India. Agrarian Relations under British Rule, 1860–1935* (Wiesbaden, 1978). The problems of the revenue system have been discussed by D. Rothermund, 'The land revenue problem in British India', in *Bengal Past and Present*, Vol. 95, No. 1 (1976); this article and other essays on agrarian history are reprinted in D. Rothermund, *The Indian Economy under British Rule* (New Delhi, 1983). Indian land prices are discussed by R.W. Goldsmith, *The Financial Development of India, 1860–1977* (New Haven, Conn, 1983), pp. 46, 63.

The data on agricultural production are derived from the book by G. Blyn, *Agricultural Trends in India, 1891–1947: Output, Availability and Productivity* (Philadelphia, Pa, 1966). The data on Japanese rice production are from G.C. Allen, *A Short Economic History of Modern Japan* (London, 1981). For the famines, cf. B.M. Bhatia, *Famines in India* (London, 1963).

5 THE LIMITS OF INDUSTRIALISATION UNDER COLONIAL RULE

5.1. For the stages of industrialisation in Europe, cf. A. Gerschenkron, *Economic Backwardness in Historical Perspective* (Cambridge, Mass. 1962). India's retarded industrialisation is discussed by R. Ray, *Industrialisation in India — Growth and Conflict in the Private Corporate Sector, 1914–1947* (Delhi, 1979); the scarcity of capital and the bottlenecks of money supply are analysed by Chandavarkar, *CEHI 2*, pp. 762 ff. A detailed survey of investment in Indian industries is provided by A.K. Bagchi,

Private Investment in India, 1900–1939 (Cambridge, 1972).

5.2. For the cotton textile industry, cf. Morris, *CEHI 2*, pp. 572 ff. An interesting comparison of cotton textile production in terms of the different qualities of yarn and cloth is contained in the article by H. Kawakatsu, 'International competition in cotton goods in the late 19th century: Britain versus India and East Asia', in W. Fischer *et al.* (eds.), *The Emergence of a World Economy*, Vol. II, pp. 619 ff. For the recruitment of millhands etc., cf. M.D. Morris, *The Emergence of an Industrial Labour Force in India: A Study of the Bombay Cotton Mills, 1854–1947* (Berkeley, Ca, 1965); see also R.K. Newman, 'Social factors in the recruitment of Bombay millhands', in K.N. Chaudhuri and C. Dewey (eds.), *Economy and Society*, pp. 277 ff. On Jamshed Tata and his enterprises, cf. R.M. Lala, *The Creation of Wealth. A Tata Story* (Bombay, 1981); see also Morris, *CEHI 2*, pp. 588 ff.

5.3. The jute industry is discussed by Morris, *CEHI 2*, pp. 566 ff; see also A. Dasgupta, 'Jute textile industry', in V.B. Singh (ed.), *The Economic History of India, 1857–1956* (Bombay, 1965). For coal mining, cf. D. Rothermund and D.C. Wadhwa (eds.), *Zamindars, Mines and Peasants. Studies in the History of an Indian Coalfield and its Rural Hinterland* (New Delhi, 1978).

5.4. The data cited in this section are from R.W. Goldsmith, *Financial Development*, pp. 45, 52. The TISCO investment is discussed by Morris, *CEHI 2*, p. 591; for the policy of the Japanese finance minister, Prince Matsukata, cf. G.C. Allen, *Modern Japan*, pp. 48 ff. For the land prices, cf. R.W. Goldsmith, *Financial Development*, p. 63. The working of the managing agency system is illustrated in a detailed case study by H. Papendieck, 'British managing agencies in the Indian coalfield', in D. Rothermund and D.C. Wadhwa (eds.), *Zamindars, Mines and Peasants*, pp. 165 ff.

6 THE IMPACT OF THE FIRST WORLD WAR

6.1. The price history is discussed in detail by McAlpin, *CEHI 2*, pp. 890 ff. The impact of the war on the structure of the Indian economy has not yet been studied in detail. Some useful points are made by R.W. Goldsmith, *Financial Development*, pp. 68 ff.; see also B.R. Tomlinson, *The Political Economy of the Raj, 1914–1947* (London, 1979).

6.2. For the industrial development during the war, cf. Morris, *CEHI 2*, pp. 600 ff.; for coal mining, cf. B. Guha, 'The coal mining industry', in V.B. Singh (ed.), *Economic History*, p. 312; for Tata, cf. Lala, *Creation of Wealth*, p. 25; for the cement industry, cf. Morris, *CEHI 2*, p. 606.

6.3. The data on agricultural production are based on Blyn, *Agricultural Trends*, pp. 260 ff. (appendix); the price data on McAlpin, *CEHI 2*, pp. 890 ff.

6.4. A detailed discussion of wartime monetary problems is contained in the report of the Babington Smith Committee of 1919, reprinted in Government of India, *Reports of Currency Committees* (Calcutta, 1931), pp. 235–323; the evidence given by J.M. Keynes before that committee is reproduced in *The Collected Works of John Maynard Keynes*, Vol. XV (London, 1971), pp. 272 ff.

6.5. The assessment of the national income in this section is based on Heston, *CEHI 2*, pp. 398 ff.

7 ECONOMIC CONFLICTS IN THE POST-WAR PERIOD

7.1. 'Fiscal autonomy' is discussed by Kumar, *CEHI 2*, p. 906. For the Babington Smith Committee and Keynes's evidence, see the notes under section 6.4 above. The subsequent development of the currency was analysed by the next committee, the Hilton Young Committee (1926), whose report is also included in Government of India, *Reports of Currency Committees*, pp. 325–457; see also M. Joshi, 'Currency', in V.B. Singh (ed.), *Economic History*, pp. 375 ff.; for prices after 1920, cf. McAlpin, *CEHI 2*, p. 904; for foreign trade and the balance of payments, cf. K. Chaudhuri, *CEHI 2*, pp. 841 ff.

7.2. The data are from Blyn, *Agricultural Trends*, Appendix. The impact of rainfall on the production of food grains and of price on the production of cash crops is discussed by D. Narain, *The Impact of Price Movements on Areas under Selected Crops in India, 1900–1939* (Cambridge, 1965). The significance of the no-tax campaign in Bardoli is highlighted by S. Mehta, *The Peasantry and Nationalism. A Study of the Bardoli Satyagraha* (New Delhi, 1984).

7.3. For the cotton textile industry, cf. Morris, *CEHI 2*, pp. 616 ff., 661 ff. (on millhands); for data on textile workers, see also Krishnamurty, *CEHI 2*, p. 539.

7.4. For the jute industry, cf. Morris, *CEHI 2*, pp. 611 ff.

7.5. On 'discriminating protection' in general, cf. B.P. Adarkar, *The Indian Fiscal Policy* (Allahabad, 1941); see also Tomlinson, *Political Economy*, pp. 61 ff. On Tata, cf. Lala, *Creation of Wealth*,

p. 27; see also Morris, *CEHI 2*, pp. 624 ff.

7.6. The political context of Gandhi's eleven points is discussed by D. Rothermund, *Die politische Willensbildung in Indien, 1900–1960* (Wiesbaden, 1965); the importance of these points for the Indian business community is highlighted by G.D. Birla, *In the Shadow of the Mahatma* (Bombay, 1953); see also Birla's speeches and writings of this period reproduced in G.D. Birla, *The Path to Prosperity* (Allahabad, 1950). The history of FICCI is presented in its *Silver Jubilee Volume, 1927–1951* (New Delhi, 1952). The earlier development of the economic thought of Indian nationalists has been described in detail by Bipin Chandra, *The Growth of Economic Nationalism in India* (New Delhi, 1966).

8 THE CONSEQUENCES OF THE GREAT DEPRESSION

8.1. For several specific articles on India in the Great Depression in the context of the contemporary history of other countries in Africa, Asia and Latin America, cf. D. Rothermund (ed.), *Die Peripherie in der Weltwirtschaftskrise: Afrika, Asien und Lateinamerika, 1929–1939* (Paderborn, 1983); see also the papers on the Great Depression in Rothermund, *The Indian Economy under British Rule*, pp. 114–210. For a general study with special emphasis on international trade and commodity prices, cf. A.J.H. Latham, *The Depression and the Developing World, 1914–1939* (London, 1981). There are hardly any specific regional case studies of the impact of the Great Depression on various parts of India, but the comprehensive study of C.J. Baker, *An Indian Rural Economy, 1880–1955. The Tamilnad Countryside* (Delhi, OUP, 1984) contains several references to the depression, cf. pp. 115 ff., 249 ff. (on rice prices), 262 ff. (on the marketing of cash crops), 297 ff. (on credit contraction), 437 ff. (on the collapse of the zamindars), 457 ff. (on the plight of village officers). Similarly, the book by S. Bose, *Agrarian Bengal. Economy, Social Structure and Politics, 1919–1947* (Cambridge, 1986) contains information about the depression in Eastern India. I also owe some specific information to A. Satyanarayana, whose thesis on the agrarian history of the Andhra districts of the Madras Presidency I supervised (publication forthcoming).

8.2. British financial and commercial policy is described in detail in Rothermund, *The Indian Economy under British Rule*. The Swedish experience is analysed by L. Jonung, 'The depression in

Sweden and in the United States: a comparison of causes and policies', in K. Brunner (ed.), *The Great Depression Revisited* (Boston, 1981). British monetary policy is discussed by I.M. Drummond, *The Floating Pound and the Sterling Area, 1931–1939* (Cambridge, 1981); Drummond mentions the views expressed by Montagu Norman, Wedgwood Benn, George Schuster, Henry Strakosch *et al.* For Schuster, see also his autobiography: G. Schuster, *Private Work and Public Causes. A Personal Record, 1881–1978* (Cowbridge, 1979). For a recent study of Japanese policy during the Great Depression, cf. R. Dore and R. Sinha (eds.), *Japan and World Depression. Then and Now* (London, 1987).

8.3. For a discussion of protection, cf. Rothermund, *The Indian Economy under British Rule*, pp. 181 ff.; see also Adarkar, *Indian Fiscal Policy*, pp. 131 ff.; the situation of the cotton textile industry is analysed by H.J. Leue, 'Die indische Baumwolltextilindustrie: Wachstum trotz Krise, 1929–1939', in Rothermund, *Die Peripherie,* pp. 145 ff.

8.4. For the jute industry, cf. S. Mukherjee, 'Das restriktive Krisenmanagement der indischen Juteindustrie', in Rothermund (ed.), *Die Peripherie*, pp. 171 ff.; see also Government of Bengal, *Report of the Jute Enquiry Committee*, Vol. I (Alipore, 1939).

8.5. The data on the steel industry are taken from Government of India, Department of Commercial Intelligence and Statistics, *Statistical Abstract for British India, 1930–31 to 1939–40* (Calcutta, 1942); see also Morris *CEHI 2*, pp. 624 ff.

8.6. The rise of the sugar industry is discussed by Adarkar, *Indian Fiscal Policy*, pp. 194 ff.; see also Morris, *CEHI 2*, pp. 635 ff.

8.7. The data concerning the import of rice mills, oilpresses, motor vehicles, etc. are from the *Statistical Abstract* (see section 8.5).

9 INDIA'S WAR PROFIT: THE DEBTOR TURNS INTO A CREDITOR

9.1. The general political situation of India during the Second World War has been described in the comprehensive study by J. Voigt, *Indien im Zweiten Weltkrieg* (Stuttgart, 1978) (English edition forthcoming). For the expansion of the currency, cf. Joshi, 'Currency', in Singh (ed.), *Economic History*, pp. 404 ff.; see also Goldsmith, *Financial Development*, pp. 115 ff.

9.2. For the 'Stores Purchase Department', cf. S.K. Sen, *Studies in Economic Policy and Development* (Calcutta, 1972); the position of the cotton textile industry during the war is described by Fukazawa, 'Cotton mill industry', in Singh (ed.), *Economic History*, pp. 245 ff.; for the jute industry, see Dasgupta, 'Jute textile industry', in Singh (ed.), *Economic History*, pp. 271 ff.; for the steel industry, see Bisht and Namboodripad, 'Iron and steel industry', in Singh, *Economic History*, pp. 207 ff.

9.3. The letter by Lord Linlithgow to Governor Haig of 1 December 1939 is preserved in the India Office Library, Mss. Eur.F 115/22a. The food crisis has been described in detail by the civil servant who was in charge of food control in the Bombay Presidency during the war: Sir Henry Knight, *Food Administration in India, 1939–1947* (Stanford, Ca, 1954). The graph in this section is based on the price data provided by Knight. More recently an economic analysis of the Bengal famine has been attempted by A. Sen, *Poverty and Famines: An Essay on Entitlement and Deprivation* (Oxford, 1981), pp. 52 ff.

9.4. For a study of the beginnings of economic planning in India during the Second World War, cf. D. Rothermund, 'Die Anfänge der indischen Wirtschaftsplanung im Zweiten Weltkrieg', in P. Halblützel *et al.* (eds.), *Dritte Welt: Historische Prägung und politische Herausforderung (Festschrift R. von Albertini)* (Wiesbaden, 1983), pp. 81 ff.

The text of the Cripps-Bevin plan has been published in N. Mansergh (ed.), *The Transfer of Power*, Vol. III (London, 1971), pp. 374 ff. The full title of the 'Bombay Plan' is *A Brief Memorandum outlining a Plan of Economic Development for India* by Sir Purushottamdas Thakurdas, J.R.D. Tata, G.D. Birla, Sir Ardeshir Dalal, Sir Shri Ram, Kasturbhai Lalbhai, A.D. Shroff and John Matthai (Bombay, 1944). For contemporary criticism of this plan, see G.D. Parikh and M.N. Roy, *Alphabet of Fascist Economics — A Critique of the Bombay Plan of Economic Development for India* (Calcutta, 1944).

The documents concerning the Department of Planning and Reconstruction have been published in N. Mansergh (ed.), *The Transfer of Power*, Vol. IV (London, 1973), pp. 847, 967, and Vol. V (London, 1974), pp. 526, 1099 ff., 1218 ff.

10 INDIA'S DILEMMA: DYNAMIC INDUSTRIALISATION AND STATIC AGRICULTURE

10.1. For a general evaluation of economic policy, cf. W. Malenbaum, *Prospects for Indian Development* (London, 1962). For the problem of taxing agriculture, cf. T.M. Joshi *et al.*, *Studies in the Taxation of Agricultural Land and Income in India* (Bombay, 1968). For land reforms, cf. Government of India, Planning Commission, *Reports of the Panels on the Land Reform* (New Delhi, 1955). On the problems of implementing the reforms, cf. W. Ladejinsky, *A Study of Tenurial Conditions in Package Districts* (Planning Commission, Government of India) (New Delhi, 1965).

10.2. For a critical analysis of the first two five-year plans, cf. S. Subramaniam, *Die Wirtschaftsentwicklung Indiens, 1951–1961* (Tübingen, 1965). A more recent study with special reference to foreign aid has been published by H. Tischner, *Die wirtschaftliche Entwicklung Indiens 1951–1978 unter besonderer Berücksichtigung der Auslandshilfe* (Berlin, 1981). The third plan document contains an encyclopaedic survey of the planning process: Government of India, Planning Commission, *Third Five Year Plan* (New Delhi, 1961), see also A.H. Hanson, *The Process of Planning. A Study of India's Five Year Plans, 1950–1964* (London, 1964).

10.3. For the data, cf. Tischner, *Wirtschaftliche Entwicklung Indiens*, pp. 188 ff.; see also Vaidyanathan, *CEHI 2*, pp. 961 ff.

10.4. Cf. Tischner, *Wirtschaftliche Entwicklung Indiens*, pp. 109 ff.; see also Vaidyanathan, *CEHI 2*, p. 960. For a discussion of the role of cattle in India, cf. J. Lensch, *Problems and Prospects of Cattle and Buffalo Husbandry in India with special reference to the Concept of 'Sacred Cow'* (Hamburg, 1987).

10.5. On the price trends before 1947, cf. A.K. Ghosh, *Prices and Economic Fluctuations in India, 1861–1947* (New Delhi, 1979); for the subsequent period, cf. D. Bright Singh, *Inflationary Price Trends in India since 1939* (Bombay, 1961). Wages are discussed by R.S. Papola, *Principles of Wage Determination. An empirical Study* (Bombay, 1970). For the PL 480 programme, cf. Tischner, *Wirtschaftliche Entwicklung Indiens*, pp. 162 ff.; see also the special study by J. von Plocki, *Auswirkungen der Nahrungsmittelhilfe unter PL 480 auf den Agrarsektor der Entwicklungsländer dargestellt am Beispiel Indiens* (Wiesbaden, 1979). On capital aid, see Tischner, *Wirtschaftliche Entwicklung Indiens*, pp. 20 ff.; see also P.J. Eldridge, *The Politics of Foreign Aid in India* (New Delhi, 1969); for a very critical assessment of foreign aid, cf. H.L. Bhatia, *Does*

Foreign Aid Help? (Birla Institute of Scientific Research) (New Delhi, 1981).

11 THE 'GREEN REVOLUTION' AND THE INDUSTRIAL RECESSION

11.1. For an evaluation of the political situation in 1965–7, cf. Kulke and Rothermund, *A History of India*, pp. 321 ff.

11.2. For a general analysis of the 'Green Revolution', cf. F. Frankel, *India's Green Revolution. Economic Gains and Political Costs* (Princeton, NJ, 1971). For the data on which the calculation of the quinquennial averages are based, cf. Government of India, *Economic Survey, 1981–82* (New Delhi, 1982) and *1986–7* (New Delhi, 1987). This survey also contains the data on the production of the different states of India. The Agricultural Prices Commission and agrarian policy in general are discussed by Tischner, *Wirtschaftliche Entwicklung Indiens*, pp. 134 ff., 318.

11.3. For the data, cf. *Economic Survey* (see section 11.2 above); for a discussion of the recession, see also Vaidyanathan, *CEHI 2*, pp. 969 ff. Several aspects of the recession are discussed in A. Bagchi and N. Banerjee (eds.), *Change and Choice in Indian Industry* (Calcutta, 1981); the contribution by P. Patnaik to this volume ('An explanatory hypothesis on the Indian industrial stagnation') is of special significance here; see also the contribution by the editor, A. Bagchi ('Reinforcing and offsetting constraints in Indian industry'). Recently a detailed study has highlighted the dwindling of public investment after 1965 as a cause of the recession: I. J. Ahluwalia, *Industrial Growth in India. Stagnation since the Mid-Sixties* (Delhi, 1985). Problems of the steel industry and, by implication, of the public sector in general are discussed by S.S. Sidhu, *The Steel Industry in India* (New Delhi, 1983). The role of Soviet help in the exploration of India's oil resources is analysed by D. Rothermund, *Indien und die Sowjetunion* (Tübingen, 1968), pp. 79 ff. For the data on the generation of energy, see *Economic Survey 1981–82*; the latest data quoted are based on the *Economic Survey 1986–87*. For a discussion of the revision of the index of industrial production, cf. *Economic Survey 1986–87*, pp. 33 ff. (The old index — 1970 = 100 — did not give proper weightage to new industries like chemicals, garments, electronics, whereas some of the old industries were given too much weight. The new index — 1980 = 100 — has corrected this and accordingly shows a much higher growth rate.)

11.4. The consequences of devaluation are discussed by Tischner, *Wirtschaftliche Entwicklung Indiens*, pp. 367 ff. The problems of inflation are analysed by A.M. Khusro, *The Indian Economy. Stability and Growth* (New Delhi, 1979); strategies for fighting inflation are presented by L.K. Jha, *Economic Strategies for the 80s* (New Delhi, 1980), pp. 79 ff. On foreign trade, cf. Tischner, *Wirtschaftliche Entwicklung Indiens*, pp. 350 ff. For the data, cf. *Economic Survey 1981–82* and *Economic Survey 1986–87*; see also Reserve Bank of India, *Report on Currency and Finance, 1984–85*, 2 vols. (Bombay, 1985). For the role of the Reserve Bank's credit to government and 'monetary targeting', cf. S. Chakravarty *et al.*, *Report of the Committee to Review the Working of the Monetary System* (Bombay, Reserve Bank of India, 1985).

11.5. For the data, cf. *Economic Survey 1986–87*.

12 POPULATION GROWTH AND ECONOMIC DEVELOPMENT

12.1. The data are from the *General Report, Census of India 1981*. The structure of the workforce is discussed by Krishnamurty, *CEHI* 2, pp. 533 ff.; the latest data are derived from *Economic Survey 1981–82* and *1986–87*. For the theory on the unlimited supply of labour, cf. W.A. Lewis, *Theory of Economic Growth* (London, 1972).

12.2. For a detailed discussion of the various attempts at measuring the national income of India, cf. Heston, *CEHI* 2, pp. 376 ff.; see also M. Mukherjee, *National Income of India. Trends and Structure* (Calcutta, 1969), as well as his more recent study in U. Datta Roychaudhury and M. Mukherjee, *National Accounts Information System* (Delhi, 1984). The graph included in this section is based on the data presented in the latter volume. I am grateful to Professor Moni Mukherjee for reading an earlier draft of this section and discussing it with me; I am, of course, entirely responsible for all mistakes that may still remain in the text. The latest data are taken from the *Economic Survey 1986–87*. For the contribution of the service sector to national income, see also K.L. Saxsena, 'India: a critical appraisal of estimates of national product for the service sector', in *National Accounts in Developing Countries of Asia* (Paris, OECD, 1972).

12.3. For data on the process of urbanisation, cf. A. Mitra *et al.*, *Indian Cities. Their Industrial Structure, Inmigration and Capital Investment, 1961–1971* (New Delhi, 1980); see also H. Kulke *et al.*

(ed.), *Städte in Südasien* (Wiesbaden, 1982); the following contributions to that volume are particularly relevant for this section: H.C. Rieger, 'Bombay or Nasik? Urban overcentralisation in India's industrialisation process' (pp. 193 ff) and H. Nissel, 'Jüngste Tendenzen der Zuwanderung nach Bombay' (pp. 213 ff.). For a typology of Indian cities with regard to the pattern of in-migration, cf. Q. Ahmad, *Indian Cities: Characteristics and Correlates* (Chicago, 1965). The 'push-back' factor is discussed by A. Bose, *India's Urbanization, 1901–2001* (New Delhi, 1978), pp. 191 ff.

12.4. For the Physical Qualify of Life Index, cf. M.D. Morris, *Measuring the Conditions of the World's Poor: The Physical Quality of Life Index* (New York, 1979). For an evaluation of the data provided by Morris for different regions of India, cf. D. Rothermund, 'Die Dimensionen der Armut: Indien und der Lebensqualitätsindex' in N. Wagner and H.C. Rieger (eds.), *Grundbedürfnisse als Gegenstand der Entwicklungspolitik* (Wiesbaden, 1982). An excellent survey of regional disparities in agriculture as well as in industry is provided by A. Kundu and M. Raza, *Indian Economy: The Regional Dimension* (New Delhi, 1982). Whereas Kundu and Raza provide a striking outline of such disparities, Kumar and Krishnamurty, who examined highly aggregated data, came to the conclusion that India shows less regional disparities than other countries: cf. D. Kumar and J. Krishnamurty, 'Regional and international disparities since the industrial revolution: the Indian evidence', in P. Bairoch and M. Levy-Leboyer (eds.), *Disparities in Economic Development since the Industrial Revolution* (London, 1981).

12.5. For detailed reporting on environmental problems, see Centre for Science and Environment, *The State of India's Environment 1982 — A Citizens' Report* (New Delhi, 1982) and its sequel: *The State of India's Environment 1983–85* (New Delhi, 1985). For a general assessment, see D. Rothermund, 'India 2000 — perspectives of a near future', in *Asien* (German Association for Asian Studies), No. 10 (1984). The study emphasising water control is by James K. Boyce, *Agrarian Impasse in Bengal: Institutional Constraints to Technological Change* (Oxford, 1987). For an analysis of the social base of the political system, see V.A. Pai Panandiker and A. Sud, *Changing Political Representation in India* (New Delhi, 1983). For Gunnar Myrdal's pronouncements on the 'soft state', cf. G. Myrdal, *Asian Drama. An Inquiry into the Poverty of Nations*, 3 vols. (New York, 1968), Vol. I, p. 66; Vol. II, pp. 895 ff.

Index

Note. Where relevant, sub-entries are in chronological order.

This book is a compact synthesis of the economic history of India. It describes an ancient peasant culture subjected first to military feudalism, at its height under the great Mughals, and then to the essentially parasitic East India Company which imposed a form of capitalism that paralysed the economy of its host. In the twentieth century, India has come into the world market and the book charts the impact of the two world wars and the great depression. Since independence, India has improved her economic position in spite of further population increase. Recent industrial growth and surplus production of cereals may be signs of a more economically secure future.

Much has been written on the Indian economy but this is the first major attempt to present India's economic history as a process and to place the development of agriculture and industry in political context. Currency and monetary policy have also been discussed as they are of central importance in all periods of Indian history.

Dietmar Rothermund is Professor of History at the South Asia Institute, Heidelberg University.